six weeks to better parenting

six weeks to better parenting

**The complete guide for creative
raising of children two - twelve**

by Caryl Waller Krueger

BELLERIDGE PRESS
Box 970
Rancho Santa Fe, California 92067
(714) 756-3756

Printed in the United States of America
First printing 1981

Library of Congress Cataloging in Publication Data:
Krueger, Caryl Waller, 1929-
    Six weeks to better parenting.

    Includes index.
    1.   Parenting — United States.   2.   Play.
    3.   Home & School.
    4.   Education; Preschool — United States.
    5.   Education, Elementary — United States.
    I.   Title.
HQ755.8.K7   1981   649'.1   80-26457
ISBN 0-938632-05-1

The author has made every effort to make the information and suggestions in this book practical and workable, but neither she, nor the publisher, assumes any responsibility for successes, failures or other results by those putting these ideas into practice.

Contents

WEEK THREE
Can Order and Helpfulness Be Fun? 109

WEEK FOUR
The Important Mess of "Do It Myself" 137

WEEK FIVE
Education As A Home Responsibility............................ 217

The next six weeks...

can be exciting ones for your family. In this book you'll learn new ways to have fun, work creatively, teach obedience, and help your child get the most out of school and play. You'll feel more successful yourself and your child will be happier.

Read a little each day or a section each week. The reading for some weeks is shorter than others — that's because you'll want to be spending more time putting certain systems or ideas into immediate use. There are no educational prerequisites for parenthood, so it's up to you to learn all you can to make home life more satisfying.

In these pages are hundreds of helpful ideas for better parenting. As your child grows older, you'll want to go back and reread certain chapters. And you'll refer to the lists and charts often in the days and years ahead.

Now get started with your first week...

Week
One

1
1
1
1
1
1
1
1
1
1
1
1
1

Meet Wendy,
Kent,
Karen and Mark

What child likes to be used as an example for good or for bad! Yet in a practical "how to" book such as this one, there are countless experiences and examples that involve children I have known — my own children, my nieces and nephews, the children of good friends, and of course, children that I have taught in school and Sunday school.

In this book you will get to know four children rather well: Wendy, Kent, Karen and Mark. Please understand that these children are not mine. The are a composite of hundreds of children and I hope you will find in them something of your own children.

Let's start by meeting Wendy, the oldest of the four children. She has had that precious experience of being the "only child" for the first several years of her life. As the oldest, she has been experimented on and is the pioneer in the family's job of child raising. She would be the first to tell you that she isn't a child anymore, and in many ways her responsibility and maturity would make you doubt that she had a collection of dolls still hidden on a closet shelf. As a competitor and a doer and a protester she keeps busy at home and at school. Studies are not difficult for her and words written and spoken are her forte — she knows her ability to talk you into things. Still, there are times when the "little child" shines through once more.

Next there is Kent. What can one say about the first boy in the family — that unfortunate soul who follows in the footsteps of a well-behaved and orderly older sister? He is charm and innocence, confusion and disorder, all rolled into one lovable ball. His is the room that defies weekly cleaning. He is the one searching for his gym shorts while waving a piece of bacon in the air. He may not remember the multiplication tables, but he can recite the contents of the latest *National Geographic Magazine*. And when you finally get through to him that he has done something wrong, he is the one who secretly places an intricate

3

construction of his favorite Lego toys on your pillow at night.

Every family needs a Karen, one of those free birds who lives every moment to the fullest. Impulsive, demanding, even bossy, she prances through the day singing, dancing, playing the piano, organizing dramas in the playroom, restaurants in the kitchen, and animal hospitals in the garage. Though proud of her accomplishments, she still needs parental reassurance. She finds herself in that enviable feminine position — between two boys. At home she alternates competing with Kent and prodding Mark. She has mastered the 3 R's in school but must learn patience with her peers.

Finally there is Mark, the roly-poly fellow whom everyone took care of as "baby in the family." Cheerful and lovable, he still finds value in a pout or a "stretched truth" and has quickly learned the politics of playing one sister against another. In an effort to grow up he is willing to try everything and eat everything, and while he wants to enjoy more grown-up advantages, he is not totally willing to give up that advantageous post of "littlest" in the family.

Well-intentioned parents of children older than yours will often say: "See how your life changes when he gets to the *walking* stage!" Later you hear, "It's misery when they learn to argue!"..."Wait until they're old enough to go places on their bicycles alone!"..."It's nothing until they're about to enter their teens — if you think things are bad now, prepare for the worst." Actually, no stage of a child's experience needs to be painful or boring or discouraging. Each progressive stage of childhood can be pleasant and profitable. Both parent and child should strive to enjoy *where they are* without longing for the time past or fearing for the future.

Most of the creative life of the family stems from parental ingenuity. Our children give us daily opportunities to choose between living routinely or creatively. The purpose of this book is to encourage you to follow-up on the instincts you and your children already have to live that creative life.

1
Living
Spontaneously

We came home from the drive-in with a big sack of hamburgers, milk-shakes and french fries. I had thought, "We'll just gather around the table and each can eat his favorite food." Wendy had other plans. She had seen a colorful bird in a tree earlier in the day and decided that it would be more fun to eat supper in a tree. Her enthusiasm sparked the others. Within seconds they had all scrambled to leafy perches where they precariously sat and supped. I put a paper bag at the bottom of the tree and as the meal continued, unwanted wrappers, pickles and other debris provided an excellent game of "toss into the bag," with plenty of misses.

Thus the tradition of supper-in-a-tree was started at our house. It has since been expanded to include supper-in-your-bedroom, a privilege, not a punishment; supper-on-the-roof, a marvelous place to eat and have a good view of the neighbors; and supper-under-the-table, Mark's invention after reading a book about having a private little house of one's own.

How easy it would have been to spoil the spontaneity of the moment with the usual parental phrase, "Please sit down, put your napkin in your lap and eat your hamburger carefully." But the importance of the experience was the spontaneity of it — the fact that it was a new idea, tried and proved successful. Shouldn't childhood be filled with a variety of experiences, many of them created by the child's own imagination? Children are not miniature adults. Their habits and desires often run counter to ours. How much fun supper-in-a-tree gave us! As evening came on, we watched the sky change colors, the birds enjoy a dropped french fry and the ants attack the sweet stickiness of a spilled shake.

A child's creative nature needs room for expansion and the parent's response to what may seem whimsy should be, "Why not?" rather than "Why?" Children needn't give you ten good reasons for doing things that intrigue them. If there is no good reason why they shouldn't be allowed to do it, let them go ahead and have fun. Life will, all too soon, become so organized that opportunities for spontaneity and change diminish and often are entirely lost.

The important thing to remember is that *you* have to fit the day. Don't make the day fit you. If one child is in a very cozy and confidential late afternoon mood and wants to build a fire in the fireplace and sit in front of it and talk with you, that's far more important than that plumbing repair or prompt supper. Times for an intimate talk with your child are rare and precious. A half hour of talk and "doing nothing" may sound like a luxurious experience for parent and child, yet it's a luxury that we can't afford to miss, even after a hard day at work.

Do things just because you feel like doing them! We sometimes give "just-because" presents, a hair-bow or a ball tucked under a pillow at night "just-because we love you." We may suddenly decide as supper ends to postpone dessert and go for a family walk. Or one child may be invited to stay up long past his bedtime to read or play cards with Dad or Mom or a visiting grandparent. Once in a while, when we have an especially exciting dessert, we serve it first! It's called a "Backwards Supper." Who says supper can't occasionally start with dessert and work its way back to meat and potatoes?

Of course there's a place for routine in our living, but the routine should never stand in the way of an exciting experience. Let your children hop out of bed at night to see an especially beautiful full moon, the crashing waves of the ocean, or one of our satellites tracking by. Plan to waken early and huddle silently in blankets to watch the glories of an orange and lavender dawn.

One evening we had mentally mapped out a time schedule for dinner and the evening when Karen called us to the living room to watch a "preformance" that she and her best friend had been working on all afternoon. Of course it meant changing our plans, but what merit did our plan have other than the fact that it was ours? Flexibility is the key quality for parents who want to give the most to their children and still maintain parental individuality.

2
The
Prepared
Parent

One night Mark and Kent were put to bed without the usual story, hug, kiss and prayers. Instead, Mother delivered a lengthy lecture on the importance of tidy rooms. Tears and shouts resulted, at which point Father entered. He immediately soothed the boys and privately reminded Mother that this was not the time for education. The children were at fault, yes. They were told to straighten their rooms and had failed to do so. A strong reminder was in order but bedtime was the wrong time for it.

A PARENT'S MASTER PLAN

The prepared parent has to treat the day as a good executive vice president would treat the business day, whether both parents are employed outside the home or not. When both are gone much of the day, the plan may be even more crucial. There must be a time and a place for seeing that assignments have been carried out, for the origination of "new business," for the educational sharing of ideas, for the comradery that builds loyalty and bonds of devotion. Diplomacy must be part of that plan.

Most every home has 30 to 90 minutes of frenzied activity at the beginning of the morning: bedmaking, face washing, breakfast, dishes, getting the laundry going. Suddenly there comes a time when the school children are off, the toddler has happily discovered some toy forgotten from the day before. At that point, a parent can sit down and make the master plan for the day. The following concerns the at-home mother, but it will also be adaptable to the homemaker father.

1. The time for business work or home tasks (sometimes both).
2. The time for one's personal self.
3. The time with the children.
4. The time with spouse.
5. "Outgoing" time.

Time with the children should not be leftover time. How sad is the parent who "does good" for every activity within the community while his/her own children long for love and companionship. "Outgoing" time, away-from-home activity, can be organized so that it falls into school hours as much as possible. While committee meetings are important, meetings with your family are equally important — perhaps even more so.

In our busy culture and with both parents often working, togetherness has to be planned. Kent and Karen love the after-school snack-and-tell time, the opportunity to sit down for a quiet moment and share the day's experiences. Whichever parent is at home has a rare opportunity to hear firsthand, while the impressions are still bright, the things which make the difference in a child's school day. Having invested these moments of interest in the child, the parent lets the child go about his own play, work or homework. But it is important to return to the child in another hour or so to see that the time has been well spent either in play or in work.

If Mark and Kent had been told to tidy up their rooms at 5 o'clock in the afternoon, 6 o'clock would have been the ideal time to check on the project and give further direction if it hadn't been completed. This would have avoided the bedtime scene which left ugly feelings for boys and parents.

The parent can look ahead and see that if the family is going somewhere after dinner, then homework must be finished beforehand. The hours from after school to suppertime are important for parent and child. Many working parents phone their children after school to get a capsule comment on the day, to learn if the child's plans have remained the same, and perhaps to give a simple instruction on starting the potatoes cooking for dinner. Even the at-home parent will not spend all these hours *with* the child but should be *aware* of what the child is doing and express deep interest in his play or homework. When both parents come home, the day shifts and takes on a whole-family atmosphere. As the evening progresses and the children go off to bed, parents have time for each other, time to share the details of their respective days, only some of which could be shared at dinner with the children.

A TIME FOR YOURSELF

Looking at such a typical day, there is one essential element that we haven't discussed. The success of the other three divisions of the day depends on it. This is time for yourself. In order to give of yourself to children, to spouse, to community, you have to be selfish about your own time. If not careful, you could spend the whole day in work — at home or office — laundry, meetings, child care, or chatting with spouse. But as a priceless *individual* you have to have a time for yourself each day.

Most of us have the energy to get quantities of work done in the morning. For the parent at home with preschoolers this is an active time. But, I have always found that "my time" follows lunch. When the children are young this is their usual nap time. When they are older, they are in school. So you as a parent can set aside at least an hour for yourself in the early afternoon. At this time you solely concentrate on yourself — enriching your own life, increasing your own intellect, doing something for yourself that you enjoy doing. It might be painting a picture or reading a book. It's an active time, not for a nap, but for conscious refreshment and personal progress. Whatever you choose to do during that precious hour, it should be something you can do only by yourself. Fixing a leaky faucet, making a cake, weeding the flower garden, are all tasks that can be done in the company of someone else. *This* is the hour of self-development, when you see, use, and augment your own capabilities and talents and learn something new, exciting and possibly worth sharing with the family.

It is especially important that the at-home parent's intellectual growth doesn't stagnate. In business, you are often learning new things, talking with interesting people, reading and expanding your horizons. "Meanwhile back at the ranch" is it only changing diapers and making casseroles? If so, there is trouble ahead! A regular schedule of reading, an outside class, a worthwhile club or sports activity, all give mothers and fathers added topics of conversation, and help keep them abreast of each other. The more worthwhile these "extra-curricular" activities, the more interesting and varied the things you'll be able to share with each other.

Personal care, of course, is important, and the busier you get, the more important it is. Neither age, sex nor business is an excuse for mistreating yourself. Take time, grab the time, insist on it. Nothing is as refreshing as a face scrub and a clean shirt or blouse before dinner. This aids your outside. But also insist on time for your inner self, the calm and collected soul gained in moments of quiet. This can be yours in the bath tub, in a porch chair, on a private five-minute walk — your time to meditate, contemplate, pray and appreciate the joy and beauty of life.

A DAILY CALENDAR

Each November we buy an appointment planning calendar, much like that used by busy executives. Into the spaces of the day we put all the routine things that have to be done: people to call, tasks to perform, errands to run. Writing them down helps to group them and certainly saves time, energy and even gasoline, because similar things can be done at one time or on one trip. Equally important, we parents schedule daily time for ouselves, whether it be writing a letter, reading in the sun or making a flower arrangement.

Writing everything down for the day and week shows us how it all can get done without that hopeless feeling of too much to do and too little time to do it. The planning calendar relieves us of trying to remember, and feeling guilty if we forget. It is a marvelous record of past purchases, appointments, entertaining, correspondence with grandparents. The book sits open on my desk, and everyone in the family is welcome to list activities. This way, I know when my husband has a late afternoon meeting, or a child is going to be at another friend's home for supper, when a teenager has a babysitting date, or when special large school assignments are due.

HEADQUARTERS

I mentioned my desk, and I sincerely feel that every organized parent needs a central headquarters. It can be a real desk in the family room, or as simple as a counter and cupboard in the kitchen or workshop. Efficiency in home management deserves good equipment: if possible a typewriter and telephone, file folders, plenty of sharp pencils.

This can be the family message center — no missed calls when everyone leaves on the desk written phone messages and notes as to location and return time. Here is your purchasing center, the place for discount coupons, the grocery list, a plan for the upcoming meals, the repair/maintenance list, social schedules for all members of the family.

An idea that rescued me from desktop clutter is this: Buy an expanding file marked 1 - 31 for the days of the month. File all those miscellaneous items under the dates this month when you intend to handle those matters. Invitations, meeting notices, bills to pay, theater tickets are safely tucked away for the right date. In the last pocket accumulate things for the following month. These files are available at office supply stores.

Proper parenting is a position of such magnitude that it requires a real office or headquarters. See that you have it. It's a good place to start.

3
The Orderly Child

When the grandparents came for their yearly visit, the children enjoyed chatting leisurely with them in the guest room. Mark, we noticed, would slip out of grandma's and grandpa's bedroom once a day with a mysterious, satisfied look on his face. It was soon discovered that he had taken it upon himself to line up all their shoes in neat rows. When asked why he did this, he explained in a matter-of-fact way to grandma, "If you want to go out to play fast, it helps to have your shoes in pairs so that you can put them on quick."

Prior to that, we had thought all our lectures on the importance of keeping one's room neat had fallen on deaf ears. We were secretly pleased that even a small child could learn order, but Mark had not only learned order, he had also learned a reason to be orderly. Without the reason "why" being taught to the child, order becomes mere blind obedience and as such has less value.

Age two is none too soon to teach a child to tidy up his toys at the end of his play day so that he can find them and discover them anew the following day. As soon as order in one's personal possessions has been taught, it's easy to transfer this trait to orderliness and method in study —a far more important lesson for our children.

FIRST THINGS FIRST

A child must be able to see what he has to do ahead, and he must have the confidence that it can be done. Order helps him do this. Order is not restricting to a child. It gives him the ability to whiz through the routine things of the day and thus gives himself freedom to spend time on unregulated activities, creative play, spontaneous fun. When I was a child, my mother's motto was, "First things first," and although the oft-repeated words came to make me shudder, they at least taught me that there were certain things that should be accomplished before I could go on to the more interesting things of the day.

11

In our own family we have labeled these first things as "The Morning Sevens." In the first 30 minutes of the morning, there are seven things that every civilized person does. When you get these over with, you are free to go on to anything else you choose. What a nice investment of time! Merely 30 minutes and you can do as you wish.

THE MORNING SEVENS

1. Wash
2. Make bed
3. Dress
4. Tidy bedroom and bathroom
5. Put clothes in hamper
6. Brush teeth
7. Do assigned helps (i.e. feed the cat, bring in the paper)

Get these seven things over with first thing each day and be free to go on to really interesting things!

Write your own list — make it six, seven or eight. Be sure to interpret them to your children at first, but later refer to them by brief words such as above.

You can decide what are the basic essentials for your child to accomplish in the morning. For the younger child, draw a picture of each of the things expected done. For example, a bed indicating to make one's bed, and a toothbrush to remind the child to brush teeth. On school days "The Morning Sevens" should be done before breakfast. On Saturdays and Sundays you can relax the time. "The Morning Sevens" have become a saying around our house for I heard my husband say, when the boys wished to borrow tools to make a small boat, "It's all right with me, as long as you've done your Morning Sevens."

The entire purpose of teaching a child to have certain *unimportant* areas of his life organized and routinized is so that he can function properly without parental presence. I am sure that if we stood over our children and said to them: "Wash your face," "Put your dirty clothes in the laundry," "Pack up your school books," that these things would get done. But the test of our teaching comes when the child does these things without reminders. This is the essence of teaching a child obedience and order. How will he behave *without* your standing at his elbow?

Later in this book we will take up the matter or orderliness and helpfulness in detail, but for now, remember that organization brings happiness and freedom. Much of the unpleasant family conversation is over things forgotten or left undone. How nice to be free of the morning parent-child inquisition and to cover it with one title, "The Morning Sevens!" Without order, a child will still be bed-making at 3:30 in the afternoon. With order, he is out playing with friends.

4
The
Three S's

It was Easter and I was about to frost an elaborate cake I had made in the shape of a rabbit when five-year-old Karen came in and exuberantly requested the right to give the bunny his ears, eyes and tail. I was pleased she wanted to take part in holiday preparations but recognized that the rabbit might not have that professional touch I thought I could give it.

I gave her the job. She dobbed the white and pink frosting over him with the finesse of a Renoir. She got the tail lopsided and managed to give him a pair of crossed eyes. When she was finished, she stood back and admired her work and announced it was the most beautiful rabbit in the world. The frosting dripped off the edge of the plate as she showed it to Kent, who said, "Yes, that doesn't look like any old ordinary rabbit at all." After dinner we served the rabbit cake and everyone commented on how good it tasted and what a spectacular job of decoration had been done on it.

Later I mentioned the incident in a letter to the Grandparents, who happily wrote back how wonderful it was that Karen was learning to frost cakes so beautifully. She just beamed and kept the letter in her desk as a sign of approval from thousands of miles away. Although Karen didn't know it, she was glowing over the three S's: success, satisfaction and security.

SUCCESS

Karen felt success. She was able to do something that perhaps seemed difficult at the beginning. I could have spoiled her feeling of success by insisting that I finish the project or that she was too little to do it. On one hand we want our children to grow up to be successful. On the other hand we may keep them tied to us and then wonder why they are inept and dependent.

Too often we underestimate the abilities of our children. If a child wants to try a task that seems beyond him, consider the request seriously. If there is no danger in doing it, let him go ahead. Don't be a doubter and

13

an "I told you so." Respect his enthusiasm and confidence. Encourage him, show him, guide him, let him alone when he's ready for it. What sweeter shout than "I did it, I did it MYSELF!" Don't deprive your child of that joy of success in a false desire to be important or necessary yourself. Your self-importance is unimportant and the child's need for you still manifold.

SATISFACTION

Having succeeded at frosting a cake, Karen still required the satisfaction of knowing that she had done something special. How often we forget to give the child that feeling of satisfaction. He has done the job well, or at least he has *done* it, but in a busy world we forget to take time to recognize that success. In a family situation, there are so many ways to let the child know that he has done a satisfactory job.

Verbal praise, of course, is the most common. Ask yourself each day if you have found as many occasions for praise as for criticism. Praise in front of someone else makes it doubly satisfying. On the other hand, criticism in front of someone else is much to be avoided.

It may sound corny, but applause can be used for praise also. We have a monthly supper at which we consider our achievements for the past 30 days. The children set certain goals for themselves, and we liberally sprinkle the commendations with applause for one another and an occasional toast of milk.

So often, if there's good news from school, only the person at home at three o'clock hears it. How nice to repeat it in front of all at dinner so that both parents and sisters and brothers can know the good news. School papers pinned up on the family bulletin board or scotch-taped to the refrigerator door are additional reminders of a job well done.

When Wendy, Kent, Karen or Mark come home with one of those inevitable clay pieces from school, I see that it has a place of honor on the coffee table in the living room or on my desk for a week or so. In many schools each child annually makes a clay piece that is glazed, fired and given out at the next holiday. With four children you can imagine how many of these clay pieces we have collected! Some of them are moderately grotesque. None of them indicates that we have a Michelangelo in the family. However, they were all done with love and gusto. Once each year I clear a shelf at child's eye level in a prominent spot and display these several dozen items. Then there is much discussion as to whose dinosaur is the greatest or just how a particular glaze was achieved. After looking at them for a few weeks, we are all content to put them away for another year.

More recently we have adopted a new method of showing approval to a child. One of us writes him a letter. It can be short and to the point but by putting it in writing, busy parents are sure to remember that needed praise. For example, here's the note I wrote one day.

Dear Wendy,

I just wanted you to know how very much I appreciated the beautiful job of cleanup you did for me in the kitchen after Friday night's party. You didn't leave any of the icky pans for me to do the next morning. You remembered to wipe off the counters, and I especially appreciated the fact that you did it ungrudgingly. One of our friends commented on how gracious you were about it all. Having a daughter like you makes entertaining extra fun.

Love,
Mother

SECURITY

The third *S* is *security,* that confident feeling of being loved whether or not you have achieved success and satisfaction. Going back to Karen and the rabbit cake, at one point the head fell off and the frosting hit the floor. What would be the response to this? Would we say, "Karen, you are clumsy and stupid and I knew you'd make a mess of it." Hardly. A child at this point sees his success and satisfaction slipping out of his grasp but still needs to hang on to security. The wise parent calmly tells the child how to clean up the spilled frosting and then considers with the child the best way to salvage the headless bunny. Why should we *not* make an issue of the damaged cake and the spilled frosting? I base the decision to criticize or not to criticize on the child's motive. In this case, the motive was a good one. The child was trying to be helpful and to make something that would please the entire family. That it was not a success does not change the motive.

The child needs more direction, and this is where mother or dad steps in and helps to salvage the mess. They need not say that it was a good thing that the frosting was spilled. That would not be honest, and children respect truthfulness and see through deceit. In fact, the parent might well say, "It's too bad that we've wasted all that frosting" or "How sad it is to have a decapitated bunny." However, it's wise to point out to the child that this is *not* one of the earthshaking events taking place in the world today. We must keep it in its proper perspective.

Parents must remind themselves constantly of their aim and not be sidetracked. The aim at this time is to have a happy holiday meal, climaxed by a rabbit cake. It's not to have a miserable child sitting sobbing at the dinner table. A far more valuable lesson for the child is how to clean up a mess.

Several days after the rabbit cake experience, with friends coming for dinner, I tried to elaborate on a cream torte by making it one tier higher. You can imagine my horror when I opened the refrigerator and found the top layer sliding off the cake and down amid the other items on the

15

shelves and leaving behind a trail of sour cream filling and raspberry frosting. Karen was at my elbow and said, "You can shove it back together and put more frosting on it. Aren't you glad it wasn't the bunny cake? This is lots easier to fix and I know you can do it. Besides, it tastes so good, and that's what counts." I hugged her! The tables had been turned on me. But the lesson had been learned and made her own — and easily, too! Despite the slipping cake and sloppy refrigerator, I felt like a great mother!

Now what about the child who seems to do more things wrong than right, the child who experiences few successes during the day and has little satisfaction? Handling this child is a real test for a parent. How easy it is to praise and love a child who does everything right! There are some children who move along from success to success, get everything right the first time, are never forgetful and rarely make a mistake. As parents, we hardly seem to be needed.

The challenge lies in how useful we can be to the child who appears to be slow or naughty or forgetful. This child requires more of our time and more of our guidance. When he comes to us and requests to frost the rabbit cake, we should be wise enough to say, "O.K., I'll put the white frosting on if you concentrate on the eyes and the tail and the pink in the ears." We make the goals smaller, the jobs easier, gradually increasing them when the child has tasted the success and satisfaction of having done a small job right. Goals work best when built upon success. We go from one success to another, forgetting the intermediate non-successes. We emphasize what is done right and while we don't condone or ignore the wrong, it is de-emphasized. Here is where we really look for the good, so that we can compliment the child on something that he has done right.

Kent had a particularly fierce homework session with me one night. Nothing was going right. He had forgotten his spelling words at school. He didn't comprehend the multiplication system any better than I could cope with new math. He was about 1,000 years off on all his history dates and a book report due the following day had not even been started. The homework dragged on from before supper right up to bedtime. What could I say to this child? The situation seemed so hopeless that I attempted to write down the ideas that would express my feelings to him.

When Kent was clean and sitting pajama-clad in bed, I'm sure he expected a lecture on doing better on his school work. I sat on the edge of his bed and we chatted — well, mostly I talked.

"We didn't seem to get as mad at each other today about your homework. I guess it's because we saw that there was an awful lot to do and no time to waste in being angry.

"I'm certainly glad that you confessed right off the bat that you had forgotten the spelling words. That, at least, gave us time to call your friend and get them. That's really a sign of growing up, that you were willing to own up and find a solution. And I noticed tonight that although you had to erase and re-write some of your sentences two or three times, you really didn't grumble over it.

"We'll have to do better about these book reports. You like to read, so would you like me to remind you to read over the weekend so that you won't have so much to do the night before the book report?

"And I did notice that you cleared the table of all your books and papers and pencils and scraps. I really appreciate your tidying up after your homework.

"I think you're sleepy tonight. Remember how you told me that you never like to go to bed? I think tonight you really welcome your nice, cozy bed."

Never in the conversation did I suggest to Ken that I approved his homework methods. Instead, I pointed out those small areas where some improvement had been made. The important thing we realized was that there was a problem to be tackled and overcome, but despite it all, I loved him.

He threw his arms around me and kissed me goodnight. In the morning he remembered to thank me for the help of the night before and even asked me to test him once more on the dates! The following week he remembered the spelling words and also showed me the library book he intended to read over the weekend. We'd made some progress — not a lot — but progress nevertheless... and so often our gains are small ones.

With children like Kent, it may take many such sessions to see actual progress. But we can't give up. If parents lose faith in the child's ability, how can they expect the child to have self-confidence? How important to give our children the hope that they can do things right, that they are improving even though the improvement may seem infinitesimal to us.

Whether a child is slow, average or fast at catching on to the challenges of growing up, we must see that he has an appetite for and a healthy portion of success, satisfaction and security. These are not the "desserts" of the meal we prepare for him, but the very "meat and potatoes" on which he grows.

5
Creating The Right Home Atmosphere

We have a family meeting each Sunday afternoon. This is an hour or so of conversation among children and parents on important events of the week, matters of religion and ethics, plans for the future and comments on the successes or failures of the past. (We'll talk more about the family meeting in a later chapter.)

The topic one Sunday was, "What does the family mean?" Each child was told to write down in advance what family and home meant to him. Mark was in kindergarten and when it was his turn to read, he rose seriously, unfolded his paper and read this sentence, phonetically printed out: "HOEM IS A PLACE WARE YOU CUM TO BE LUVD WEN THEY CALL YOU FATSO AT SKOOL." We didn't know whether to laugh or weep! There followed an interesting discussion on the difference between living in a home and living in a hotel. Both places provided beds, meals, protection from the elements. But what was the difference between the relationship of the people living in the hotel and those living in a family? Of course, the difference the children noticed was that the people in the family loved one another. They did things for each other, sometimes with no apparent return, and could even help one another. This mutual love and concern needs to be built into our family relationship from babyhood onward.

Kent was late for a soccer game one day and looked for a sister or brother to help him finish his home tasks so he wouldn't hold up the game. Karen gave him that line, "Why should I help you?" He was quick to tell her, "We don't live in a hotel, you know." Unselfishness is quickly taught!

The right home atmosphere includes relatives and friends beyond the home center. In growing up it is important for our children to know older people so that they can be at ease with them and learn from them. When our children were young, we lived thousands of miles from any relatives. Since this was the case with many of our friends and neighbors, it was not uncommon for children to have what are called PGPs — Proxy Grandparents. Among our friends our children had three or four couples that were like aunts and uncles, and the children of those couples became proxy cousins.

Many of our simple family activities can include other children and often other families. Our children need to know other families as a whole and see other parents in action. School teachers, Scout leaders, Sunday school teachers, elderly neighbors, childless friends, and those with grown children can help our own children to see many points of view, ways of life, interests and talents. A child shouldn't grow up thinking his family's tastes and ways are the only and best! Association with other adults and families is not an occasion to compare (and show how good we are) but to broaden our child's outlook and to put him at ease in a large setting.

HIS OWN ROOM

An essential element in creating the right home atmosphere for a child is his own room or a place of his own within a room that he shares with another child. If a child cannot have his own bedroom, then it's important that there be a definite division of space in the room that he shares with a brother or sister. This is not only emotionally essential to the child but it also helps to avoid arguments if children sharing a room know exactly which drawers and shelves belong to each. You may want to label the drawers and shelves so there is no doubt!

A child's bedroom should be more than a place to lay his head at the end of a busy day or to sit at his desk and knock out his homework. In essence, it is his own little house. His room should be exactly as he wants it within the limits of your guidance. In other words, order should be restored once a week and the bed should be made and clothes picked up daily. The room itself should reflect the creative abilities of the child. Often the child's room in a newly-purchased house has carpet, wall colors and draperies. The child is given some furniture. And that's it — without any consideration for his tastes. But his own personality can be overlaid on this set scene.

If he wishes to rearrange his room in a unique way, let him do so. See that he has a wall area on which he can express himself, whether it be a corkboard or an area where he's permitted to tape or tack items even though the wall may be damaged. If he has a bulletin board or display area, help him keep it fresh and timely.

Take a yearly look at each child's room to see how it can be upgraded. Sometimes a new bedspread, a picture on the wall or just a change in a chair cushion can add zip. After a big housecleaning, help him figure out a new way to arrange his desk, bureau, bed and toys. We usually think one room plan looks best but a child will want to try three or four different arrangements.

A child should be encouraged to really *use* his room. With a comfortable chair in it, it should be a place where he can go to enjoy himself in quiet. Rather than throw away some old tables, we spray painted them for each child's room. We cut the legs down so that a child can sit on the floor to play at the table. Kent built an entire city on his table one week and turned it into a race track the next. Karen usually had her dollhouse on her table. Wendy cut out many a new dress on hers, while Mark used his for showing off a collection of shells. By encouraging our children to really use their rooms and not merely keep them for sleep or show, we give them places to express their creativity and ability to make their own cozy spots.

A child's room is definitely not the place he's sent for punishment. If a child has to be given solitude, don't make him sit cross-legged in his own room. Let him go to the corner of the laundry room, so that if he has any unhappy associations, they will be about the laundry rather than about his own personal castle!

A PLACE FOR PROJECTS AND HOMEWORK

There are two important spaces that every child needs and these should be established in his own room, in a family room or other room of the house. These two areas are his creative corner and his homework spot. Don't try to combine work and play! The creative corner should be in an area where his materials need not be frequently moved or removed. He should be allowed to have some place where he can make a mess if he chooses and not have to clean it up immediately or even at the end of the day or week. A place for continuing projects is essential to reinforcing the creativity of children.

Equally important, though, is a spot conducive to doing homework. Some children work well at a desk in their own bedrooms. If a desk cannot be provided, a card table and a shoe box for pencils and rulers is good. It should be an area free from distraction, a table cleared of everything except the project at hand. Let's be sure not to place obstacles in the path of our student by making toys or TV convenient during the homework session.

Kent had a difficult time keeping his mind on homework. For this reason, we established what we call "study hall." We had a large table in our family room, an old dining room table, in fact, and for an hour each day, before or just after dinner, all the children did their homework together in the quiet atmosphere of a study hall. The children who had no homework were invited to sit and read quietly. The discipline of one quiet hour is good, and we parents, in the same room, were able to catch up on our correspondence, pay bills, read the newspaper, and have some leisure time for quiet thought. TV time might follow but did not preceed study hall. We found that well-established study habits gradually paid off in higher grades and more joy in the subjects being studied.

In support of education in the home, a modern encyclopedia is essential. It is expensive but will save endless trips to the library as the children grow older. Sometimes a set in good condition can be purchased secondhand from a family where the children are grown. Some encyclopedias have yearbooks and referral stickers for the existing volumes to keep them up-to-date. But encyclopedias don't go out of date rapidly and even a ten- to twenty-year-old set is useful, both for children and parents. An atlas or a globe is helpful; and if there's a place where a large map can be pinned to the wall, this is a good idea, too.

Here, then, is a checklist to see how your own home rates as having the proper equipment for a growing child.

1. The child's own room, or area of a room
   A. Drawers or shelves for his own clothing
   B. Cupboards or shelves for his personal belongings
   C. A display place. This can be shelves or a cork board on which the child can show off things that he has made or drawn. Celotex or cork insulation tacked to the wall of a child's room will give him a place to put up his important drawings and papers and his favorite pictures and posters. A shelf for models or dolls or other collector's items is also advisable.
   D. A place for precious things. A child can be taught to respect another's privacy. One way to do so is to provide a really secure place for valued items. Some children like a box with a little padlock. Others are content with a file folder or a shoe box they can tape shut. In this can be diaries, old pictures, that important library card, the key to one's piggy bank, a special letter from a friend, membership cards and awards, and other items the child deems worthy of keeping. NOTE: These are important to the *child*, not necessarily to the parents.

2. A study area
   A. Desk or card table
   B. Adequate lighting
   C. Resource materials, such as an encyclopedia and an up-to-date dictionary
   D. A supply box or drawer with the child's own pencils, rulers, scissors, tape and crayons. He is responsible for the care of these items and for replacing them as needed.
   E. A globe, atlas or map

3. A reading corner. A cozy area with good lighting, it should be con-

venient to a shelf where the child can keep his own volumes or current library books, and where magazines of interest to him can be placed. Children love new things, and they also like getting mail. When a grandparent or friend asks for a gift idea for a child, magazine subscriptions are ideal.

4. The craft area. This can be a table or counter where a child's continuing project — whether it be drawing or model-making or sewing — can be carried on but not disturbed by other family members.

5. An outside area of his own. Except for apartment dwellers, every child can have some area of the yard that is considered his own. Here he can pitch his own tent without ruining the lawn, dig without upsetting flower gardens, make a clubhouse out of old boxes or climb a tree. Naturally, such a place is often unsightly, but the more out-of-the-way it is, the more the child likes it. Although we have purchased climbing and swinging equipment for our children, our most used outdoor toys are homemade: an old-fashioned rope and board swing in a tall tree, a wooden ramp that the boys enjoy with their miniature cars, and a commodious tent made out of old sheets and bedspreads.

Too often we think the answer to giving our children a proper atmosphere is the purchase of some toy or other object. But for long-lasting satisfaction, the making of something (maybe not as beautiful) is far more effective. Haven't you seen a creative child follow the directions for a toy or game for a while, then enjoy it far more when he breaks with the traditional rules and uses the parts of the toy for some completely different purpose? At first glance, this may seem destructive, but this stems from our old-fashioned training regarding neatness and following the rules!

For example, Kent and Mark had a small, motorized race track which they enjoyed conventionally for about a month. When Karen decided to get into the act, she added some houses from another game. Then Mark found some zoo animals and fencing from a third game, and Kent decided to build a second level superhighway over the raceway to make it more like real superhighways. A whole city was created in the playroom! Even a cablecar toy was brought in as a third dimension. The newly-created conglomeration of toys became a popular neighborhood attraction, to the point that the floor under the city was not swept for nearly six weeks. But what marvelous times they all had playing with this "new toy!"

Flexibility and cheerfulness in parting with certain areas of the house for children's activities make the difference between a home children enjoy and a home children avoid. If your child would rather play at someone else's home or always prefers to go to the park, it would be well to see what kind of a home atmosphere you've created for your child and his friends.

22

Your Week One Check List

- Live spontaneously — have fun with your family
- Prepare a daily plan for yourself including time for
  - ☐ work
  - ☐ children
  - ☐ spouse
  - ☐ self
  - ☐ out-reach
- Organize your headquarters with necessary equipment including
  - ☐ calendar
  - ☐ message-center
  - ☐ filing system
- Set up a child's list of morning priorities including
  - ☐ wash
  - ☐ make bed
  - ☐ dress
  - ☐ tidy room and bathroom
  - ☐ put clothes in wash
  - ☐ brush teeth
  - ☐ do assigned helps
- Start stressing the three S's
  - ☐ success
  - ☐ satisfaction
  - ☐ security
- Check your house and see that your child has a place for
  - ☐ personal possessions and clothes
  - ☐ homework
  - ☐ projects, crafts
  - ☐ reading
  - ☐ outside play

You've got a great start. Now, onward to Week Two!

Week
Two

2
2
2
2
2
2
2
2
2
2
2
2

What Kind
Of Characters
Are We Designing?

When Wendy had completed the first few months of kindergarten, conference time arrived and I could hardly wait to learn the teacher's impressions of Wendy. Like every interested parent, I was hoping I would hear that Wendy had caught on quickly, was obedient, cheerful, drew well, shared toys and ate lunch neatly. To my surprise, the teacher took the entire interview to tell me an aspect of Wendy of which I was unaware.

She said that early in the school year, when the children were adjusting to school routine, some spent a good deal of time sitting — or crying — in a corner of the kindergarten. Although I had counseled Wendy on her own behavior and attitudes toward this new experience, I had not particularly mentioned anything for her to do for the other children. So, I was not prepared for what the teacher said. Wendy had put her arms around one crying girl, told her she would be her friend and suggested that they go and paint together. She reminded another child that he was never alone and that even when no one else was around, God was with him. Gradually working her way from child to child, this self-designated assistant teacher was able to calm three or four children each day and interest them in the various activity areas. The kindergarten teacher said this went on for several weeks.

Of course I was pleased, even more than if I had been told that Wendy was the best artist in the kindergarten or the most ready to read. Here was a small reward for the many quiet lessons we had given the children on what sort of people we wanted them to be.

Children are great mimics. Much of their character is derived from what they believe to be the proper thing to do, as a result of watching their elders. On the other hand, much character building goes on between brothers and sisters and friends. Our reactions to what our child does with these peers, and our guidance when asked what should be done, are just as important as setting the proper example. Don't over-react to their actions nor under-react and fail to correct or praise. I'll use leadership as an example.

I once noted that Wendy was always the leader in her group's play. If someone was to build something, she'd build it. If someone was to have a speaking role, that was Wendy. When they played house, she was mother. When they raced cars, she was the judge of the winner. I realized that this was because she, being the oldest at home, was used to taking leadership. So I made opportunities for the younger children to lead and she to follow. And, at the right time, I chatted with her about the importance of letting friends lead — that we didn't want to deprive them of the opportunity to lead, even if the leading wasn't as well done. The importance of being a cooperative follower was stressed.

On the other hand, Mark, being the youngest, usually went along agreeably with the others. He never tried to lead until I began to give him leadership opportunities at home. As the older children went to school and he remained at home, he took on more leadership with his peers and in home activities. Now a collegiate, he is probably the best leader, perhaps due to or in spite of his many years of being the youngest.

Without formal classroom sessions, the home is where a child learns goodness and affection, honesty and poise, pride of ownership, unselfishness, manners, promptness, flexibility, respect for authority, good humor, willingness to be different and the desire to stand for principle. Obviously, these are not taught in a day or a week or a year, but they are aspects of character that are strengthened through daily experiences.

As you read this week, be aware of those good characteristics your child has mastered, but also be aware of where you have some reinforcing to do.

6
Is It Good To Be Good?

The standard preaching to children is: "Good has its rewards and wrong is punished." However, the child's-eye-view is: "Good has its rewards *sometimes* and wrong is *not always* punished." They see children (sometimes themselves!) getting away with wrongdoing. No matter how vehemently you insist that good has its rewards, *saying it* is not sufficient. Children are smart and quickly find what appears to be the exception to the rule. The decision to do the good and right thing, or the wrong thing, is one that a child must make dozens of times each day. And so, in his mental battles between good and evil, we have to give him plenty of ammunition for choosing the right thing to do.

Wise parents find daily occasions to point out to their children how making a difficult but *right* decision has brought its rewards:

"You remember how Wendy didn't wish to go to bed early the night before the test at school. But since it was such an important test, she finally agreed. And now look at her scores. She did very well on the tests and we are proud of her!"

"Kent took the quarter he found on the playground to the school office and how nice it was that the assistant principal complimented him on his honesty."

"Karen befriended a new girl who arrived during the middle of the first term, and now she has an invitation to attend her birthday party."

"Mark didn't argue with his friend over the sand toys at the beach today. What a good time they had! They were so pleasant that we stayed even longer than we'd planned."

As children become older, we can point out that sometimes good has no apparent reward, other than the satisfied feeling of knowing that we've done "the right thing." There need not and should not be a reward for every good deed.

When we point out that we do not always see the reward of doing good, it's easy to follow this by saying, contrary-wise, that we also don't always see the punishment that comes from wrong-doing. Sometimes it appears that something unpleasant happens after a child has done the

29

"right" thing. How important, then, to compliment him, to give him affection, and to reassure him that at least he has the satisfaction of having done what *he felt* was *right*.

Important to the relationship between parent and child is the child's realization that his parents are not infallible. A child should have faith that his parents are usually doing the right thing. However, when we have made a mistake, it can be an example of how doing the wrong thing brought the wrong result. Making supper one night, I used a baked round steak recipe, but I didn't bother to get the recipe out. At supper, when no one could cut the meat, I had to admit I had done the wrong thing. Everyone was good natured about it and in a few moments we were all eating hot dogs. However, it has proved a worthy example, both in the kitchen and in other areas of the children's experience, to point out that following the rules and doing the right thing usually bring about the right conclusion.

Remember the importance of praise for the obedient child. Having done the right thing, he must know we recognize and appreciate it.

Sometimes it helps children decide between right or wrong if we give them a few questions to ask themselves:

1. Does it make you feel happy?
2. Does it accomplish the job we are trying to do?
3. Does it make the others involved happy?
4. Would I do it again this way?
5. Would I do it this way if Mom and Dad were watching me?
6. Am I proud of what I'm doing?

Note the question: "Would I do it this way if Mom and Dad were watching me?" This may involve an element of fear. Don't teach a child to be good merely out of fear of what would happen if he is bad. Rather than making him afraid of what will happen to him for wrong-doing, give him the security that is his from doing the good and right thing. Sometimes when a child has done something wrong, rather than punish him, you can merely say, "I would certainly never praise you for doing that," or "I know you won't wish to do that again," or "Could we have forseen this bad result?"

History and literature provide ample examples of people who have done what might have seemed wrong or difficult, but what they knew in their hearts to be right, and how eventually, sometimes years later, they were rewarded. From Dick Tracy to Don Quixote we have to emphasize "doing good" and the happiness and satisfaction that it brings.

Sometimes our children do wrong unintentionally or because of clumsiness. We should differentiate between these mistakes and purposeful wrongs. Our handling of these unintentional errors is entirely different from the discipline we invoke when a child has willfully made a wrong decision. This discipline can be as light-handed as a suggestion as to how to do it correctly. Teaching goodness to a child is basic to teaching all character traits.

7

I Love You!

One night when Karen was going to bed after a day when she had frequently been naughty, she said to me, "Tell me that again, about how much you love me." She wanted to hear the words "I love you" and "I like you best when you're good but I love you even when you're naughty."

It is never the child that we dislike but the wrong that he has done. The minister who married us had many wise things to say but the one that I remember particularly is his statement, "Never end a day without reaffirming your love." This is certainly true of the husband-wife relationship, but equally true of the parent-child relationship. No matter what experiences the day has brought, at the end of each day we should reaffirm to our children our love for them.

Love is taught daily by example and by observation, in many little and big ways, in the things that we do for each other, and the things that we let others do for themselves.

PRINCIPLE AND LOVE

A dear family friend and I were chatting about the importance of discipline in raising children. She said, "Principle without love is an iceberg; but love without principle is a jellyfish." This has become a favorite saying of mine, for in raising children we cannot be all principle — like an iceberg — nor can we let our love for our children permit us to be jellyfish and let them do wrong.

What do I mean by *principle?* Start with the dictionary definition: a basic truth or standard, especially of behavior. Thus, principle embodies our teachings concerning standards, home rules, ethics, morals, rights and wrongs, obedience, and to some extent conformity to basic social graces.

Picture an old-fashioned scale. In the balance on one side we put principle. However, for perfect balance it must have an equal portion of love. It says in the Bible that love is the fulfilling of the law, and of course

32

modern children are bombarded with the message of love for one another. How then, as parents, can we take these urgings to be loving and combine them properly with principle, with law?

Within the family circle love takes on three aspects: love between parent and child, love among the children, and love between the parents. The love between parent and child should start at the earliest moments of life in order to have a strong foundation. Loving a child is sometimes all we can do. When words fail, when a child's world has fallen apart about him, to love him may be our only needed response. More than any other facet of character, love is shown by example. It isn't something that we can easily lecture children about at the dinner table.

More difficult is encouraging love from child to child. Love doesn't need to be an embarrassing collection of words, for if you can't say it, at least you can show it. It's a parent's responsibility to point out to children opportunities for them to show love and affection for one another. A parent may prompt one child to praise another for something fine that the other has done. When Karen and Mark were both of the toddler age, they usually played together and were very close. It was easy to suggest to the older Karen that she express affection and love for Mark. When he fell down while playing in the same room with me, I would very easily say to Karen, "Will you please comfort him for me," and to this day she naturally throws one arm around his shoulder when something is bugging him.

Being "our brother's keeper" is an aspect of love. It is gratifying to see one child helping another to complete a project, clean up a room, or get dressed to go somewhere.

A device I once used to teach concern and love for one another was to be a "secret friend." For several weeks, every one in the family, parents and children, was encouraged to secretly do surprising little favors for one another. There were no goals as to how many secret deeds one had to do. There was no recounting later of who had done the most. It was merely an unselfish act. During this time, one could expect to find one's bed made by a secret friend, a batch of cookies in the kitchen, a flower on the desk, the message "I love you" on a pillow at night, toys unexpectedly cleaned up, or the newspaper on Dad's chair. The number of things the children thought of to show love to another member of the family was spectacular!

The younger children were especially ingenious in doing secret deeds. Over several weeks of having secret friends, there was only one mishap. Mark must have felt he was behind in being a secret friend and was truly searching the house for good to do. When I checked an angel food cake baking in the oven, I found it a soggy mass at the bottom of the pan. Mark's good deed was to turn off the oven to "save electricity." Too bad he hadn't bothered to look inside! (It was rather good spooned over ice cream.)

Love from parent to parent should be natural and not confined to a farewell kiss in the morning and a welcome home one at night. Friends of ours with only one child have what they call "the family three-way hug" in which the father scoops up both his wife and his daughter for a welcome home greeting or "just because" kiss. Children need to be reassured that their parents love each other. Sometimes, when the only things that they hear are disagreements and reminders between parents, they may sincerely doubt that mother and father love each other. They may get the impression that marriage is dreary.

Much of our loving attitude can be shown in the way we speak to one another. If everything is a command or a shout, a child learns little about the importance of pleasant speech. We may have to remind *ourselves* daily at first, until the habit of expressing love to our children becomes natural. Certainly, we don't intend to be iceberg parents!

Physical expressions of love should start in early childhood, and many of them continue easily up through the teen years. Little children like lap sitting. How easy it is to read a book to a child nestled in your lap. Dad can watch an exciting TV show with both arms around his young son. A mother can say, "Here, sit on my knee while I brush your hair." When going for a walk or shopping, to hold a child's hand or, in the case of an older youngster, to put your arm around his shoulder, can become natural and normal. A morning kiss is easy to give and receive with younger children. But most every child enjoys the love expressed at the end of the day. The good-night hug says "I love you" despite everything that has happened during the day. There is something precious about going into a child's dark room at bedtime and reassuring him of your love and interest in all that he is doing. And if it's been forgotten before, this is an ideal time to express appreciation for the good the child has done during the day. Sometimes in the darkness of the bedroom, those who find it difficult to say "I love you" find it comes more easily.

We know a family who created a lovely tradition of replacing "Goodbye" with "Remember, I love you." This was the standard farewell to those going to work and school in the morning and was used at the end of telephone conversations and letters. We first became aware of this tradition when my husband was in this father's office and noticed a photograph of his family with the inscription, "Remember, we love you." We were so impressed with this family's affection that we have adopted this idea into our own tradition.

LOVE AND HATE

Children find it especially difficult to be loving when love meets no return. This is one aspect of love that we can teach — that even if it meets hatred, love is still the right response. The reaction or non-reaction of others doesn't change it. Despite what a mean or unloving playmate does, our child's responsibility is to be careful of his own reaction; and children must be taught that the loving thing is always the right course.

A young child and his friends often become entangled in noisy arguments during the course of an afternoon's play. Occasionally a parent is drawn into the discussion and asked to be the judge, even though not a witness to the incident. The parent may have sincere doubts whether either side is giving the true story. A simple, effective way to end these unpleasant occasions is merely to ask a child the question, "Did your actions show that you were loving?" Or, more simply, "Was that a loving thing to do?" The child wants a solution to the problem! And so it's easy to say to him, "What would be a loving thing for you to do?" This is a simple rule for action that the young child can grasp.

Children's books are full of marvelous examples of a child's love for animals, his less fortunate peers and the unloved of the world. From *Heidi* to *The Jungle Book,* children read stirring stories of the intrinsic rewards of love. Pointing out these examples to a child can reinforce his natural desire to be loving. The opposite of love — meanness and hatred — are foreign characteristics to a child and have to be taught to him.

Let us not go so far with love as to forget to combine it with the integrity of principle. We certainly wish to be neither iceberg nor jelly-fish. Many times during the day we must say or do things that may appear to our children to lack love. It is important that a child know why he is being punished.

Whenever possible give the child a reason for those requests that appear unreasonable to him. Add these lines to your vocabulary:

1. "I want to teach you this, because I wouldn't be a loving parent if I overlooked it."
2. "If I didn't love you, I'd just forget about this."
3. "I love you too much to let you do that."

There are times when a child feels so hurt or so wronged that the most beautiful explanation or rationalization in the world is meaningless to him. At this time, what he needs is our love. And when the love has healed the wound, then and only then can we speak to the wounded and try to correct whatever has caused the damage.

Children watch their parents very closely and so we in turn must be careful to realize how they may interpret our speech and action. Children forget that parents have their own disappointments, are often tired at the end of the day, and need reassurance themselves. A child may feel that something is wrong within himself and that he is unloved. We must be alert that our own upsets, pride or desire for obedience do not stand in the way of our true feeling of love for the child.

8
Are You
Telling Me
The Truth?

A trail of chocolate crumbs and foil candy wrappers led from the kitchen through the hall, up the stairs, and directly into Kent's room. I knew that Kent had not asked permission for any snack, and he was aware that I disapproved of eating while walking through the house. Distressed over brown chocolate smashed into green carpet, I followed the trail into his room where he sat placidly, chocolate on face, reading a book.

To a young child, the fear of being caught in wrong-doing is far greater than the fear of telling a lie, and in many cases a lie seems to be the easiest way out. Would you, at this point, ask the child if he had eaten candy and tempt him to lie? In the formative years, we want to make it as *easy* as possible for a child to be *truthful*. We don't want to set traps for him when we know he has done something wrong, nor do we wish to play district attorney and make it exciting for him to see how long he can withstand our barrage of skillful questions.

If Kent is asked at this point about the candy, he may feel it is necessary to deny that he's been snacking and even blame it on someone else. It's better in this case not to tempt the young child, but merely to say, "You must have been very hungry for a snack. You forgot to ask my permission to eat between meals." This makes it easier for the child to be honest and to admit that it was a matter of forgetfulness, not sneakiness.

However, the question of honesty versus lying is not always so easy. Sometimes we are not 100 percent sure of what we are being told by our children. So we have to create at home an atmosphere where telling the truth is always known to be better than telling a lie. Few parents have a perfect record here, and it is a daily challenge to make the telling of the truth attractive to a child. He must make many confessions that seem distasteful to him: "Yes he is the one who left the bike outside"... "Yes he does have homework to do"... "Yes it did seem like a good idea to hit his little brother."

Parental self-righteousness rises within us when a child has lied. We sometimes vehemently zero in on the fact that a lie has been told and we fail to find out why the child felt it necessary to lie. If we can get rid of the cause for the lie, we can get rid of the need to lie. Perhaps the child has left the bicycle outside because he has no respect for his property and he knows that when this bike is rusted, we will gladly buy another. Perhaps he is afraid that if he admits the quantity of his homework, he will not be permitted to see his favorite television program. Or perhaps we have not helped him to think ahead to see that he has adequate time to do all he wishes to do. Perhaps he finds it easier to lie about hitting his younger brother than to admit that they were arguing over a particular toy. The circumstances which caused the lie are important to discuss.

However, the lie itself must be pointed out to the child, with distinctness and clarity, as being the second mistake. In countless incidents between parent and child, the parent must reinforce the child's understanding that it is always better to tell the truth and to tell it as soon as possible. When a child has told the truth to the parent, the parent must acknowledge the fact that the truth was told and perhaps even say, "I know it was hard for you to tell me the truth, but I appreciate it. Now let's see what we can do."

LYING AND PUNISHMENT

When a child has found it difficult to tell the truth, but has told the truth, we must be sure that our reaction is more generous than it would be if the child had lied. Thus, he will see the benefit of having told the truth. This doesn't mean that he goes free for having done something wrong merely because he confesses it. But he must see that having confessed what he has done brings him less trouble than if he had lied about it.

We should verbalize this difference in punishment to our children. For example, we may say, "Because you admitted to me that you spilled the paint on the carpet, your punishment will be to clean it up completely. However, had you lied about it, you would not only have had to clean it up, but you would also have had the additional punishment of having no paint for your models for a month."

Sometimes children are just trying us to see if we're alert, and it is well to laugh and say, "You didn't really think I would believe that, did you?" By making it easy to tell the truth and by reminding children that a lie brings further trouble, we will find fewer and fewer lies being told.

Admit to the children that you are aware that there are some lies you never catch, but point out what continual lying is apt to teach them. Simply ask the question, "Since you got by with telling a lie that time, what would you do next time?" A child may be quick to answer, "I would do it again." And here he can see how one mistake can lead to another.

A child who has told a lie should not have it held over his head forever or be suspect to further lies. However, an honest parent can sincerely say to a child who has lied in the past, "I really want to believe what you are telling me now, but you disappointed me yesterday when I believed you and it turned out to be untrue. Can I really count on you this time?" Sometimes words are tumbling out of our children so rapidly that we need to ask them to stop and carefully recall exactly what happened, not what they *think* happened.

Occasionally we get dishonesty all out of proportion. We found that Kent disliked dessert but enjoyed small candy snacks. (This was aside from the after-school juice and crackers.) Remembering the ask-for-a-snack rule was difficult for Kent. We didn't want him to feel sneaky or dishonest about having his extra snack. Finally we reached an agreement: He would be permitted to take a certain amount of what he wished as long as he ate his meals and kept his teeth thoroughly brushed. In this case, we removed the need to lie until a time when he would be more able to control his desire and remember to ask for an extra snack.

We don't want a child to have obstacles placed in his way or to feel tense about being watched every moment. Telling the truth should become natural.

In a disagreement between two children when one is telling a lie and the other the truth, the question to be decided is not who is right or wrong, or who is honest or dishonest, but what is the right thing to do, what is the honest thing to do, what is the loving thing to do. Sometimes we can say to a child, "Would you feel that was fair and honest if you were in Mark's place?"

The main reason most children lie is fear of the consequences of telling the truth. So we have to let a child know what the consequences of admitting the truth or telling a lie will be. When he sees clearly that his punishment is little or nothing for telling the truth, then he can easily make the choice for himself. He can look at the situation and say, "I can tell the truth and this will happen," or "I can tell a lie and that will happen."

Young children often lie out of habit. They deny anything you ask them. It is important to make the telling of the truth a serious matter. Try removing the child from the situation, finding a quiet place where he can carefully think over what he has said or done. Give him the opportunity to change his mind or to tell the story again or to reconstruct the truth. Give him every opportunity to correct the mistake. We must be sure that we, deep in our hearts, *want* the child to tell the absolute truth and that we do not wish to trip him up on some minor fault so that we can give him a punishment out of proportion to the offense.

EXTRACT NO PROMISES

When the child has admitted the lie or been caught in it, don't make him promise never to lie again. This gives him a burdensome assignment. Merely tell him how disappointed you are and ask him to try hard not to lie again. The conversation should end with an affirmation that you appreciate all the times he tells the truth, even when it's difficult. For certainly, out of the thousands of statements that every child makes during the day, he is telling the truth the great majority of the time.

If you have several children, you can practice truth-telling. Have two children stage a little incident, no more than 30 seconds or a minute in length. A conversation or an exchange with a toy will be sufficient. Then have everyone write down or tell exactly what he saw and heard. You will find that everyone forgets part of what happened or sees it from a viewpoint that makes it appear different from others. This is a good way to point out the importance of being aware of all that is going on and the importance of not telling half truths.

Be sure to be as honest as possible in dealings with the child. He sees parents in charge of everything important in the home — very influential people in his life. But if he notes that we are dishonest in our relationships with him, he may assume that this is the best way to get the grown-up power and authority he desires.

Sometimes we are busy and forgetful, but the child doesn't realize this. With him we have to be honest about where we're going, whether it's to church or the hospital or a meeting. We must be honest in answering his question as to what we would do if he came home with a bad arithmetic grade, and we must be equally honest when we have promised him a reward. When a child says, "But Mother, you said...," we often wish to defend ourselves and deny that we have said certain things. However, if you are not absolutely sure, be gracious, defer to the child and respond, "I don't remember saying that, but if you say I did, I trust you — I must have said it." We have to be careful when we use this line, but it certainly is a morale builder for a child.

Let's tell our children regularly that we do trust them. Start with small things and say, "I trust you to put away your glass and plate after your snack...I trust you to go to bed obediently when the baby sitter tells you to...I trust you to go and take the 50 cents out of my purse."

Letting each child know that we believe in him and in his ability to be honest and good builds in the child the desire to be the very person we expect him to be. It makes him proud that he can be honest even when it is most difficult.

9
The
Poised Child

Because they enjoyed our company and liked conversing with the children, an older childless couple had invited us to dinner. On the way home, Wendy, then age 10, said, "We left just in time. I was on topic number five."

She was referring to our suggestion to the children that when going into a social situation they have five topics to discuss. Even a three-year-old can prepare to tell several items of interest. Wendy had done well. She had remembered to comment favorably on the special German pancakes and to inquire how they were made. She had shared a happening at a recent Camp Fire Girls weekend. She had asked what the cat and kittens did during the day and described a new pink dress she was sewing. Finally, after describing the differences between new math and old math, she had run out of topics.

Ability to cope with new situations determines poise in both children and adults. Much of this depends on verbal skills. A child or adult need not be able to give a two-hour monologue to fill a social evening. But how pleasant it would be if everyone we encountered had five interesting topics to discuss!

A child does not gain poise in social situations merely by going through the situation itself. Practice and preparation at home are essential. A child who acts deaf and dumb in public or conversely puts on an hysterically embarrassing and loud show (or even worse, a temper tantrum) is a child who has fears to be mastered. Lack of poise comes from the fear of looking foolish or the fear of making a mistake or the fear of the unknown.

A child seems natural and poised among his own friends in his own living room, at a movie theater where he has been before, or among loved aunts and cousins. However, that same child will seem like an entirely different person the minute he is placed in unfamiliar surroundings.

How important it is to give a child home opportunities that challenge him to think on his feet, to show his flexibility — his ability to speak and to act spontaneously. The testing of ability comes best on the home front

40

rather than in public. We should encourage our children to speak up at home, and, in turn, we should listen to them. Then, as uncritically as possible, we should suggest ways of improving.

This poise includes the knowledge that his appearance is acceptable and that he can cope with special events. Thirty seconds before a child goes out the door to a party is no time to tell him that his hair is messy and his package poorly wrapped.

ADVANCE PREPARATION

A good time to check out a child's preparedness for a strange event is in the car on the way to that event. Car time is greatly wasted, and if some preparation has been done at home, reminders in the car can help the child avoid embarrassment and mistakes. However, the preparation has to start at home. In the final moments before the event, let the child tell you what he thinks is expected of him.

For example, if we are taking a child to a travelogue in a large auditorium, at home we check in the encyclopedia to give him a little basic knowledge concerning the history of the country and some of the sights he may look forward to seeing in the film. We make sure that he's been to the bathroom and has on comfortable long pants so that the scratchy upholstery doesn't bother him. We run over with him how to greet friends that we meet at the travelogue, and of course we'll cover the basic social graces such as sitting still and not talking during the performance. We also remind the child that on the way home we'd like to hear what he thought of the film and what he learned from it. Having given this small amount of preparation at home, we can easily say to the child in the car, "Tell me how you think a good listener would behave at the travelogue tonight?" or "What do you think the man presenting the travelogue will expect of us?" In a few moments, most children will repeat back to you the need to be attentive and quiet, polite and appreciative. Experiences such as these, repeated time and time again, add to the child's poise, both at public functions and at home.

HOME TALK

The art of conversation need not be a lost art and we should encourage our children to give longer than one-word answers to questions. Be pointed in telling the child that no conversation consists entirely of commentary on bad news: hurricanes, automobile crashes and wars. Their conversation should include good news, questions on current events, and comments that show their awareness of other's interests.

Often a child misunderstands what a parent has said, has uneasy feelings, and so lacks poise. Or a child overhears only part of a conversation or hears parents losing their tempers and saying things that even they themselves do not believe.

When there is an emergency in the family, when someone is not feeling well, when father or mother is changing jobs, when there is some major worldwide upset — these crises should be discussed frankly with a child so he understands what is going on and what it will mean in his own sphere. While we don't dramatize trouble, we must not lie to children or try to whitewash what is going on. All too soon they will know as much as we do and lose confidence in us if we have not squared with them. If a parent knows the child is to have a tooth extracted, it's a great mistake to tell him the dentist is only going to clean his teeth.

For example, I once sent Kent off on his own to the dentist, with the understanding that one very loose tooth was to be removed, since the new one was already behind it. Unknown to me, the dentist found three loose teeth with three new ones already crowding them out and made three extractions. You can imagine that Kent did not quickly let me forget this particular incident and how I had led him into a strange situation unprepared.

COPING BRINGS POISE

Although one parent — or surrogate parent — usually tries to be home when the children return from school, a child should be prepared to know exactly what to do if no one is at home. Working parents should have definite plans for the child if their return home is later then the child's. I found that if I'm doubtful about my exact return hour, a cheery message on the kitchen table, along with glasses and a box of cookies, will reassure the children that all is well.

Once I had to be away unexpectedly and knew that six-year-old Kent would have no way to get into the house. With chalk I drew footprints from the back gate to the porch where I put a book, cookies and milk, so that he could occupy himself until I returned.

It's easy for a child to be poised in familiar home situations. The test comes when your child is involved in a crisis. This is when the poised child is the greatest asset and the panicky one a hazard to himself and others.

KEEPING CALM

One windy night a neighbor's home caught fire. Because the wind was so strong, sparks and flaming pieces of the roof blew our way with great ferocity. Because our roof was wood shake, we saw the need of defending our property. Without any panic, everyone was quickly organized into our own private fire brigade. In the darkness of the night, with sparks falling like rain, the older children worked on the roof with hoses, putting out any flaming material. The younger children filled pails with water to put out burning leaves and debris. It was an exciting and confusing time, yet none of the children expressed fear or panic and each one went about his assigned task with confidence and diligence. At one point I noticed Mark, whose pail was empty, calmly using his shoe to stamp out a small piece of flaming material that had landed near him.

Neighbor children were far more excited, but seeing the calmness of our household, they started to help. Thus occupied, they forgot their fears for their own homes. Karen gave watchful care and soothing conversation to a one-year-old baby who was rigid with fear.

When the fire was out and we not longer needed to protect our property, the children returned to their beds and a peaceful night's sleep free from fear. We later discussed and relived this experience and collectively applied its lessons for the future.

Clearly, poise is a quality we can give our children through example. Poise comes easily when a child knows what to expect or how to react to the unexpected. If lack of poise comes from fear of the unknown, we can give poise to our children by making them as knowledgeable as possible.

A little rehearsal of an event is often helpful to the child. When Karen was to perform in her first piano recital, we staged a mock recital in the living room. Karen, who usually went barefoot, put on the very shoes and ruffled dress in which she would be performing. She walked gracefully to the piano, seated herself, played, rose, bowed and left the room. She did this twice just for the family. During the second rehearsal, she completely stopped in the middle of the piece and said, "Oh, darn it!" This was a good opportunity to point out to all the children that when performing music or spoken word, the audience rarely catches our mistakes if we do not call attention to them ourselves through comments or facial expressions. An older Karen has proudly told me that when she has made a mistake in a play, she has remembered this first lesson and continued without being fazed.

SOCIAL TALK

Even four-year-olds can practice what to do when meeting and introducing people. Other procedures to rehearse are: shopping alone, what to say at supper and breakfast when staying overnight at a friend's, and appropriate comments to make when opening birthday presents or at a wedding.

Before his eighth birthday I had told Kent that he should say more than a mere "thank you" after opening the presents, and that he should think what to say should he get duplicate presents or something he already had. Later when he opened a game he already owned, he gave me a wink and announced proudly to the group, "This is a wonderful game. I really can't wait to play it."

A child who appears sullen, silent, shy or unpoised often may feel he doesn't have anything important to say. In some cases, a child's life is so passive that this may truly be so. Encourage him, then, to live adventurously so that he will have topics of interest to share in pleasant conversation. Ways to enrich his life is a topic we'll cover later.

Today's children have many opportunities to speak at school and at youth club meetings. It's easy to ask them to give us the talk the day before or at supper following. It's good experience and lets them know their assignments are important to us.

At our afternoon snack-and-tell times, I sometimes ask the children to share the highlight of their school day or something good that has happened. It's so easy for children to relate small, unhappy experiences on the playground and tales of mean teachers. How much more important that we help them recall the better events of the day! If a friend has sent a particularly interesting letter to the family, even the youngest readers can share in reading paragraphs from it —good practice in reading aloud.

When we traveled in Europe with the children, we did a great deal of advance study. Each Sunday afternoon in the two months beforehand, we met for an hour to cover some of the details of the forthcoming trip and the children reported on assignments given the week before. Making notes from travel folders and guide books enabled them to talk intelligently on the things we were going to see. This enriched the experience itself, but it also gave the children poise in sharing with others the countries and sights they had seen.

Upon our return, each of the four children presented an hour-long program to his particular classroom. Karen went further in giving her program to other grades, an auditorium convocation and finally an adult class.

Poise, of course, is much more than merely knowing what to say. Poise is knowing what to *do* under a variety of circumstances in strange places and in new experiences. Remember, we can't simply tell a child to be confident. We strengthen his confidence daily by being willing to listen to him; by letting him know that we feel his opinions are important; by assuring him that he is important to us and of value to the world. A poised person has self-esteem, and a child loses that when a parent is constantly criticizing or demeaning him.

FEAR

Fear erodes poise, so we must work closely with children to overcome fear. Wendy at one time was upset and afraid because she was going to a party where she knew only her hostess. The solution was simple: I saw to it that she arrived at the party five minutes early and thus was the first person there. She then had the opportunity to talk with her young hostess alone and to compliment her on her dress. As each additional girl came, she went out of her way to talk with the new arrival and to say something pleasant and complimentary to her. Arriving early put her on the inside track and let her meet the girls one at a time. The girls responded to her friendliness and she had a wonderful time at the party.

Kent was to stay overnight with a friend when he was still young enough that, excited and filled with several bottles of soda pop, he was apt to wake up wet in the morning. I could see that he was wondering how one would handle this problem in another person's home. I gave him several suggestions concerning the amount of liquid to be consumed in the afternoon and evening. I also told him that since it was the practice of boys at that age to keep their underpants on under their pajamas, he might just quietly wear three pairs and a pair of heavy pajamas. Should there be an accident, no one would notice. He slipped a plastic bag into his case so that should he be wet or damp in the morning, he could quickly roll up the underpants or pajamas and put them in the plastic bag in his case. He certainly didn't want to be made fun of by having a rubber sheet or plastic pants, and these precautions gave him the necessary confidence. They weren't even needed.

Karen often climbs into her father's lap if they are seeing a TV show that has a few scary moments in it. When the re-run of *Snow White and the Seven Dwarfs* came to town, Wendy reminded everyone of the terrible moment when the animated trees reach for Snow White. We decided when this point of the picture came on, it would be popcorn time. The younger children were so excited to have popcorn that they really couldn't wait for the spookiest part of the movie. When it came, it didn't seem as bad as the first time.

One of the most common fears of children is of the night. From babyhood, we have told our children that darkness is merely the absence of light and is nothing in itself. Don't succumb to the request to leave full lights on in bedrooms. See that the child's bedroom and bathroom have night lights. We have made little of dreams and nightmares and have expressed a great deal of love and affection to the children at bedtime.

Darkness should certainly not be feared. Take your children on moonlight walks to look at the stars and the night will take on a new dimension for them. When building a home we often came over in the evening before the electricity was on. The children were amazed at how much they could see and how well they could make their way around the house in the dark.

Each of our children has a flashlight in his night table since the area in which we live has frequent power failures. Because we spend time talking together in the dark and because our home is plunged into darkness several times a year, darkness has little effect on them except for the fun of using candles and flashlights.

One of their favorite games is hide-and-seek in the absolute dark. They are becoming so sure of themselves in the dark that having someone pop out of a shower stall or closet is no longer a fearful event for them. Nighttime hide-and-seek was played out-of-doors with another couple and their children on a vacation trip. This time we gave everyone a partner. Since we played this game on the first evening, the fear of going to the outhouse in the dark or sitting outside in the twilight evaporated.

Another fear we should be sure to settle with our children is that something could happen to the family unit. We should not emphasize the possibility of chaos and disaster, separation and death. Our words and actions should stress devotion and permanence. A child can be given the ability and poise to cope with almost any situation with youthful dignity.

When a child's importance and value has been reinforced for him by the parents, poise will be as natural to him as breathing.

45

10
"It's Mine!"

In an affluent society, teaching children pride of ownership and care of possessions is almost a daily battle. Many a child has such a variety of toys that if one is broken he can merely toss it away and play with another. Some children are restless and don't know what to do because they have so much.

Let's start with the child's observations of what his parents do. If he sees us casually denting our car, loading our closets and permitting home repairs to pile up, the child is likely to be numbed by this atmosphere and unthinkingly follow this pattern. So, we have to start with our own example.

Next, see that your child has really adequate places to keep his possessions. These need not be expensive cabinets. Plain shelving and boxes can do much to bring order to a child's room. Although many parents shudder over spending time in a child's room to help him organize his possessions, this is an investment that will pay off in years to come. When I make my twice-yearly "room search," with child-help, I come armed with spare boxes in which to place obsolete toys, rubber bands to put around cards that have lost their boxes, and even a label maker so that boxes can be marked to make locating toys easy.

For the child who keeps his clothes in a scramble, I have found that the shelf just above the hanging rod can be easily labeled "Shirts," "Pants," "Jackets," "Dress Clothes," "Jeans," etc. And don't forget to lower the hanging rod to let kids reach their clothes easily.

A child wants to keep many things just for the sake of keeping them. Sentimental as he may be over them, he probably will never again play with them. They clutter up his room and keep popping up unless we provide him with a good final resting place such as a box or a scrapbook.

When a child seems to lack pride of ownership, merely scolding him is not sufficient. We parents, older and wiser, should be able to look over the situation and find out what is causing the problem. Does he have too little time to put things away? Does he have inadequate storage space? Does he have too many toys?

START EARLY

A toddler in his playpen may start throwing and breaking his toys. Even at this age let him know that you do not approve of his purposely trying to break toys. There is a big difference between wearing out a toy by use and willfully destroying it. Our disapproval should also be shown when we see what others have done to destroy and deface our world. We can be seriously incensed when we see litter, graffiti, carved tree trunks and abandoned cars. Even the youngest child is now aware of ecology and pollution problems, and it is easy to show him how he is "polluting" his own home atmosphere.

To teach pride of ownership, punishment and shouting are rarely needed. This is one occasion where the punishment can well suit the "crime." Kent has finally learned he can't save time by tossing clean clothes, or clothing worn briefly, into the dirty laundry. He knows that mother's eagle eyes will spot this and because he has made extra work, he will be asked to be the great folder-of-the-laundry that week.

Mark is learning that shorts and jeans should not be sent into the wash inside-out, and it is just as easy and proper for the wearer to turn them right-side-out. After continual reminders on this irksome habit, I told him that I would no longer wash trousers that appeared in the laundry bin inside-out. He didn't take me seriously. Even after the threat, eight pairs of shorts and slacks appeared inside-out. I put them in a large grocery bag. About a week later, Mark appeared at breakfast in shirt and pajama bottoms. He could not imagine why his laundry had not been returned to him. With a straight face, I told him he was welcome to check the laundry room. He discovered the grocery bag with his entire wardrobe of pants inside-out. He spent breakfast-time turning them. I then promised to wash this special load that very day, but he would have to pick the cleanest of the dirty lot to wear to school.

The lesson was sufficient. Out of a dozen pairs of slacks and shorts that he turns in each week, rarely is more than one inside-out. He had learned that failing to care for possessions causes extra work.

Your child should know that you will not buy a continuous supply of belongings for him. Tell him you will buy his first bicycle (if you wish to do so and are able to do so) but afterwards the maintenance of the bike and the replacement of it if lost are up to him. The same goes for that all-important first wrist watch or doll buggy. Understanding this, your child is more apt to bring his prize possessions in out of the rain and to remember that important rule concerning jewelry: THERE ARE ONLY TWO PLACES FOR YOUR JEWELRY: ON YOU OR IN YOUR BOX. Any other place that a watch or ring or bracelet is found is wrong. I do not hesitate to collect jewelry left in bathrooms, on stairs or on counters. I give it back with a free lecture which always ends with the same lines: "There are only two places for your jewelry: On you or in your box."

47

Repetition will get the message through.

ROTATING TOYS

Don't hesitate to set aside some of the child's possessions for another time. After the joy of all the new Christmas or birthday gifts has worn off, sit down with your child and decide what he can conveniently play with in the next month. Then, in a box or on a top shelf in his closet, put the other items with the understanding that he can have them whenever he wishes, but also that this gives him something to look forward to, some new toys in a month or so.

Kent's birthday is near Christmas and the double windfall is great. He is most agreeable to stow away part of it to celebrate a second time, about the Fouth of July, with the bringing out of a big box of new possessions.

Encourage your children to rotate their toys. Often a child plays with the first thing he stumbles over! Sometimes it is well to put away all cars and trucks for a week and bring out puzzles and games. At our house the train set is considered a special toy, but one that gets out of whack quite easily. We bring the train out just twice a year. During that time the entire playroom is taken up with the train and all its accessories. When everyone is surfeited with playing with the train, we are content to put it away for another six months.

When a toy is new, it's a good investment to spend five minutes so *you* understand how the toy works or how a new game is played. Encourage the child to read the instructions to you and then let him demonstrate all that the toy can do or how the game goes. Children get the most out of toys when they follow directions. They can be inventive and do other things with toys and games later, but it's well first to understand what the wise inventor had in mind!

Now, what about the familiar sight of two children, each holding on to the same toy and yanking it back and forth between them? Too often, parents rush in to settle these childish arguments when there is no need to do so. Children will quickly find that there is something else to play with and that fighting over one toy really doesn't settle the question at all. Of course, if you're dealing with a stronger child who is constantly taking away things from a weaker or younger child, then the parent should step in.

However, there comes a time when there is a one-of-a-kind family toy and a parent may have to legislate by saying that a child can play with it for ten minutes and then it must move on to the next child. We have found this especially necessary with large water toys such as swim rafts. We suggested the ten-minute rule. Now the children legislate the sharing themselves.

Let grandparents know that they need not give identical toys to their grandchildren. Make it clear to the children that they are equally loved and equally "gifted" but the gifts are different to each child. When children argue over toys, settle it quickly with the question, "Who owns it?" The owner has the right to do with the toy as he chooses. (Sharing it is something we will talk about in the next chapter.) Or a parent can say, "Isn't this something that you could play with together?" Bring out similar toys. If the boys are fighting over one truck, finding several other trucks creates a far more interesting game or play.

SHOWING OFF

Pride of ownership can also be built by giving the child opportunities to show off his possessions. A wise parent might say to a visiting child, "Have you seen Karen's new puppet? It's very precious and tangles easily, but I'm sure she'd be happy to show it to you." Or "Did you see Mark's setup of cars and trucks? He spent a great deal of time making garages and parking places for all of them, and it's certainly something that you will want to play with."

When grandparents or older interested friends visit the home, encourage the children to take them to their rooms or play area to show a new game or doll. Wendy collects dolls and keeps a record of the date, place and giver for each one. The grandmothers have been generous in buying elegant dolls for her, and she is careful to see that the dolls are clean and perfectly clothed, with coiffures in shape.

While pride of ownership is essential, teach the child also that possessions are merely tools for increasing intelligence, happiness and usefulness and that *possessions* are not happiness or usefulness in themselves. Thus when the child has outgrown a toy, it is time to pass it along to another. Or when it is sufficiently worn out, it is time to throw it away.

Kent is our best example of the unimportance of worldly wealth and possessions. Several years ago his housekeeping was extremely bad, to the point that every gimmick or threat or cajolery that we could think of did no good. One day it was just beyond me, and I took all his things and packed them into several boxes. All that remained in his room were his bed, empty shelves and his essential clothing. You can imagine how surprised Kent was when he first discovered that I had had enough of his messy housekeeping. However, not being particularly interested in his material possessions, he certainly was not at all upset. He found in the corners and crevices of his room rubber bands, paper clips, a battery, etc. and being an other-worldly creative child, he played for more than an hour with make-shift toys. Next day he began to miss some of his possessions. I let the first comments come from him.

His first question was when was he going to get his belongings back. I quietly told him that he could earn them back by taking good care of what he had. Thus, if the paper clip or battery or rubber band contraption was not in the middle of the doorway so that I slipped on it when I entered his room, he could at the end of that day request a particular toy's return. Each day it would be the same. If he had taken care of what was in the room, he could retrieve one more item. This sytem gave him an opportunity to think over carefully what he owned and earn and request what meant the most to him. I never objected to toys on the floor as long as they were part of an on-going game or project. I would, however, take the toy back if I found it abused or just left in a mess somewhere.

It took Kent only a few weeks to see that I was serious about his not taking seven or eight card games and mixing up all the cards and leaving them scattered throughout the house; that I did not like finding books in the bathtub or hidden under the bed; nor would I abide dirty underwear rolled up and stuffed into camping packs. As his toys gradually came back, Kent found convenient places for each of them. Thus the order in his room was not something handed down to him but something he created himself. This was far better than my placing his possessions where I thought they best belonged. What he wanted for reading or play in bed before going to sleep, he put in his night table. Other projects he intelligently distributed to his play table, desk, cupboard, shelves and closet. At last he had a clear picture of everything he owned. Some of his belongings he had forgotten. Others, outgrown, he was willing to hand on to his younger brother. Still others, he discovered, were so far demolished that it would be best not to waste storage space on them but to merely consign them to the junk pile.

The proper ending to such a story would be that Kent turned out to be the neatest person in the family and that I never again had to speak to him on the subject. As every parent who reads this book realizes, this of course is not true. Of the four children, Kent is perhaps still the most disorderly. He does, however, value his possessions more and while conditions in his room are rarely perfect, they have never reached anywhere near the chaotic condition of the day I acted so drastically. The lesson was observed by the other children and even the youngest has been known to remark that he certainly does not wish me to come in and pack up his room!

In teaching pride of ownership to our youngsters, we want to be sure we never place the value of an item so high that they feel it best never to use it but rather just horde it. We should show that it's normal and natural that items become worn, broken and need to be repaired or tossed away, also, that a toy that has been loved and used is fulfilling its purpose. There is nothing shameful about a worn book, a well-loved doll, or a truck with chipped paint.

11
"It's Yours!"

It was a party day for Wendy. Her six friends gathered eagerly around the table to watch the opening of the gifts, each child pushing her gift forward in hopes that it would be opened next. One guest stood back from the group with seeming disinterest. She appeared to be worried. As each package was opened, it was such fun to see the happiness of the giver when Wendy expressed pleasure over the selection. Many of the children knew how to operate the toys and games and were eager for Wendy to share their enjoyment. Finally, she reached the package brought by the reluctant guest. When it was opened the guest said, "Oh, so that's what Mother wrapped!" We then realized that this guest had not known what she was giving and had missed all the fun of choosing, wrapping and waiting to share her pleasure with another.

One of the most satisfying character traits is the joy of making another person happy, not merely by giving something to him, but, even better, by doing something for him. Unselfish concern for others can be instilled in the youngest children by the careful parent who creates opportunities for putting others first.

When young friends turn up for our afternoon snack-and-tell time, it's our tradition that the host child asks his guest to choose from the variety of snacks that we keep on hand for this fifteen-minute session. The guest chooses the kind of fruit we all eat and whether we will drink juice or milk. In dozens of small ways we can help our children to be unselfish. Sometimes the lesson can be emphasized by asking our children what they hope would be done for them in a similar situation.

One day when Mark was rushing to get ready for school and had forgotten to feed the fish, Karen graciously offered to do it for him. We were pleased to hear him shout down the hall, "I'll do something for you sometime!"

When we were visiting friends in Switzerland, Karen was playing with her Swiss counterpart at our friends' summer home. Few toys were available for the two girls, but there were dolls and some doll clothes. For two hours these two, who could not speak each other's language, played together without a single raised voice or attempted argument. As we rode back to our hotel that evening, we questioned Karen as to how the play had gone on so well. She answered ingenuously, "We just loved each other so we knew what to do to make the play happy."

USING THE GOLDEN RULE

The Golden Rule, "Do unto others as you would have them do unto you," is a good guide for unselfishness. However, children are quick to point out that often they do an unselfish thing and never see the good deed come back to them. And so it is well to point out that unselfish acts are in themselves the right thing to do, and that they may not always be returned immediately and equally.

As a child grows up, he comes to his parents for many things that can be referred to an older brother and sister, thus encouraging one to help another. An older child can help the younger comb his hair, learn to tie shoelaces, wash and press doll clothes, or use a hammer or pliers.

Sometimes we shield our children from the world and they do not see the importance of unselfishness because they think everyone has as much as they have. However, some children tend to give away their possessions to friends and almost complete strangers in an attempt to buy friendship. One week Mark came home from school every day with a new, small wind-up car. After some calm questioning I found that the boy providing Mark with the toys was hoping he would be invited over to play. Mark wasn't particularly keen on this boy and it took a bit of encouragement on my part to have him return the toys. Some weeks later, Mark, without any bribery, had the boy over to play and the relationship has been a happy one.

In teaching sharing and putting others first, be alert to occasions when our young ones confuse generosity with letting themselves be intimidated. Wendy associated with a small group of girls who picnicked together. Because of her outgoing nature, she seemed either to volunteer for or be assigned to bring the homemade cookies for every picnic, while the others brought a loaf of bread or a bag of potato chips or a hand of bananas. When it was pointed out that she was depriving them of the opportunity to create and share something, she gained enough courage to suggest next time that another girl be the gourmet cook.

GETTING AND GIVING

Wendy said to me one Christmas, "You know, Mother, I must be growing up. I'm most excited *this* year about the things I'm *giving* — even more than about the things I hope to *get!*"

Sometimes parents do so much for their children and *legislate* sharing to such an extent that the child doesn't learn spontaneous sharing.

Youngsters can be taught to share the same bathroom and to leave the counter and washbowl in good shape for the next user. They can be taught to share hymnals at Sunday school and hold them at a desirable distance for both children. When one box of caramel corn is available for several children, parents need not make the division. This is a good opportunity for children to learn equitable portions. In teaching two children how to "divy up," there is merit in the old system of letting one child divide the "goodie" and giving the other first choice.

Children know instinctively what is fair. I overheard an amicable conversation in the playroom one day when several boxed games were brought out. The two players decided that the one who selected the first game to be played would not choose again until the fourth game. Thus, the person who didn't get first choice got both second and third choices.

Sometimes our interference in arguments where selfishness prevails can best be settled by *not* solving the problem for the children but merely telling them to work out among themselves what seems to be a fair decision. Rather than legislate, say to the arguers, "You work out a fair plan and if you wish, check it with me before you put it into action." Children thus learn to be problem-solvers without shoving decisions onto others.

With unselfishness as with other character traits, our own example is important. Sometimes parents need to "toot their own horns" to show that a family has to be unselfish if it is to be a happy and efficient unit. Mark was being stubborn about picking up a game he insisted he had not brought out. It helped to point out that Mom and Dad shared their earnings with the whole family; that whoever was cooking that night did not make just a lamb chop for himself but cooked enough for all; and that the table-clearer took everyone's dishes, not just his or her own. The other children jumped into the conversation to tell what they did for the good of the group. It wasn't long before Mark sighed and went off to pick up the game.

DON'T BE THE LITTLE RED HEN

How many glasses of milk are spilled in the years of raising children! I used to leap up to get paper towels and mop up the mess since I knew I, like the little red hen, could do it best and quickest myself. A child who has knocked over a glass is usually too stunned by the mess to move! But, I can be especially complimentary to the other child who first sees the need and fills it. Let's not move so fast that we deprive our children of opportunities to be helpful.

In looking for something good on which to compliment a child each day, the child that has done something unselfish or not strictly necessary is one who gets a great deal of praise at our house. Unselfishness should become so natural that a child's goodness doesn't take you by surprise. Truly unselfish acts are never done with the idea of getting something in return. Wendy set the table one afternoon and when I complimented her on it in front of the family at supper, she blushed and said, "I just saw you were busy —the others would have done it if they'd been home." The other children quickly agreed and the point was not lost on them.

Unselfishness cannot be taught in a few moments. Sharing can't be taught in the car while delivering a child to a friend's house to play. It has to be taught in the minutiae of daily living. All that can be done at the last minute is to remind the child of the rewards of an unselfish nature.

12
Thank You
And More

The polite child is a joy to his parents and a shining star to other adults. But politeness is hardly a quality which means much to children. Politeness is a learned trait that must become second nature to the child, for he seldom sees its direct benefits.

The teaching of politeness starts in babyhood and "thank you" should be among the first words a child learns. Since toddlers are mimics, we have to say thank you to them to teach them to say thank you to us. The many polite phrases used in our society should become so natural to our children that they don't even need to think about them. This means that phrases such as "thank you," "excuse me" and "please" have to be used at home so that they become automatic away from home. Why should we be any nicer to our friends than we are to our family?

Here are six opportunities for parents to teach their children "thank you" and more:

1. **Written Thanks.** When a child has received a gift or been taken to a play or granted some other special favor by someone outside the immediate family, the child should write a brief thank-you letter. See that he has inexpensive stationery and envelopes suitable to his age, with lines for the younger ones. These thank-you letters need not be a chore. If a child is used to having a quiet time or study period each day, this activity fits in easily. Even a six-year-old can do the entire project himself — the licking of the stamp, the sealing of the letter, and the searching out of the proper address in the family address book. The youngest child, speaking in the simplest sentences, can dictate to you a short letter of thanks. A few questions from you will stimulate his prose. As to length, a good guideline is one sentence per year of age of the child. Use this as a minimum requirement and even the youngest can figure out how long his letters should be. Teach your child that a thank-you letter sounds best when appreciation for the favor or gift is expressed both at the beginning and again at the end.

Writing letters should be fun for the child and not necessarily an exercise in good grammar, spelling and penmanship. The child should be alerted to these three areas, but a sincere message is more important. If the child's letter is legible and fairly neat, the recipient can figure out what the message is despite misspellings. I would rather receive a spontaneous letter that I knew the child wrote happily than one that had been erased so much that I knew the child was nearly in tears by the time he finished thanking me for the gift.

A friend of mine makes note writing fun for her children by using the letters of the child's name or the person to whom the child is writing. If the child has been on a trip, he might use the name of the place he has visited. These letters are printed vertically down the left side of the paper. The child then fills in sentences after them. My friend says this method produces spontaneous and amusing letters. For example, Dick Jones might write:

Dear Grandma,
I hope you can visit us again soon.
Can we go swimming?
Kite flying is starting now in our neighborhood.
Just wait until you see my new skateboard.
On Monday we went shopping and bought it.
News from you is always welcome.
Eat lots of those good strawberries for me.
Sincerely, Dick

You can do the same thing using the letters *Dear Grandma* or *California* or *Happy New Year.*

Pre-school children can be shown the words "Thank you" to copy and can illustrate their notes with original drawings. This means far more to the giver than a letter from the parents or a heavily erased letter that appears to have been written under duress.

Letters pile up at the year-end holidays, so several days after Christmas, I list for each child those letters he needs to write. Then I figure out how many days until school starts again. The child is given the option to write his notes all at once or to write at least two or three a day so that by the time he goes back to school all are done. Writing the letters right then, while the toys are being played with, makes them much more creative and spontaneous. Even amid holiday fun, most children are willing to give 15 or 20 minutes daily to this obligation. Make letter writing a pleasant time, with many of the family writing simultaneously, perhaps with a background of good music, a favorite television show or a fire in the fireplace.

2. Verbal Thank-you's. Sometimes written thanks are unnecessary if the child remembers to give his thanks in words -- more risky if you come from a forgetful family! Few things are more embarrassing than the well-phrased question from friend or relative, "Did Mark enjoy the little gift I gave him?" This, of course, tells us that Mark never said thank you. When you are sure that Mark will soon see Aunt Nell, you can run over the ground with him, prior to their meeting, to make sure he remembers what he received and has something intelligent to say about the gift. Again, the "Thanks" and "Thank you again" are important. A really appreciative child will also remember to mention the gift or favor at some later date. While he may have been reminded to say thank you or to write a letter the first time, if the favor is brought up again, the giver knows the appreciation is sincere.

3. Saying Thank You In Other Ways. Wendy loves to sew, not one of my talents. Among our close friends are several who sew beautifully and on occasion they have helped Wendy with patterns, difficult shirring, buttons and zippers. Wendy often bakes cookies for our family and finds it easy to take a few dozen to her sewing assistants. Kent doesn't particularly enjoy writing but he does love to draw, and so his thank you's are often an elaborately drawn horse in action — a sketch that he thinks is worth keeping — along with a few words of thanks.

4. Responding To Compliments. Children are often flustered when someone compliments them. Compliments are opportunities to teach children to accept praise graciously, without belittling themselves or appearing falsely modest or shy. Karen loves to give speeches, present plays, put on musical programs. At first it was difficult for her to know what to say when someone praised her efforts. Here parents can help by giving a few simple suggestions:
    "I worked very hard on it. I'm glad you liked it."
    "I enjoyed doing it, too. It really was fun."
    "Thank you for telling me."
    If we help the children through these experiences the first few times, they will soon get the knack of responding on their own with sincerity and spontaneity.

5. At The Homes Of Friends. When our children are away from our sides, we hope they remember all their good home training. A child should be taught to ask permission to use the telephone at a friend's house, to check with home if invited to stay for dinner, never to ask to stay for a meal, to offer to help put away toys and games when through playing, to say goodbye and thank-you to all concerned. These few simple rules will make the child welcome in neighborhood homes.

6. At Parties. As the host or hostess for a party, the child has far more to do than to select the menu, prepare games, wrap and award the prizes. An essential part of the preparation is his response to gifts or compliments at the party. Children should be taught not to race through the opening of packages. They should learn to give adequate time to the card, the gift and the giver with an immediate and enthusiastic "Thank you." When a child is a guest for a meal, he should be taught to comment favorably on some food. This comes naturally when a child has been taught at home to appreciate the work that goes into preparing even the simplest meal.

Children learn best by example. It is easy to comment favorably, and occasionally unfavorably, upon the manners of their peers. I told Wendy that she could invite Lisa to supper often, since Lisa was so polite and helpful it really was no extra work. I don't know if the word got back to Lisa, but she has never forgotten to make a special point of thanking me and the rest of the family for her visits at our home.

Mark said quite disgustedly one day, "I'm never going to have Jerry to play again. He wants to bring everything out, and when he goes home, he doesn't even say thank you. He just runs out the door and leaves me with a mess."

Many brilliant, wealthy and witty people have the worst manners and cannot find the words "thank you" in their vocabularies, but in a world needing love and appreciation, let's teach our children the words that show we care.

13
Who's "The Boss?"

One afternoon my husband and I went out on errands while his parents were visiting us from afar. The only one of the children home was Karen. When we came back, although they had had a happy time, Grandma reported that Karen did the things she chose to do without particular attention to Grandma. Not being familiar with grandparents, since they lived so far away, Karen had assumed that Grandma had no authority. In fact, when questioned about her behavior, Karen said, "Well, I didn't know Grandma was the boss." It was our mistake in not transferring our authority to Grandma when we left.

Infants quickly learn authority by parental tone of voice: soothing, encouraging tones when a child obediently swallows the mashed-up peaches; quicker, displeased voice when the child throws his training mug from his highchair for the third time. Parents become the first authority in a child's life. As the child grows older, he is exposed to babysitters, teachers, counselors, policemen and countless other authorities that he must learn to respect.

With respect for authority rapidly diminishing in our world today, we must give it a logical basis for acceptance. Children are obedient to the parents because this makes for a happy and safe home. They are obedient to teachers because then they learn more and function better in the community.

The parents' place as chief authority exists not merely because of age or relationship, but because they are the ones who know most about the situation and can best control it. If the children are to respect parental authority, parents must have something worthwhile to say, must mean what they say and must, in most cases, give adequate reason for insisting on a particular action.

WELCOME QUESTIONS

Welcome a child's questioning of your authority and try to answer those questions. Explain why you are an authority and why you have made a particular rule or decision. Teach children that since parental authority is correct in most situations, it is wise not to doubt it in *critical* moments.

A familiar old story points out that there are times a child must accept parental authority on faith. Two fathers with their sons were on a mountain hike. One son was trained to respect his father as an authority. The other doubted everything his father said and would only respond after much arguing and if given the specific reasons. As they hiked, they became lost. When darkness fell, they found themselves moving through unfamiliar mountainous territory. The boys were walking just ahead of the fathers. Suddenly the fathers became aware that directly in front of their sons was a steep precipice. The sons did not see it. Both fathers cried, "Stop!" The one son stopped immediately. The other was heard asking, "Why, Dad?" as he and his voice disappeared over the cliff. Whether the story happened or not isn't important. It does show the need at times to rely unreservedly on authority.

Conversely, we must teach our children that blind acceptance of authority can be equally wrong. While traveling with our children in Israel, we saw memorials to the millions of people who were murdered in Germany during the days when the Nazis were systematically exterminating the Jews. This was a vivid lesson to our children, who asked repeatedly, "But why did the officers do it just because they were told?" Here then is the problem: We must teach our children to think through the acts they are about to commit, and yet we must teach them that there are some authorities that they must accept.

1. **Parents.** Father and mother are authorities on homelife because, as heads of the household, they pay the bills and understand how the family money should be spent; they know the importance of nutrition, cleanliness, safety and getting one's homework done; they have been through all these early stages of life and have had experience in many areas. Thus the children should be willing to accept parental authority to avoid "re-inventing the wheel."

There are two pitfalls in parental authority. The first occurs when one parent contradicts the other in front of the children. The other is parental disregard for law. Naturally, parents will disagree at times, but when this happens openly, it should be quickly settled. Dad says Kent should do his homework; Mother says he should practice his baseball if he ever wants to play for her favorite Chicago Cubs. Parents must realize that they have contradicted each other and, without argument, settle — perhaps compromise — on a plan for the child. When their unified decision is announced, the child finds it easier to obey parental authority.

Beware of the child who asks one parent, the one from whom he hopes to get the wanted answer, and then if not receiving that answer, puts his request to the other parent. It's an unwritten law in our house that if you've asked one parent and gotten a "No," you don't try for a better opinion from the other parent without giving the first parent's opinion. This double dealing, playing one parent against another, is something that must be squelched quickly.

Parents should support, not undermine, each other's authority. Such remarks as, "Oh, Mother didn't really mean what she said," or "Dad is tired and will feel differently about it tomorrow," or "You just go ahead and do what you think is right; I'll speak to Mother about it," make children uneasy. They need the security of knowing exactly what the laws of the home are. Despite a child's rebelling against parental suggestions, he likes to know where he stands. It gives him added security to know that a certain behavior is acceptable and another behavior is wrong and punishable.

When parents establish no basic home rules, children flounder and make mistakes. As adults, we function within the broad framework of the law, and we usually do not feel inhibited by the laws of the community. If there's a law we do not like, we set an example, not by breaking the law but by obeying it while working to change it. Point out to your children news items in which public opinion has helped change outdated laws. They will learn how even home rules can be peaceably altered.

We set an example by respecting the authority of police and government in our community and by not trying to circumvent the law. We do not speed because no one is watching. We do not go through a red light because it's one o'clock in the morning and no one is waiting at the intersection. We do not double park because we think we can get by with it. We do not take our short thirteen-year-old into movies by paying the twelve-year-old admission.

Each day in countless ways we either support or tear down the respect for authority we are trying to build in our children. One afternoon when we took the children to a circus, Wendy was in charge of getting the tickets. When she came back with them and the change, she realized she had two dollars too much. She sped back to return what wasn't hers. When she returned, she looked glum and reported that the ticket seller had merely said, "Humph," and grabbed the two dollars back. Here was an opportunity to point out that we do not do the right thing in order to win approval or praise; we do the right thing because we know that it is the correct way to act. All the indifference of the ticket seller, as opposed to the expected gratitude, should not diminish Wendy's satisfaction in doing what is lawful.

In teaching children respect for law, we must show them early and consistently that we *mean* exactly what we say. If we have said to a child, "Either eat your dinner or you will sit there until you do," we must be willing to go through with our demand. Otherwise, our words are value-less. This gives an added responsibility to parents not to make an ultimatum they are not willing to carry out. I always cringe when I hear parents in stores threatening toddlers with the line, "If you don't come immediately, I'm leaving you." Although the child may respond, he is quick to learn that mother or dad would not follow through.

Because we want to spare our children punishment, we are often tempted not to carry out a correctional plan. Kent was promised a cassette tape recorder for bringing his grades up to a certain level. As an added incentive, he was given a tape of a much-loved TV theme and heard it played on his dad's recorder. When the grades came excitement ran high to see if Kent had earned the tape recorder. Unhappily the grades were not up to the desired level. Our love for him would have made it easy to say, "Well, you did almost as well, and since you want the tape recorder so much, we'll give it to you now." This might have *seemed* like love, but we had set a certain goal and had to stick by it. In teaching children to respect our words, we must be sure we are willing to follow through.

In selecting a punishment let's be careful that in carrying it out we don't punish the entire family! We were at a friend's home once when the mother said to her youngest, "Finish your hamburger or no one here is going swimming!" We were *all* elated when the little one stuffed down the last morsel.

2. Teachers. If the child has been taught good manners in regard to his elders at home, he can easily transfer these to his school teacher or day care attendant. Parents should not under-cut the authority of teachers but should be alert to the fact that teachers are human beings. Occasionally we may have to explain some of their actions to our children as being somewhat less than wise but nevertheless well-intentioned.

We want our students to be obedient and to learn as much as possible. But, there can be the occasional person in the teaching field who does not belong there, and we do not wish our children to be blindly obedient or swayed by the teaching of this person. If a situation arises in which we feel that the teacher or school authority is in error, we have a duty as parents to carry this to the administration and to see the situation straightened out. Although this happens rarely, it is important, for we know the profound effect one influential teacher can have on young people.

In seventh grade, Wendy was in a private school that required a Bible course. Because the course was not popular with the students, the teaching of it fell to an inexperienced teacher who, although he had theological training, had lost his faith in God. He began each session by having those who believed in God stand up. Then he would see how many of them he could badger into disbelief before commencing the day's lecture. One by one, the students, overwhelmed by his clever articulation that made them feel ignorant or ineffective in their own beliefs, fell by the wayside. Wendy was the final student to remain standing for many days, and although she argued her beliefs and stood firm during the class session, at the end of each class she would run to the girls' room in tears. Although this was a fine private school and Wendy knew the importance of listening to and learning from teachers, she also learned early how wrong some people's tactics can be and how pugnacious they may be in presenting their own opinions to students.

As parents we brought this situation to the attention of the administration. They were understanding and put up mild arguments as to the importance of teaching children to stand up for their beliefs. We could understand the teacher's wanting to make the children verbalize their reasons. On the other hand, we could not approve of the daily humiliation and badgering. Finally, the administration agreed to give the teacher some direction. The daily faith-down ended and the class improved slightly. At the end of the semester, the teacher chose to take up the study of his true love, modern drama.

Sooner or later our young people must learn to judge "authorities" on the basis of what they themselves feel to be right. However, in teaching them to make these decisions, we must also show them the proper channels for change and the way to disagree.

3. **The Sitter.** For young children, the babysitter or a good friend or the lady who does the weekly cleaning — if you have that luxury — often becomes an authority in the house. For the hours that parents are away, that person represents the parental authority. When we first introduced our children to the idea of other people taking care of them, we made it absolutely clear that in our absence this person was the authority, the person in charge, and that he or she represented us. The same courtesies and obedience that a child gives parents should be given to the sitter. The first time that children encounter a new person in charge at home, they test this new authority. Say to a new sitter, "They may try to see if they can stay up a little later or eat in the living room or monkey around before bed. They'll be testing to see how far they can push you, so it's important this first time that you be extra firm." This works wonders in getting sitters started in a position of strength.

Before going out, have a little pep rally with all children and sitter present. Everyone then hears the rules for the night. It's also a good idea to write them down. Reiterate what the children are to do in your absence, what they may eat and what time they are expected to be in bed, so that no doubts exist. Most important, always say, "Now when we return home, Susie, I will want a report about the children from you." Then be sure you ask her for it. The following morning, it gives you something on which to compliment the children: "Susie reported that you cleaned up your toys nicely, ate your ice cream at the kitchen table and were in bed on time."

Let's be sure, however, that we don't put words into her mouth. To say, "Everything was fine, wasn't it?" puts the sitter in a difficult position. Better to say, "Did the children go to bed immediately when told?" "Did Karen turn off TV when the murder mystery came on?" As with children, we want to give our babysitters every opportunity to tell us whole, not half, truths. Sometimes it helps a child to respect the babysitter's authority if you let the child write down the rules to be followed while parents are away. Then no misunderstanding arises over what is expected.

Children are sometimes near enough to the age of the babysitter to feel a bond so that you can ask them to put themselves in her place: "If you were a babysitter, what would you want the children to do?" Children enjoy knowing the rules of the game and what's expected of them. When parents are away, family routine need not disintegrate.

4. **Their Peers.** Our youngsters are growing up to be authorities in certain areas, so in teaching respect for authority we also need to give our children practice in *being* "bosses." No matter how young the child, give him the opportunity to be in charge of situations. If I leave the table to answer the telephone, it's easy to say, "Karen, will you be in charge of conversation and second-helpings until I return?" When I run next door to a neighbor, Kent can be chairman of answering the phone and seeing that the younger children are not into mischief. Wendy is old enough to occasionally supervise study hall and express her authority by seeing that homework is done correctly and neatly. Such experiences help our children to develop leadership abilities, to learn to be the right kind of boss and both to lead and to follow their peers.

Finally, what are the qualities that a mother or father must express as a good supervisor? The first is confidence — the conviction that you have the knowledge and ability to be in control of the situation. You are smart enough to know when children should go to bed; you understand sentence structure sufficiently to correct homework; you have lived long enough to see that certain ways of doing things are best.

The second is patience. If our children could learn in a year all the lessons we are trying to teach them, our usefulness as parents would end quickly. We must be willing to lead, remind, show again and tell again.

The third is grace. It is not necessary to be militaristic or gruff in order to express authority. Often a calm, quiet statement of how things are going to be is much more effective than shouting, "Do it because I say so!"

The good boss expresses appreciation for obedience and points out the benefits that result from following a plan or a law or a rule.

One afternoon the children had been playing happily with a large new ball when it came time, at 4:30, for them to spend a quiet hour on homework. Loud grumblings. But I was convinced that this was the right time since they seemed less able to concentrate in the evening and I could better supervise now. So, without loud insistence, I quietly announced that this was the plan and that we were going to follow it. Conviction, patience, understanding and grace went into the decision to assert my authority, despite the many pleadings. The reward came quickly, for about 45 minutes later, when the homework was nearly done, Father suggested a quick trip for hamburgers and the six o'clock movie that would get us out by eight and home in time for 8:30 bedtime!

We can't always point out immediate rewards to our children for doing the right thing at the right time. How great it was to have this instance on the very day they were resenting my authority!

In teaching our children respect for authority, let's try not to present ourselves as the supreme all-knowing commander of every human situation. We must gently and firmly point out that in matters of home conduct, parents generally know what is right but that parents make mistakes, too. Being an authority doesn't mean infallibility! We strengthen our position by readily admitting our wrongs and showing our children that we don't lose dignity or authority by upgrading a poor decision.

14
"I'm Sorry!"

Karen had ample time before leaving for school one morning to play her phonograph, create a new dance, pack herself a four-course lunch, make a phone call to plan the afternoon's playtime with her friends and rear-range something in the doll corner. However, she left her spelling words on the window seat when she went off merrily to school. Five minutes before the tardy bell rang, she remembered them and got permission to phone me to ask if I could make the three-minute drive to school with the words. The quiet tone of her voice, her gentle pleading (rather than demanding), her sincere "Oh, thank you , Mother," made me smile as I grabbed the paper and jumped into the car. This is not something I do frequently. As I pulled to the curb and handed the paper to Karen, her eyes sparkled and she said, "Thanks, Mom. You're a life-saver. So sorry I forgot my paper."

How easy it is, under such circumstances, to forgive a child for some small trespass. The lesson had certainly been learned and further embel-lishment of the experience was unnecessary. Nothing would have been accomplished by roaring up in front of school, tossing the paper out the window and chiding the child. There are times when those speeches fall on deaf ears and this would have been one of them. Instead of starting Karen's school day the wrong way, I had the satisfaction of having done a favor for her and she had the glow of knowing that Mother cared enough to bail her out of an unhappy situation. Her genuine sincerity on realizing that she had done the wrong thing was sufficient to bring forgiveness.

How long should we be angry over a child's misdeeds? First, it is never essential to be angry. We can be disappointed over what the child has *done* or unhappy over what he has *said*, but anger is not a helpful quality.

Disapprove of what has been done but do not disapprove of the child himself. This helps us to forgive the child, for as soon as he has seen that what he has *done* is wrong (that the wrong was not part of *him* but what he *did*) we can forgive the child for having been forgetful or unkind or thoughtless. Forgiveness of the child should come as soon as we have seen that he has understood his wrong-doing.

Our first assignment in teaching forgiveness to a child is to show him why we are unhappy with his actions. Then, calmly and gracefully, we help him to see what wrong has been committed. Next, the wrong is righted. Somewhere along the way the child says, "I'm sorry." Then he's ready to be forgiven, and this forgiveness should be immediate, complete and final. It gives a child an insecure feeling to think that he has been partially forgiven and that in the future the experience will be saltily rubbed into the wound. By quick and complete forgiveness, we teach a child a better sense of values. We teach him to bounce back from a bad experience, reap its lessons and get on to the next project. We don't wish him to dwell unhappily on bad experiences or to feel that minor infractions are evidence of major character faults.

Sometimes a family will let petty mistakes get out of proportion so that the angry periods which follow become a great part of family life. Someone in the family unit is always "mad" at someone else. Holding of grudges becomes a major pastime. Parents must set the example in playing down mistakes and being quick to forgive.

As parents, do you battle and refuse to make up; revive past mistakes; refuse to forgive and forget; find it difficult to say those precious words, "I'm sorry?" If so, you may find the same unbending qualities in your children.

No matter what our religion, whether we feel the Bible is a religious or historical piece, we can remember Jesus' words concerning those who had done him the greatest of injustices: "Forgive them for they know not what they do." This is a good basis for teaching forgiveness to our children. When a child experiences meanness at home or school and feels unforgiving, a quiet analysis of what has happened often shows that the wrong was done by someone who really did not realize what he was doing. The wrong-doer has acted either out of ignorance of the true facts, as a result of his own envious or prideful feelings or because some entirely different experience has caused him to lash out at the first person he finds. When we see what has motivated people to wrong us, it is difficult to hate them and far easier to love and forgive them — "for they know not what they do."

But, every time a child says, "I'm mad at Mary," you needn't have a great ethical discussion. These little phrases about being mad at friends, or boys hating girls, or intending never to speak to so-and-so again, pass and are quickly forgotten. Unless we find that our children regularly have these feelings and are burdened by their own sense of hatred toward others, we can let such comments go unnoticed, without the dignity of a hearing.

We should teach that forgiveness is the response to a wrong done. This may be hard, for many a child feels that when a wrong has been done, the proper response is to do a wrong back. This is the reaction that we should quickly discourage, for this is letting the wrongs others do govern our lives and actions. Teach your child that no matter what another does, he must do what is right to set a good example — and that being good will benefit him in the long run.

Many people find it difficult to say, "I'm sorry," for they believe that it means they have admitted doing something wrong. This is not necessarily so. "I'm sorry" *can* mean, "I'm sorry that I've done something wrong" or "I see I've done something wrong and I'm sorry about it." However, "I'm sorry" can also mean "I'm sorry if you thought I did something wrong" or "I'm sorry that what I did upset you." Often the person refuses to say "I'm sorry" because he thinks this tantamount to admitting guilt. However, we can always afford to be sorry that someone is upset by or misunderstands our actions. How soothing it is for the other person to hear us say that we are sorry!

What about the second offense? If there is a repeated offense and it is apparent that the lesson has not been learned, our forgiveness comes more slowly and the time spent educating the child out of the mistake increases. Not speaking to a child only makes him resentful and does nothing to bring about a solution to the problem and reconciliation. By being willing to talk over the wrong done, we create an open and frank atmosphere with a child and enable him to see his mistake.

When a child has made a mistake and corrected it, we might ask him where the mistake has gone. The mistake really has gone nowhere because it had no real validity in the first place. Like the wrong answer to a math problem, it has been erased. There is no need to remember the mistake or attach it to the child forever. Don't make forgiveness so difficult and mistakes so earth-shaking that the child is fearful of living his life to the fullest. If we are innovating and creating and living adventurously, it's not uncommon, along with a busy and full life, that, in retrospect, there be some actions we would change. Such mistakes lose their importance if the more positive experiences are stressed and forgiveness made easy and sweet. What a joy it is for a parent to take a remorseful child into his arms and tell him sincerely that he forgives and loves him.

15
Smiles
And
Laughs

Late one evening as we were driving home from our soon-to-be completed shopping plaza, a weary Kent began discussing the wonderful places he would visit when all the new shops opened. Being a lover of small cars, airplanes and models, he rambled sleepily on to say, "And the best place of all is going to be Pete's Shobby Hop." As soon as the words were out, everyone burst into laughter and began repeating the wonderful phrase, Shobby Hop. Kent was on the brink of tears or laughter and happily chose laughter. He saw that by repeating the phrase in several more sentences he brought more guffaws from children and adults. Everyone began inverting initial sounds and, by the time we had completed the drive home, everyone was cheerfully exhausted.

This proves two points. First, a simple incident, as every comic knows, can become humorous when elaborated and repeated. And second, the ability to laugh at oneself is essential. It's something we either cultivate or ignore.

The purpose of humor is far more than amusement. A sense of humor is necessary to one's mental health. We've heard people say that they would not have been able to survive certain sad or discouraging situations if they hadn't had a sense of humor.

A good sense of humor helps us put things in proper proportion. In the course of the family day, many things are shot way out of proportion and we may find ourselves stressing the petty and ignoring the important. Encourage laughter and fun! But, what is considered funny? With the very youngest child, joy and fun are interrelated. If we take a small child's hands and clap them together, he smiles and then laughs. If we make funny faces, he laughs more.

As a child grows older, making faces, putting on costumes, originating funny words and sayings or repeating some silly action are laughable. The school child begins to see the humor in take-offs, satires and mimicry. Soon he can appreciate cartoons and the better comic strips.

LAUGH AT YOURSELF

Too much stress cannot be placed on teaching children the ability to laugh at themselves. Parents should not be ashamed of being funny or doing something that is slightly silly. As your young children begin to do things that are funny, encourage them by laughing at their attempts. When a child unintentionally does something that amuses others and is on the brink of tears, be quick to be laughable and happy. This encourages him to laugh at himself and to see the humor in what he's done. Enjoy and value any childish attempt to be funny.

Be sure to distinguish between smart aleck and genuine humor. When Kent was little, he often made fresh remarks that could easily be mistaken for smart aleckness. But, these were his first attempts to be funny. When we showed him better ways of being funny and how some people might misinterpret his humor, he gradually learned other amusing ways and has become the family comic.

Teach a child what is NOT funny. In this department are bad jokes and dirty words. Be strong in your disapproval of such attention-getting devices. It is never funny for a child to lie. Jokes and mimicry about other people's handicaps, ignorances, traditions or age should be shown in poor taste. Even small children can be taught that if the laugh hurts someone, it really isn't funny.

Some of the funniest things to laugh about are things children and parents do unintentionally. Make the most of these easy mistakes so the child sees that minor mistakes are not disgraceful. Taking a child to truly funny movies and reading humor aloud will enhance his comic sense. On the other hand, TV shows in which one character spends most of his time trying to clobber another are not the highest form of humor.

Wendy and Kent enjoyed riddle and joke books when they were young, an early exposure that is good training. Mark had a difficult time grasping puns, the so-called lowest form of wit, so Dad took time to explain their humor by showing the double use of the word.

Young children grasp humor gradually, so work patiently to make the most of humorous family events. Some of the funniest things that have happened in our house are really only funny in the re-telling, and with each re-telling, they get funnier. We don't hesitate to embellish the humor for the sake of telling a story well, and we use specific details, correct pauses and good timing, an art we can cultivate in our children.

During supper-time conversations when you share the day's events, ask occasionally if something funny happened today. The children will go out of their way to tell you what they thought was funny. Sometimes children are embarrassed to attempt humor because they think others will not find them funny. Encourage the child to exercise his sense of humor as he would any other skill, to improve it.

One year, Mark wanted to have an Easter rabbit give out prizes at his yearly party. He wanted Kent to be the rabbit, dressed in white ski underwear. Kent refused. Although he was four years older than most of the boys, he had no desire to appear before them in his underwear. We showed him how comical he could be and how he could have a funny photo made with each guest. Finally he agreed but wore a vest and tie over the underwear to make himself a fashionable rabbit. He even wore his cowboy hat and attached to it, as if poking through, a pair of bunny ears. He was the sensation of the party and with the first laugh became more bold. He soon enjoyed the adoration of all the younger boys. With a Polaroid camera, we took a picture of each guest sitting on the Easter Bunny's knees. The boys were encouraged to make crazy faces. Seeing how humorous they looked, they continued being funny throughout the whole party.

TEASING

One of the earliest attempts at humor by small children is teasing. Some parents condemn teasing. However, teasing is not all bad. The only child, with no brothers or sisters to tease or be teased by, is often treated in such an adult manner that he is surprised and upset when he goes into a school or play situation and is teased. He doesn't know how to cope with it.

The solution: Even we adults do a great deal of teasing around our home to give our children a sense of humor when they meet teasing situations at school. This gives the teased child an opportunity either to tease back or to show his sense of humor and poise. The teaser learns to know just how far to go before his words become hurtful and no longer funny.

When a child sees something memorable or funny, encourage him to imitate. Our children saw a rerun of Walt Disney's *Fantasia*. Later when we were playing the ballet music to which the hippopotamuses had waltzed, I was surprised to see the boys perform a satirical dance like wallowing hippos in short ballet skirts. They had caught the humor and knew their ability to copy.

Finding humor amidst adversity is an asset. We were in a potentially dangerous situation in a foreign country when the gloom was lifted by young Mark. Late one night when we were returning to a large city through a no-man's-land, we were stopped at a roadblock and a soldier entered our Volkswagon bus to protect us. The presence of a fighting man carrying his machine gun at the ready caused an uneasy quiet to settle over the entire family. Our happy day became gloomy as we inched our way toward the lighted city. Mark sensed the chill and out of the absolute quiet said, "Let's all sing so we won't hear any shots fired at us!" Everyone

71

laughed at his solution. But we began to sing and soon our solider friend joined in the songs he knew. To think we had almost left Mark at home beause we felt he was too young to gain much from the trip! However, as it happened, his naive and lighthearted remarks were highlights each day.

THE SOUND OF LAUGHTER

In encouraging happy times around home, help a child to feel free about laughing. On the other hand, we don't want a child to develop an hysterical or shrill laugh. How wonderful it is at a gathering to hear sincere laughter. In turn, the mirthful giggles of children are music to our ears when they don't sound forced or put on. When we hear laughter around our home, we can remind the children that we approve of their fun.

By letting children know how much we enjoy hearing their laughter, we encourage a certain amount of harmless mischief around the house. One night I was reminiscing and told the terrible things we did during college days: hiding the silverware, putting ditto machine jelly in beds, stitching coat sleeves shut. At first the children were shocked that parents could do such things. In the weeks that followed, I noticed that they tried to repeat some of our collegiate pranks. I found scotch tape over my toothbrush, spaghetti in my bed, a noisy old alarm hidden back in a cupboard and canned goods with the labels removed. (These made an interesting meal one night.) So when Wendy's Camp Fire group went on a camping trip, we appointed two girls to be solely in charge of mischief. They had little trouble coming up with great ideas! Wendy still tells of frogs in sleeping bags and green food coloring in the milk.

Don't forget April Fool's Day! It's a good occasion to pull pranks and learn how to be on the receiving end.

When Father was teaching an adult class Tuesday evenings, our Tuesday suppers consisted of take-out hamburgers or chicken pies and TV dinners from our freezer. The casual approach to the meal made everyone humorous, and it was on a Tuesday that the famous Backwards Supper was invented: dessert first, then a casserole, then fruit cup.

Another Tuesday invention was "The Gorilla." I suppose most mothers see themselves as charming and witty and pleasant in appearance. However, one winter night when we came bustling into the house with hamburgers, I had on a tacky-looking dark mouton lamb coat. One of the children said I looked like a gorilla in it. Happily, I was not offended. It was then that the gorilla was invented. I responded that as soon as everyone had finished supper, I would show them how a real gorilla looked. They needed no encouragement to finish eating that night. With suitable facial expressions and dangling arms swinging back and forth, I put on what came to be known as Mother's Gorilla Show. I was well aware

72

that I looked quite ugly and fierce and so told the children that Mother's Gorilla Show was a secret from Dad since he wouldn't wish to be married to a gorilla. The children thought this a great secret and every Tuesday night when supper was over, we would have a gorilla show.

Each Wednesday at breakfast, when Dad inquired how things went Tuesday night, he was mystified about the gales of laughter. It was months before we shared the gorilla story with him but I have never had the nerve to actually show him his gorilla wife. When I quit the act, Kent picked it up and has been an admirable substitute.

Teasing, wrestling, rough-housing, chasing the children to bed, (rather than ordering them to bed) and genuinely enjoying their humor will help to develop fun in your children's lives. We think of childhood as a happy time of life, but some children are so serious that they have lost the joy of youth and respond unsmilingly when they have so much to be happy about.

We carried a children's joke book in the car for awhile. One child read the jokes aloud but soon the others began to anticipate the punch lines. In many cases they came up with even funnier lines than those in the book.

Some parents feel that if they provide their children with comic books and give permission to see "sick" TV shows, this will develop the child's humor. Actually, most "funnies" are no longer funny and much of the humor in the entertainment world is so low that it is beyond an innocent child's comprehension.

When a revival of Laurel and Hardy and W. C. Fields movies showed at our local theater, our children sat through several hours of vintage slapstick comedy and pantomime. Although they laughed at the shows then, only in the weeks that followed did I realize the great impact these true comedians had had on our children. They saw the importance of exaggeration, repetition and surprise and that humor need not be at the expense of someone else.

Karen often finds it difficult to laugh at herself when things go wrong. One Thanksgiving, she had planned an elaborate pageant about the pilgrims and Indians. As we and our friends watched our combined children acting out their roles in this great saga, one thing after another went wrong. A pail of water was knocked over, the peace pipe broke, someone's costume fell to the floor and finally one of the young guests forgot his hastily-learned lines. At this point, Karen shrugged her shoulders and sighed to the cast, "If you can't do it right, at least be funny about it!" What followed was a much less stilted performance about a stolen turkey. Both the cast and the parents had an hilarious time. When the day was over, Karen had to admit it had been one of her best productions.

16
Sticking Up
For Yourself

Kent came home from school with a muddy shirt and an unhappy face. A boy in a class two years ahead of his had commanded all the younger kids to get off the sidewalk or be beaten up. Everyone quickly removed themselves from the disputed area. However, Kent could not resist putting just the toe of his shoe back on the sidewalk and for this the older boy knocked him to the ground and, as Kent reported, nearly strangled him. Another student called Karen to come to Kent's aid. She was too late. The tiny battle was over. The humiliation of being pommelled brought tears to Kent's eyes.

Later in the afternoon, I heard him relate the story to his younger brother with a bit more bravado. By the time Dad got home, the story went like this: "This huge boy got me down on the ground and I was just about to kick him, and I was just about to pinch him, and I was just about to hit him with my books; then he realized how strong I was and let me up."

The decision whether to fight or run starts at home when children are two or three years old, when they first haul off and sock each other to get their way. If fighting is not discouraged as the first and only means of settling disputes, rational decision-making is ignored and disputes are settled solely on the basis of who is the strongest. In home training a child should be taught that the winner is the person who is right, not necessarily the one who can beat the other one.

If our community, nation and world are ever to come to the point where differences can be settled peacefully and rationally, we must start by teaching children that the wisest way to settle arguments is to reason them out.

A child must be willing to be different and not fight over every disagreement. On the other hand, when a child is being choked, he must know that he has some defense. Even in these severe situations, brute strength need not be the answer. A mother told this remarkable story of her college-age son: He had given much thought during his college years to the world's underprivileged and oppressed and felt the answer to these problems lay in the expression of loving concern no matter what the response. One night he was walking through a park when he felt he was being followed. Moments later he was jumped by two men about his age, both bigger than he. They demanded his wallet. Seeing that human strength would benefit little, he tried to talk his way out of the situation. He obediently got his wallet out and handed it to the men and then said to them, "Really, what you are seeking in life won't be found in my wallet. In fact, taking my money will only deter you from getting what you really want." Since he wasn't clobbered at this point, he took courage and spoke more concerning brotherly love and his interest in his fellow man. His sincerity evidently began to impress his two oppressors. They had earlier threatened to knock him unconscious; however, they took the wallet and merely ran away.

In seconds, one man returned, tossed the wallet at his feet and shouted, "We don't want your wallet." The student picked it up half expecting to find his money gone and was amazed to find not only his credit cards intact but also all his cash. This more rational approach to violence is what we should all strive for. We must give our children courage to take a moral stand when they feel strongly impelled to do so.

THE BULLY

One Sunday we had a discussion as to what makes a child resort to physical force. We even wrote down the qualities of a bully. The children described a bully as somebody who was unsure of himself; someone who did not know enough to understand and discuss the problem; someone who didn't have enough friends and was disliked or unloved; someone who would be so unfair as to threaten and fight smaller children. I made notes on their comments and then read back their description of a bully. The decision was unanimous that they never wished to fit this description.

There are verbal as well as physical bullies. They can talk others into doing almost anything. In teaching a child to defend himself, we must teach him to withstand wrong suggestions as well as wrong actions. It is no excuse to say, "But Wendy told me to get Dad's aftershave and spray it all over the dolls." Parental response to this sort of defense is, "But, did *you* think that was the right thing to do?"

Since children eventually must argue out a code of behavior with themselves, you can be the devil's advocate, persuasively presenting all the opposing arguments and thus giving them the mental drill of defending their actions.

Since we do much friendly wrestling around our house, the boys and the girls know a few good ways to free themselves from strong grips and

75

terminate fights. But they have also been taught that there are certain parts of the body that we don't kick or hit nor do we attempt to strangle one another, even in jest. Young children need to know their physical capabilities; how much weight they can safely lift; how they can suddenly wrench free; the use of ingenuity in a friendly tussle.

Teach children to be considerate of their friends and to stick up for them physically and verbally even when such action may be unpopular with the rest of the playground. Parental example is the best teacher. How do you score on these points?

1. Are you willing to be different?
2. Can you settle a dispute using logic, not lung-power?
3. Do you praise the child that seeks to be the peacemaker?
4. Do you disapprove of bullying tactics in children and adults?
5. When a child speaks up for himself, do you refrain from verbally slapping him down?
6. Do you listen to his arguments and play no favorites when you are called upon for solutions?
7. Do you give your children the opportunity to settle differences without your having to step in?
8. Do you honestly believe it's right to speak up when the viewpoint is unpopular?
9. Do you practice what you preach?

17
The
Ten O'Clock
Scholar

Karen, stamping her feet and making bad faces, burst in from school. She had wanted one of her good friends as her May Day dance partner but had drawn a girl she hardly knew. She explained that this other girl didn't catch on quickly, was clumsy and couldn't remember the hand movements in the dance. Her disgust highlighted the parental need to teach the bright child to be patient and supportive of the ten o'clock scholar, the slower learner. Within the family circle we often find that one child does most things with adeptness, speed and brilliance, while another, born of the same parents, appears slow, sloppy or sullen.

How, then, do we include the ten o'clock scholar in the activities of school and home without making him feel any less desirable or loved or intelligent than the rest of the family? Parental insight and patience are required in working with this seemingly slower member of the family.

How easy it is to love the child who does exactly what we wish promptly and perfectly. That child needs parental support less than does the ten o'clock scholar. The brighter members of the classroom or family must realize that each of us excels in certain areas. Ability to do the multiplication tables in one minute doesn't necessarily determine the successfulness of our lives.

The slow child has certain good qualities that we must reinforce. It may take much looking to find something to compliment, to find what he does well and to give him opportunities to do it. We must also help him excel in the things he does only moderately well. Every child must feel the exhilaration of success.

Many of our household tasks are handled by our children. Some are able to do more than others in less time. For example, a task assigned to Kent may be accomplished only half the time, while tasks assigned to the other children will be done almost all the time. Kent's goals must be set so there is good chance of his achieving them. If his monthly goal is to make his bed 15 days out of 30, is it fair to set Karen's goal at 28 out of 30?

Yes it is, because it would be unfair to Karen, who organizes her time well, to achieve less than her capacity. Explain this to children and they won't feel that parents are being unfair when they demand more from one child than from another.

Children are individual. While we may be satisfied with C grades from one and reward him for those, we would be unhappy if another came home with less than B's. On the other hand, we might expect one child to understand electric circuitry, repair extension cords and do simple home electrical projects. This would not be demanded of another whose small hands can't hold the pliers. That we are all different has to be made clear to children. They must know that we love them *because* they are individual.

Let the slow and disorganized child focus on one thing at a time. Decide that day or that week or that month what learning is most important for him. If he is doing poorly in school, then school improvement is his main objective. To give this child a list to write Grandma, clean the garage, get his homework done, mow the lawn and read three library books would discourage him. We start with something we know he can accomplish. When he has done it, we laud him on having achieved it and make him feel that he is a success. Then we build on this and say, "Yesterday you were able to do your two hours of homework and have time left over. Let's see if today you can do your homework *and* make your bed."

With the slower child, work out to his satisfaction a schedule showing how he should spend his time: "How much time does it take for you to get dressed? You think it takes ten minutes; I'll allow you fifteen. How much time will it take you to do your homework? You think an hour, let's count an hour and a half." Then total up the tasks and show him that even with generous allotments he still has 'X' number of hours left. Thus, if he persists in completing his work, he will have the free time he so much desires. Constantly point out the possibility of success to a slower child. Then, that hopeless feeling should never set in.

Simple lists for these children show the priority in which various assignments are to be completed. Vary the assignments: a hard one, an easy one, a serious one, a fun one.

    7:00 - Up, wash, dress
    7:30 - Breakfast
    8:00 - Make bed, tidy room
    8:15 - Leave for school
    3:30 - Snack time
    4:00 - Play
    5:00 - Homework
    5:30 - Hobby time, helping time
    6:00 - Supper

6:30 - Help load the dishwasher, free time
7:00 - Quiet time (homework, letters, reading)
8:00 - TV or free time
9:00 - Bath
9:30 - Bed

If the schedule allows ample time, the child enjoys the successful feeling of being on schedule and realizes that there *is* time to get the essentials done.

Hang onto your patience. Some children learn a routine quickly and buckle down to homework with dispatch; others may take years to master a method of getting homework done. These points are well to remember in working with a slower child:

1. Talk daily with him about his time schedule. Do not assume that he will remember from the day before what he is to do.

2. Check with him often or have him do his assigned tasks somewhere near you. You can't be angry if he has wandered away from his homework to play with a toy and has wasted 45 minutes if you have ignored him for that 45 minutes.

3. Quietly and clearly tell him the rules that he is to follow in the task. If he is to work on a language arts paper, before he starts, establish the standards of neatness, grammar and spelling you expect. If he is to set the table, tell him twice and have him repeat what he is to put on the table, and where he is to put it. Mark never remembered how the forks, knives and spoons were arranged, so I had him draw a picture of a table setting and keep it in a kitchen drawer. He no longer suffered the embarrassment of our laughing over misplaced settings.

4. Vary his tasks. The slower child often has a short attention span, so we must be alert when he is weary of one activity and ready for another. The child who has been doing close paperwork for 20 or 30 minutes can be refreshed with as little as five minutes of catch-and-throw.

5. Choose few "thou musts" and stick to them. Tell the child exactly what personal behavior you expect of him and do not depart from it. Require less than you feel he's capable of doing at first.

6. Teach him that he will bear the consequences of his own actions. If he follows the plan that you and he have devised, he gets the praise and reward of free time, a treat, TV-viewing. If he wastes his time and fails to do his work, he reaps punishment, stern parental words and the removal of privileges. Remind him regularly that this is a moment-to-moment decision and that he has the ability and the opportunity to do the right thing.

7. Praise him daily for right-doing, if possible in front of his peers so that they see that he is a valuable and worthwhile person. Never let the children in the family consider one of their sisters or brothers as an undesirable outcast.

Much time and patience is required with a slower child and sometimes parents become discouraged. We may have to give *ourselves* a lecture to determine just what we hope to teach the slower child. If he could only learn one thing what would that be? Would it be to complete his school assignments so that he would have an adequate education? Would it be to concentrate on his creative pursuits, since this may be the saving factor in his life? Although I spend much time in teaching our children the basic civilized things to do each morning, there is no punishment for those who fail. For those who *do* them, there is a reward; this is as it will be in life.

On the other hand you must not overlook the child who does conform quickly and easily to our plan. The parable of the prodigal son has a message. In this story the son who has done wrong, realizes it and returns home, is given a great feast, jewels and gifts, while the son who has remained constant through the years feels hurt that he has not received the same rewards. The wise father points out that the consistent son has had the benefit of always being in the presence and good graces of his father. In our effort to compliment and encourage the slower family members, remember that the others deserve our compliments, too.

18
Learning To Be Alone

When Mark came back from his first overnight at a pal's home, he observed that he had never been in such a noisy house. Three television sets were blaring simultaneously on different channels although no one was looking at them.

In this age of stereos, pocket radios and portable record players, quiet moments have become rare. We are a gregarious nation and want so much to be loved, appreciated, talked to, sold and entertained — never alone to face our own thoughts!

Each of us needs quiet "do nothing" time each day; and we must respect one another's need for this private time. Adult and child alike should set aside part of each day to do nothing more than be receptive to creative ideas. We mustn't be so afraid of quiet that we try to fill it with conversational drivel. Sometimes just riding in the car and quietly looking out the window is beneficial. Sitting outdoors early or late can make us aware of the many sounds of nature always in the background.

Our children attended a summer camp that gave opportunities for being alone each day. The campers were encouraged to write down their thoughts. At the end of the summer the camp published a collection of poems and stories called "Alone with our thoughts." I know that other parents learned as much as we did about our children's thinking and concerns.

PLAN A "DO-NOTHING" TIME

Make an opportunity for children's quiet time each day. Taking a bath alone, just lying there and thinking in the warm suds, can be a joyous change-of-pace for a child who normally prefers the nonsense of water-splashing with bath toys.

Every home should have a quiet place where a child can get away from everyone. It may be a branch of a tree, a corner of the living room or his own bedroom with the door shut.

In learning to respect privacy, children should be taught early that a closed door means "knock before entering." There are times when a child must store up his requests (good mental exercise) and wait until mother or dad is ready to answer them. We don't need to be immediately available to our children every moment. They can often solve their own difficulties when they find that we are occupied and cannot be interrupted.

PARENT'S "ALONE TIME"

Parents deserve "alone time" and can insist on an evening opportunity to talk with each other if they have first attended to the needs of the children. A non-working parent can say without the slightest feeling of guilt, "Dad (or Mother) has come home now and wishes to go for a walk with me after dinner." But if the home parent has ignored the children all afternoon and they have questions concerning their homework, the baseball team and tomorrow's sack lunch, it will do nothing but infuriate parents if the children keep interrupting their time together.

In like manner, working parents can get the youngsters started on homework or baths and then enjoy 30 minutes together. Later in the evening, when all children are tucked in, is a precious time for parents to talk, read or just enjoy some quiet. Often parents let young children stay up so late watching TV that the parents never have time without children.

Teach children the value of the whisper. During our 45-minute daily study hall, there is absolutely no loud talking. A child with a question comes to the parent in charge of study hall and whispers or speaks in a low voice.

Even the youngest child can respect another's privacy, such as when mother or dad are chatting with another child, when someone is using the bathroom, or when adults are reading.

Guide children into knowing when it's time for talk and when it's time for quiet. Fifteen minutes before lights out, quiet reading time in bed begins at our house. This not only gives every child an opportunity for fifteen minutes of recreational reading but it also calms bouncy natures so that sleep comes quickly when the lights go out.

I know a mother who feels that for her own well-being she needs 30 minutes of quiet before supper. She works it out so that the children are back from play and have their homework underway; that the salad is made, the vegetable in the pan and the meat ready to go under the broiler. Then she has her private time, a luxurious bath, scented and foamy, with a good magazine to read. Afterwards she appears refreshed and relaxed for the family dinner. Fathers, too, and mothers whether they work in or out of the home, should accord themselves this kind of refreshment time.

To gain time for privacy and quietude, start by letting a toddler have some play by himself in a safe place where you can check on him. Then he'll know what to do when he has no friend with whom to play. In selecting toys for a child, be sure to choose some that he can enjoy entirely on his own. If members of the family are running short of good nature, say that it is time for everyone to do something by himself. Suggest knitting, putting together a Lego city, reading a book, or going out and lying under a tree to see the pattern the leaves make against the sky.

As cities become more crowded, we must beware of "privacy pollution." Go out of your way to make occasions for privacy and quiet. Life need not be a three-ring circus. Some of a child's happiest times occur when there is nothing planned, when he can do exactly as he chooses, even if it is just stretching out on his bed and staring at the ceiling. Through so many events of the day the child moves like a robot, eating the food that is placed before him, moving from classroom to classroom with the crowd, looking down the list of tasks and ticking them off. He may be lost when faced with free time.

Parents should have a ready list of interesting solo activities for the small child and, as the children become older, should encourage them to keep such lists themselves. Some of these ideas might be:

1. Write a letter to a friend.
2. Make a scrapbook.
3. Put together a model kit.
4. Try a new recipe.
5. Read a library book.
6. Rearrange the furniture in your bedroom.
7. Sew.
8. Write a poem.
9. Manicure nails.
10. Try a new hair style.
11. Repair something broken.
12. Jog around the house.
13. Teach the dog a trick.
14. Paint or color.
15. Plant seeds.
16. Make popcorn.
17. Read a magazine.
18. Reorganize a cupboard.
19. Look at photo album.
20. Listen to a record.

The list of creative things we can do alone and in quiet is endless. Note that "watch TV" is not on the list. But we'll never get around to that list if we keep our lives and the lives of our children so filled with canned experiences, external stimulations and piped-in entertainment.

When visiting a friend's lovely mountain retreat, I expressed my joy for what a wonderful time her children must have in that magnificent setting. She responded that her children disliked the place and spent most of their time playing cards in the living room. This pointed out to me the need to teach children how to explore, how to find adventure on their own without being directed by box games or television programs. We parents sometimes make so much noise living that we fail to realize what's going on around us in an exciting world.

19
Learning To Listen

Learning to listen and follow directions brings a child success at school, at home and later in his career. Listening for verbal directions often seems boring to a young child who, in his exuberance, believes he knows how to do everything without advice. Listening is a developed art, one that we can teach ourselves and our children.

Recognize that although the ear may function perfectly, we often hear only the first part of what is said. Or we hear only what we wish to hear. Or, rather than listening to *what* is said, we are put off the track of the message by the *way* it is said.

ATTENTION, RETENTION, RECALL

The art of listening has three parts: first, attention; second, retention; and third, recall. If we are to listen, we must give all our attention to what is being said. If, for example, we are introduced to people and cannot recall their names fifteen seconds later, the ear has been functioning but we have not been fully attentive.

When we listen properly, we retain the message. This is the function of the mind or memory but we must listen with the idea of retention so that the message has meaning to us. It must be said in such a way that we can understand and store it for future use. For the art of listening and retaining is useless if we can't recall what we have heard. We have not truly listened if we cannot bring back for use what we have mentally stored. When you tell a child something you want him to hear, be sure you have his attention through the entire message. Be sure that what you say has meaning to him so that he has the ability to retain it. By giving your message meaning he will be able to recall it and put it into use. Otherwise the telling and the listening have had no purpose.

Many home and school activities involve youngsters in listening and following directions. First is homework. Kindergarten and first grade students often get written assignments. But as the child grows older, his

85

assignments are given verbally and it is up to him to be able to give attention, retain what he is told and recall it at homework time.

With the advent of audio-visual aids in school, much of the teaching is done through the ear, the eye being merely supportive. Listening corners, tape decks, phonograph records are gradually taking the place of the blackboard. Teachers today are not giving many visual directions. In fact, in many classes the teacher has moved to the back of the room where she can be heard and not necessarily seen.

Learning to listen requires practice. There are many ways we can give a youngster this practice. All of the "how-to" activities require the child to listen to directions: how to fry bacon, hem a skirt, repair a broken toy or water the plants. If the child gives us his attention, retains what he has heard and recalls it so that he can put it into practice, the task is properly done. Anything less means an unsatisfactory job.

Sometimes it is our fault if the child does not hear us properly. We should gain his attention by calling his name, taking him from distractions and requiring him to give us 100 percent attention. If we give him messages as we pass him in the hall or as he goes to bed, we do not have his attention and cannot really expect that he is listening. If, as we go off to a meeting, we shout a few directions on behavior to the children while they are giving their attention to television, we cannot expect satisfactory results when we return.

Give a child exercise in listening, not just to us but to other adults and to their friends. Let him listen to music for certain sounds, to his Scout leader for instruction, to the dentist for suggestions on better toothbrushing, to ministers, salesmen and politicians. Then let him verbalize these things to us so he (and we) can gauge his retention.

Waken the tuned-out child by saying, "Did you hear what he said?" When a child knows that we expect him to be listening, he will be more alert. When Mark got new suede shoes, the salesman gave a few ideas on their care. Mark assumed that because I was sitting next to him, I would remember these suggestions and he could turn off his listening. How sad he was when he got the shoes wet and came to me for what to do. I pointed out that he was present and being addressed at the very time the salesman explained the care of suede shoes.

The things parents wish a child to hear are often in the area of suggestions, admonitions and lists of tasks, not always of vital interest to the child. It's not without reason that they often half listen or tune us out. Be sure that what you demand of a child is important and easily understood. Then check for follow-through so he realizes that listening is important.

PRACTICE LISTENING

When you tell a child to do something, have him repeat the message so that there is no misunderstanding as to what he's heard. In giving a child directions, tell him that you do not wish to repeat them, so he must listen intently. Tax the child's memory by increasing the complexity of his listening assignment. When a child can follow simple directions, give him a verbal list of several things to do. Tell him you are giving him *three* things to remember. He will enjoy the challenge of ticking them off mentally.

When your child has done well in following directions, compliment him with "Great, you heard what I said" or "Because you listened, you finished on time" or "Because you heard me say to put your library books in the car, you don't owe any fines."

Many of the stories a child tells us may seem long and trivial. To the child they are the large events of the day. We must, in turn, listen to his simple anecdotes, the triumphs and sadnesses that have come to him during the day. But sometimes a child is trying to give us other subtle messages. If we fail to listen to what he is saying, we may miss his most important communications. Kent, for example, tells me he has nothing to wear to school. He's trying to say that everyone else is wearing cords and, although he has pants in his closet, he doesn't have any in which he feels socially comfortable.

Be alert to the child who snuggles in with his obvious message a hidden one that he hesitates to bring up. You must be an accurate listener, not jumping to conclusions but certainly sensitive to the secondary message.

Listen to your child and you will find a trend in his messages that will help you to understand what type of young person you are raising. If every one of Karen's stories tells me how she strove, unsuccessfully, to be leader of the discussion group or how she thought she would have a part in the play but didn't, she may be giving me a message that she is feeling insecure or greatly disappointed or unhappy in school. Don't think, however, that everything a child says has some deep psychological meaning! Far from it, but we should not turn a deaf ear to the more subtle messages.

You best teach your children to listen when you set the example of listening yourself. You are listened to when you have something important to say, when you show your child that you care that he listens because there is good reason for his tuning-in. You avoid having a lazy listener by creating situations that tax his ears and require that, for success, he must truly listen to what is said.

20
Little Revolts
And Big

The maverick is certainly nothing new. Young adults have always strained against school and government authority. In some senses of the word "revolt" we *want* our children to protest wrongs in society and even at home, but we want them to revolt in a positive way.

At home, most parents are not keen on having their children carry revolt to the point of disobedience and destructiveness. Youngsters become dissenters at an early age, so it's important to teach them how to disagree in a way that will bring about desired change.

Although violence has been a means of bringing about some change, civilized people must learn, sooner or later, that more reasonable and thoughtful methods of revolt produce better and lasting results. Even a two-year-old uses the vocabulary of revolt. He says, "I won't." He may sit stubbornly on the floor and refuse to move. Or he may throw his plate of food over the side of his highchair. As he grows older, he uses "I won't" more. He may lock himself in his bedroom. He may ignore us. Later he may openly attack our authority. He may choose a mode of dress that he knows upsets us or pick up drug and tobacco habits.

How do we handle a revolter, little or big, without merely insisting on the child's bowing to our will? The most effective counterbalance to revolt is reason. This active human faculty is not used enough to handle revolt because it requires more time and thought than brute force or human will. Demanding compliance may save time at first, but an early investment in the use of reason will save us both time and anguish later on. Thus, when a child first rebels and is old enough to understand our words, we must patiently determine the reasons for his revolt and help him find a way out of his dissatisfaction.

When we ignore reason and simply insist on having things done our — or society's — way, we are asking our young people not to think for themselves, while hypocritically preaching, "Think for yourself, figure it out, do something on your own." Our young revolters often do pick up the ball and make worthwhile changes. When they revolt in a responsible way, we must encourage and praise them.

Children take their cues from us. If parents live placid lives and do nothing to improve society, the children are apt to follow that lead. However, if parents are boat-rockers, fearless of taking minority positions, they will often bring these progressive qualities out in their children simply because they have been part of an adventuresome family.

RESPONSIBLE REVOLT

It is a joy to see our young people bring about change in a responsible way. Wendy is our rebel. We have tried to guide her in how to make known her dissatisfactions with school rules. Following a sixth-grade election in which she felt certain practices were wrong, she formed what she called Concerned Citizens Group for Election Reform. When youngsters are courageous enough to do this, we need not fear how they will respond to bad election policies on a state level. Wendy and her friends learned that they could effect change when they were well organized and armed with facts. From election reform, they moved on to rewrite a meaningless and archaic school constitution. Next they sponsored a dress code revolt, but hardly in the way most common today. They believed the school should set a minimum standard rather than leave it to student whims. Since this was a rather unpopular tack for pre-teens, they insisted that a questionnaire, stating both sides of the issue, be sent to parents.

A HYPOTHETICAL CASE

These practical exercises in democratic action, some won, some lost, are excellent training. We shouldn't try to talk our young people out of taking an active part in bringing about change through proper methods. A few years ago when campus revolts were popular, I was chatting with my Sunday school class of teenagers about "going along with the crowd." We discussed the will of the majority in a democratic body and also mob tactics where the will of the majority can be wrong and dangerous. I proposed a hypothetical question: the radical students on your campus have decided to burn down the administration building because a certain course of study has been refused by the principal. Would you: (1) Help burn down the administration building by lighting and throwing torches? (2) Stand on the sidelines and watch the building burn to the ground? (3) Decide it was a horrible mess and go quietly home? (4) Try to stop what was going on? To get honest answers, I asked them to respond anonymously in writing.

Out of ten students, one decided to help the fire, three would watch it, four would go home and two would try to stop it. There followed a lively discussion as to the rightness of the actions. The one who would help the fire said he would do so because he felt that all proper action had been taken to give the administration the opportunity to add the course of study. However, the others convinced him that it would be far better to keep the administration building and try again and again, after gathering facts, to have the course of study added. One pointed out that in the long run the new course would not make that much difference. The fire-lighter finally admitted that it would be the fun of doing something sensational that really intrigued him.

Those who would watch and those who would go home were the students who felt "one person can't do anything." We then discussed the power of one person to change his personal life, his community and even the world. The two students who said they would try to stop the fire were the most vocal. They admitted that against a mob they might have great difficulty. However, they felt they could *not* be quiet in the face of wrong. Those who proposed going home argued that there would be personal danger in talking against the plan. At this point, the fire-setter himself said, "Then you're the kind that's just going to be walked over by all kinds of wild people."

Everyone agreed that when a situation has reached riot stage, it is far less easy to salvage. That is also true in handling revolt with our children. It's far easier to handle the cause of revolt when symptoms first appear.

The one common cause for revolt is that a child does not wish to do what he is told. Rather than react to his tantrum or stubbornness, be calm and get his viewpoint. You may find his reasons are valid. You may have failed to convince him because:

1. You haven't told him all the facts.
2. You have not tried to reason with him.
3. He doesn't feel he has an active part in decisions.
4. You have forced him to do things that have no apparent purpose.
5. He is not finding challenge and excitement in other areas.

It's up to us to provide decision-making opportunities. Children's birthdays or New Years are good times to evaluate with your children the areas of their lives of which they have complete charge, areas where we parents do not make any decisions. Don't be afraid to say, "That's your decision." From toddler through teens, we often provide too much help, make too many decisions. Then the child revolts and takes over decision-making areas for which he is unprepared. One solution is to give him more decision-making authority each year. For example, on each birthday increase his allowance and also increase his responsibilities and privileges.

Wendy has had many years of being required to make her bed and tidy her room. Then she reached the age where, although she is still encouraged to do so, we leave this decision entirely to her. Having developed the habit, she continues in this acceptable pattern most of the time, but because *she* decides.

START YOUNG

A small child should be allowed to decide what to wear. You may wish to offer a two-year-old a couple of outfits from which to choose. This teaches him to make a decision and stick with it. What room he plays in, who he plays with and which game he plays are other decisions he can make. Let him decide if he wishes to clean up his toys before supper, and thus be able to play a game after supper, or leave all his work to the end of the evening. As a child gets older and is free in the neighborhood, he can decide where to go, who to play with and how to spend his allowance. What he eats for snacktime or dessert can be left to him. Give him the choice of reading a little for his book report each night or staying in all day Saturday to complete it.

Make it clear that some types of decisions will be made by parents longer than others but that eventually the child will have the right to make all decisions. When to go to bed, what car to buy with his own savings, whether to go to a party, what electives to take are teenage decisions.

A child may ask our opinion when he faces a decision we want him to make on his own. Give him the pros and cons, then loose him to make up his own mind. And keep quiet! He'll learn quickly that spending his entire allowance the first day of the month makes for sparse living the remainder of the month. How much better to find this out himself rather than being told in advance by an all-knowing parent.

By letting a child make many decisions we teach him how to reason and think things through. The child who says "I won't" or demands "Why?" is asking us to back up our reasons. Be quick to do so. Parents who don't make it clear what the rules are, who don't stand firm on their rules and who merely *demand* obedience, are asking for trouble in the form of big revolts.

Teach children that there's a time to be stubborn and a time to agree quickly. Certain things aren't worth an argument. There are times when we do not argue unless it is an earth-shaking issue. Mark wanted to wear his new khaki shorts to the movie. I asked him to change into jeans but en route noticed he hadn't. After sitting on the scratchy theater upholstery for two hours he said to me, "Why didn't you *make* me change?" I said that it wasn't that important to me. He sighed and said "Yeh, I know you just wanted me to find out for myself. Wow!"

How to revolt is important, too. A good revolter avoids slander, speaks with vehemence but with grace, presents what he knows to be the honest facts, listens carefully to arguments on the other side of the question, then makes his own decision or abides by the decision made for him.

When a child wants some particular change, let him present his reasons honestly and sincerely. Be fair. Perhaps you can say in good grace,

"You know, I didn't agree at first, but you convinced me." Our young revolter must see that he is not presenting evidence to a mind already made up. It behooves us to have an open mind until we have heard his facts and the child has heard our side.

The way we listen and respond, the way we present our facts, is an example to the child of how to revolt with grace. When the decision has been made, the matter should be dropped and the revolt ended. If the decision goes in favor of the child, subsequent events will prove or disprove the wisdom of the decision. If, however, the parent insists, even after hearing the child's story, that status quo is best, he should be sure to say to the child, "I do think some of your arguments are valid and I hope that you will bring up the subject again in a few months." There are very, very few completely closed issues in a family. On the other hand, do not hesitate to let the child know that you feel strongly about certain basic elements in the family code of behavior.

Next time there is an "I won't" shouted at your house, try taking the young revolter away from the situation to a quiet place. Take out a tablet and make a balance sheet of the "whys" and "why not's." This procedure, repeated several times, will soon teach even the youngest child that decisions are made on the basis of fact and reason. He can learn gradually to go through this procedure by himself before revolting.

Our kitchen is next to the children's playroom. One afternoon I heard Mark and a friend discussing a rather wild idea. The friend proposed it for several minutes. Finally Mark said, "It's no use asking Mother about it. She doesn't say yes to dumb ideas."

21
Living
With
Surprises

Mark came home from school one day in a black mood. I immediately sensed it and asked what had happened to make him kick the door and look with turned-down mouth at his favorite cookie. He answered belligerently, "They served fried chicken for lunch today. The school menu we brought home showed that it was going to be meat loaf." I said, "I know you love meat loaf, but I always thought you liked fried chicken, too." He answered, "Well, I do, but they *said* it was going to be meat loaf."

A hazard of our organized way of life! Parents say certain things will happen and they usually do. Schools announce plans and menus and children expect them to happen. When something unusual comes about, a child may have difficulty in coping unless we teach him the joy of the flexible and adventuresome way of life. Much of the when and how of a child's day is arbitrary: we decide what it's going to be. There *could* be other times and better ways to do the same things. By our own actions we can show children that when we get a better idea, we accept it and act upon it; that we can meet little changes without being upset.

Avoid a routine that excludes creativity and change. Occasionally change plans purposely so that children are not startled by the unexpected. This doesn't mean keeping home life in such a constant state of flux that there is no security. But the security we give our child is *not* in knowing exactly what is going to happen but in knowing that he is prepared to handle whatever happens.

The home offers many opportunities for teaching flexibility. Next time you rearrange the living room, include the children in the project and solicit and accept their ideas. Encourage them to rearrange their own rooms. That the new layout ignores the picture in the home magazine or the interior decorator's idea is of little importance if the arrangement adds variety and flexibility to the child's life. Kent and Karen are great room rearrangers. Only by trying out all their fabulous new systems of toy boxes next to beds, desks cozied up to windows and dressers pushed into closets can they see for themselves that some plans are more livable than others. Their trying it out is far better than our telling them the "best" way. We've found that the children have come up with some good arrangements we had never considered.

When a small child is rearranging his room, although he'll need your help to move heavy furniture, *he* is in charge. He bosses *you* around. You do as you are told. Be cooperative, don't grumble! This kind of role reversal can be profitable fun.

Be as flexible as possible about mealtimes. Depending on when parents get home, dinner can be moved around anywhere from five until eight o'clock. A candlelight supper at 7:30, with young children in their pajamas and soon going off to bed, can be a quieting, pleasant experience.

Weekends are great times for flexibility. Although anticipation is wonderful, think of the excitement that follows the announcement that in 20 minutes the entire family is going on a picnic! With such short notice, cooperation is terrific and much of the so-called work of getting ready is done with speed and enthusiasm. Doing things on short notice eliminates most wasted time in getting ready for the event. Decisions as to what to wear and what to eat are made swiftly.

WHY NOT?

"No" requires little thought. "Why not?" can be the gateway to adventure. When a child proposes a new idea or a change in the family plans, it's easy to say "no." Simply because *we* haven't thought of it or because it hasn't been done before is no reason to say "no." We stifle creativity and flexibility in our children when we say "no" rather than "let's see." "Let's see" can speed up everyone's thought processes. If the idea is a good one, we can quickly give it the "Okay, let's do it."

One Saturday lunch I was putting together a large fruit salad with Kent's help. As we finished, I asked what he thought we should serve with it, thinking he'd say crackers, chips or toast. He thought a while and replied: "What I'd really like with it is some applesauce." I almost said "no," but thinking about it, I figured "why not?" It was a great success, and not bad nutritionally, either.

A few days later when all the children wanted to sleep on the lawn in sleeping bags — on a school night — I agreed providing they actually slept rather than monkeyed around. I was getting the "why not" knack, and it was fun. With so many actions that must be accomplished on schedule "or else," we may need to work at holding onto the spontaneity of life, free-wheeling ideas, the joys of pioneering and the fun of surprises.

22
You
Can Do It!

One day a friend told Wendy and Kent a story that has meant much to them, although at the time they didn't know the meaning of the word *optimism*. A young man, trying to get somewhere, was confronted by a monumental brick wall, higher and wider than he could see. However, he didn't stand in front of the wall and say, "How high it is, how wide it is! I shall never get over this wall!" Instead, he thought, "Box, rope, ladder, shovel, bulldozer, dynamite" —all the ways of surmounting that wall! And he was successful.

This example of the "you can do it" attitude, of a hopeful and optimistic approach to problems, showed Wendy and Kent that far more is accomplished with the conviction that it *can* be done than with mental defeatism. Depending on your own convictions, you may want to teach your children that "all things are possible" with God's help. But no matter how great or small your own hopefulness, teach your child that he has definite control over personal success or failure and that positive thinking adds much to the success side of the balance.

The same is true with the problems our children bring us. It is so easy for them to toss a problem in front of us for a solution. If we let them get by with it, they will bring us a string of problems all day long. "I can't get the cracker box down." "We don't know what game to play." "I can't find my green shirt."

Start with the two-year-old child to insist that he be solution-oriented. When he's older and brings you a problem, ask him to bring at least one solution. Taught to think of solutions, he will try them and often solve the problem himself.

Don't be quick to solve the problem for the child. Ask him what he has done to solve it or how he would suggest solving it. Ask: "What have you done to reach the box of crackers?" "Have you looked in your cupboard at all the games you own?" "Where have you looked for the green shirt?" Above all, don't ridicule the solution he has brought. Say,

"Yes, that's an idea but how about…" and, when necessary, suggest a better one. Sarcasm will defeat the child's natural optimism and make him pessimistic. Sarcasm has no place in the discipline of children. Sarcasm is an adult-acquired taste. Parents communicate best when they avoid sarcasm and ridicule.

In teaching the child to view problems optimistically and seek solutions, we may at first have to go even one step further. "What can you stand on to reach the crackers?" "Find three games you haven't played this week and try those." "Move every hanger in your closet from one end to the other to be sure the shirt is not hanging on one of them."

Gradually a child will gain confidence in his own ability to solve problems and he will view experiences that others might find discouraging with hopefulness and optimism. Here are some ways we can help our children to be optimistic:

1. When you must use the phrase, "You can't," couple it with "You can." "You *can't* jump off the roof of the house but you *can* jump out of the tree. Try it from a low branch first." "You *can't* possibly do 50 arithmetic problems in ten minutes but you *can* do them in 30 minutes." "You *can't* swim across the ocean but you *can* swim across the pool."

2. Show the child how he can do it. Perhaps you have told the child that he can't play cards with his grandfather until his homework is done, and he answers pessimistically, "My homework will never be done." Don't accept a pessimistic attitude. Kent used to try this when told that certain tasks were to be done before other activities. "Impossible!" he'd say. We would simply help him do it the first time, then refer to that success the next time. It works! The child who gives the "I can't" response deserves a parent who will read a book in the corner of his room while encouraging him to clean it up. One such experience can break him of the "I can't" habit. If Kent gives me that line, I say, "Well, I will sit right next to you while you do it," and he quickly responds, "Okay, okay, I'll get it done."

3. Compliment and encourage the child. When he sees that you have faith in him, he becomes more optimistic on his own.

4. Urge him to think about the good things that happen, not just the bad experiences. We are so brainwashed by newspapers that emphasize sensationalism and pessimism that we feel all reports, to be worth hearing, have to be bad. The news media show tragedy, strife, erotica, crime to the point where we may feel pessimistic all the time. Good news is hardly news at all. We don't have to have this attitude in our own homes. When a child is telling you the events of his day, he may be inclined, at first, to tell you the bad things that happened, how he got knocked down or how he had some terrible test. Point out that balancing these two events were many hours when things went *right*. Ask him to share some good experiences from that period of time.

5. Reassure him that people care about his success—that *many* people are hopeful and optimistic about his being able to do right and be happy. Mothers and fathers, school teachers, Scout leaders—all these people wouldn't be devoting time and effort to help him succeed if they were not optimistic about the results. When things get rough and pessimism sets in, he should ask these people for help.

6. Finally, parents must help a child realize how far he has come. They must recall the things a child said he couldn't do or thought he couldn't do and show how these experiences turned out right. They must demonstrate to the child that he only *thought* he couldn't learn to tie his shoes, but when he changed his mind and decided to try, he learned how to do it. There's nothing sadder than a parent who is constantly putting his child down either because he thinks the child is inadequate or, even worse, because it makes the parent feel important.

One day I was talking with my third grade Campfire Girls about a project for which we needed a particularly difficult-to-make costume. One girl eagerly said, "My mother can show me how to do most anything." What a compliment! The statement wasn't "My mother can *do* anything," but "My mother has the know-how to show me." While we don't wish to appear super-human to our children nor lay impossible goals before them, far more things than we admit are achievable. We should teach our children that their own optimistic efforts will bring them happiness and success.

23
Try,
Try Again

Karen's young uncle decided that it was time for her to learn to water ski. She was a good swimmer, the small lake was warm, other swimmers were on the scene and all her same-aged cousins had gotten up on the skis and whizzed about the lake with great confidence. Karen put the ski belt around her waist and sat in the water with the ski tips up while the boat motor was revved up. She listened carefully to the basic instructions. As the boat took off with gusto, she plunged head first into the water.

A few more instructions, a bit more encouragement, and the scene was repeated once more. In fact, Karen plunged head first into the water about ten more times before she finally took off around the lake. Once up, her only problem was that she had slim hips and the oversized life belt kept sliding to her knees! However, she was obviously enjoying her success after the discouraging beginning.

Then from our pier vantage point we noticed Karen purposefully fall in the middle of the lake. The boat drew up beside her, she grabbed the towel thrown to her and hauled herself aboard. When the boat came back to the pier, she jumped out, hugged the towel about her, said "Don't anybody speak to me," and ran up to the cottage. She returned in a few seconds in a different swim suit. Once more she started water skiing, this time with great confidence and success. It was only at bedtime that I learned that the ski belt had moved slowly down her hips and removed the bottom half of her bikini!

Where do some children get this willingness to try and try again after failure? Karen was diligent because here was something she truly wanted to do. Those around her, knowledgeable uncles and proud parents, wanted her to do it and encouraged her. Under the watchful eye of cousins who had already been successful, she was even more eager to succeed. She had seen others do it; she could, too. So, no matter how many dunkings, all she had to do was correct her mistakes and she, too, would ski.

A child who lacks diligence in completing a project may be lazy, dis-

98

interested or lacking in parental encouragement. But, let's not forget that there are some things that are *not* worth doing. At Christmas Wendy received a long-wanted embroidery set. It was quite intricate. To begin she had to regroup all the thread in the kit from strands of three to strands of two. She was diligent in doing this. Then, finding that the needle was the wrong size, she had to get another needle. After that she discovered that part of the pattern was not correctly printed on the fabric. Later, she found that the color guide was not explicit enough to differentiate between the many shades of pink, rose and orange. She had hoped for a kit she could complete in one night with a large needle and heavy yarn. But this particular set was going to result in a year's work and produce a flowery pattern that didn't appeal to her. How relieved she was when I suggested that she put it up on her top shelf until she was a teen-age baby-sitter and could work on the project with more patience and ability.

It's well to point out that many things *worth* doing are *not* accomplished on the first try. We all agree that knowing how to walk is worthwhile; thus, when baby attempts his first steps, we encourage him despite the many times he falls. We don't say to baby, "You'll never walk," and put him back in his crib.

An older child can see the importance of diligence in learning to tie a shoe. This is a difficult and intricate experience that requires certain steps be taken in sequence. Let us be sure we are encouraging diligence in experiences that are important — important to the child as well as the parents.

When a child has tasted success and sees the benefits of completing a project, he gains the determination to try another project, so we build on past successes. Many projects that seem doomed to failure or that begin with a series of failures can be divided into smaller jobs. At spring-cleaning time, rather than say, "I want your entire bedroom put in order," divide the job into five smaller tasks. "I will look only at your dresser drawers and closet today; tomorrow I'll check out the toy chest; the next day, the cupboard; the next day, your play table," and so on. The division of a large job into smaller jobs gives the child the incentive to get it done. We can then build on the success of one day in achieving the success of the next.

Some efforts never succeed. The child diligently tries to raise his C-spelling grade into the B range quarter after quarter, but he fails. Or he strives for a regular position on the baseball team, goes out for all the practices and games but is assigned to the bench and plays only in dire emergencies. When a child fails despite diligence, we must support his determination and his desire to get the project done. Show him that although he did not receive the usual reward for diligence, he should continue to try if the goal has merit.

Diligence sometimes brings unexpected blessings. Wendy worked hard on the school paper but never got on the masthead, yet she was chosen literary editor of the yearbook. Sometimes we can see that a goal needs to be broadened, given more time to be achieved or even abandoned. Sometimes you may want to ask the child, "Do you really want to do this? Is it really important to you to receive your first-class rank?" But when a child abandons a goal, he doesn't need to be left in a vacuum. He should be encouraged to find another activity to take its place.

When you sense how important some goal is to the child, your support can be the biggest factor in his reaching it and the greatest comfort should he fail. Help him to see that the fun of *doing* can equal the joy of achieving and that failure is no cause for shame. Laziness is.

24
Religion
And The Young
Child

When Karen's father was running for an elective office, a well-meaning friend said to her, "Oh my, I can imagine how you feel about your father being in this election. It will be sad if he doesn't win." Karen chirped back, "No, it won't be sad. It will just mean that God has something better for him to do." This was no studied response on Karen's part nor anything we had discussed at home. Rather, it was part of a lifetime of teaching her that the universe is not run in a haphazard way but includes a wonderful divine plan for each of us.

In this era when "God is dead" has become a popular phrase, it's most important from infancy onward to give our children a belief in a Power superior to man. Whether you call this Supreme Being *God* or use another term, it is important to show children their relationship to this Power and how to utilize this in their daily lives. In terms of your own religious beliefs, you must give your child a framework within which to function. You must help him find an explanation for the universe and its consistency, for life, for death and for life after death. This reasoning and teaching leads the child to see the significance of what he does here rather than feel that our material life has no value or plan.

Nihilism and existentialism can degrade our children's lives during the high school and college years if we have not given them as young children the faith and the facts to understand the Supreme Being. Life is not the accumulation of brownie points; we need the conviction that doing right brings its reward here or hereafter. Children should be early taught the importance of life and how best to live it now.

How do we teach religion and the belief in a Supreme Being to our children? Through religious study in the home. This may sound dull, and you may argue that this is a field in which you are not strong enough to teach. However, the very teaching of it will strengthen you. Aids are available for teaching religion in interesting and exciting ways.

Teach an acquaintance with the literature of religion, both your own

101

and others, and respect for other religions and their symbols. Also talk about the meaning of faith, the reality of spiritual things, the importance of tolerance and brotherly love.

Explaining seeming inconsistencies in religion is important. Children sincerely want to know why babies die, how good deeds are rewarded, why some people get away with doing wrong. These are topics that should be answered with the teachings of one's own religion. Some parents may first wish to seek answers for themselves from their religious leaders.

Outside the home we should encourage participation in some form of organized religion, whether it be released time from school for religious study, reading, revival meetings, attendance at synagogue, church or Sunday school. Here, of course, the example of the parents becomes of prime importance. Where parents are unwilling or unable to set an example of religious participation, perhaps grandparents or uncles and aunts can carry out this important assignment.

Youngsters turn from religion when it is presented in a boring or irrelevant way. As parents, as members of religious groups or as teachers in Sunday schools, we've got to make our teachings practical, consistent, dynamic and useful *right now* to our young people.

Some families feel that the teaching of religion, morals and ethics can be done through the weekly session of an organized religion. But religious values must be lived and practiced daily in order to be effective. We cannot abandon our children's religious training to one hour weekly in the organized church body.

In our home we begin each week day morning with Bible study and we also have an hour "chat" on Sunday afternoons. Our morning Bible reading sessions have always been a part of our lives and so when Wendy was a baby, she was given her wake-up bottle and then put into her baby chair for Bible study time. As the children grew up, the morning 20-minute session became a natural part of their day.

For many families this is not a practical plan and religious observance may take place at mealtimes or before bedtime. The saying of bedtime prayers should be a part of daily life but not mere routine. The prayers taught to children should be varied so that they become more than a recitation of meaningless words. As a child grows up, his prayers should become deeper in meaning to him and he should be encouraged to create his own prayers. When a child reaches the age when he feels prayers said aloud with parents sitting on the edge of the bed are too babyish, he should be encouraged to pray silently by himself.

For children from two to twelve, Bible stories make excellent bedtime stories. They are often more interesting than fairy tales, just as exciting and more pertinent to daily problems. If you doubt your own story-telling ability, get a copy of *The Children's Bible*, a well-illustrated volume that can be used easily with children under twelve.

In our daily activities and conversation, we parents should not be hesitant about speaking religiously to our children and encouraging them to verbalize their religious feelings. Before Wendy was born we purchased an old Victorian chest for her room. The drawer pulls on the chest were missing so we replaced them with white porcelain knobs which we were told should be authentically painted with blue rosebuds. I got the blue paint but never having been much of an artist, I found rosebuds did not come easily to me. However, I have always been passable at printing so I selected six brief Biblical phrases as the first Bible lessons for our children. Through the years as the old chest has passed from child to child, the painted porcelain knobs have had to be repainted and reglazed in the oven. But those early lessons have been important to us and to the children. These knobs are labeled:

The Lord is my Shepherd
Peace, be still
There is no fear in love
Blessed are the pure in heart
God is Love
A little child shall lead them

When a child is eight or nine, ecumenical visits are useful. These can be made with friends of another religion or with the family. The child thus becomes aware of what other denominations are available in the area and how services differ. If often reinforces his feelings about his own religion. The important part of these church visits is the discussion that follows. One summer we attended churches with other couples who had children about the same ages as ours. Following church we picnicked together and compared the basic beliefs of our respective denominations. We discussed church teachings on marriage, death, punishment, sin, forgiveness, etc. It was a casual and friendly exchange, an opportunity to listen to others' beliefs and discuss them without being argumentative.

One of the best opportunities for learning about other religions is travel. Most major cities of the United States have spectacular churches worth visiting. In the bigger cathedrals and temples, guides explain the major points of the religion. Travel abroad exposes children to many other religions. In Italy they can see the headquarters of the Roman Catholic Church. Climbing to the top of the Church of the Nativity in Bethlehem to see the Christmas bells was an unforgettable experience for our children. Prior to this Christian trip to the Holy Land, we felt it important that they know more about Judaism so we attended a local synagogue and also had several chats with a rabbi who was willing to explain some of the basic teachings to us.

Children are interested in symbolism. The meaning of religious statuary in Catholic and Greek Orthodox churches should be explained.

Through travel our children have learned history as taught by the Star of David and the Crescent and Star of Islam. One of their travel treasures is a cross each purchased, some of rough olive wood, others of delicate pearl.

In our Sunday afternoon family meetings, we often discuss the application of religious teachings to present-day problems at home and abroad. But we give equal time to more fanciful ideas since we find the children retain knowledge when it is taught through games. One of the most popular is "Bible Charades." We take turns acting out Bible characters and stories. The person or story has to be acted out without words or props. Mark does a wonderful job of choosing his smooth stones to go forth as David meeting Goliath. Karen loves to dramatize colorful characters like devoted Ruth or Lot's weak wife turning into a pillar of salt. All by himself Kent can play the three boys in the fiery furnace. Wendy recreates the pool at Bethesda with the infirmed man attempting to get into the water. We parents are not exempt. Dad does a great job of Abraham preparing to sacrifice Isaac and my greatest triumph is as the lady with the lamp as described in Revelation.

We have also devised some fun that parallels non-religious games. We play "Bible Concentration" with a handmade deck of cards in pairs (Moses and Commandments, Daniel and Lions, Jesus and Beatitudes, etc.) All cards are faced down and we take turns exposing only two at a time in an attempt to find the match.

We have Bible Quiz-Downs using questions from a Bible magazine someone gave us. More recently, one child used the check list of things learned in Sunday School to make up a list of new questions for this game.

A favorite game is one of quotations. We typed up about 50 common religious quotes and cut them in half. We deal these out among us. Then, we take turns asking for the half we don't have. As in the game of *Authors*, popular a generation ago, you have to ask using the right words. For example, if you have the half quote that says, "Do unto others," you would say to another player, "Can you give me 'As you would have them do unto you?' " The other player must give it up if he has it. If he doesn't have it, the player having it will probably ask you for YOUR half when it is his turn. You can keep asking as long as you are successful, but when you get a "no," the next player takes his turn.

Karen and I created a game much like the popular children's games that require the move of a marker from a starting point to a finish while avoiding pitfalls along the way. Our game, drawn on old cardboard, traced the journey of the Children of Israel from Egypt to the Promised Land. All the markers started as slaves in Egypt and moved at the throw of a die along the pathway that led them out of Egypt across the Red Sea through the Wilderness and on to the Promised Land. The pitfalls included Mount Sinai, where Moses gave the Children of Israel the Ten Commandments. In passing this point, if you landed on a particular square you

104

had to say a number of Commandments. Our children learned much by making up these games.

In our travels we have collected nativity scenes from many countries. At the holiday season we join in unpacking these and setting them up in the front hall, living room, in the center of the dining table and in children's rooms. One special set is kept for opening on successive Sunday afternoons in December. Late in the afternoon, we gather to open the box. The pieces are carefully wrapped in tissue paper from the year before and numbered in the order to be opened. We take turns reading the Christmas story in three or four sections, one each Sunday. The first Sunday the part about the angels is read. Mary, Joseph and the angel are unwrapped and put in place. The next Sunday the shepherds and sheep join the story. The following week the inn keeper and barn animals are opened and put in place. On the final Sunday before Christmas, the baby Jesus and the kings and camels are unwrapped. Although we all know by now how the pieces look, there is still the thrill each year of recreating the story.

When in Switzerland one Christmas, we found some carved figures on the nativity story—all done as peasants: a Swiss barn, a Swiss shepherd, old men and women in folk dress, a seated madonna with a white-gowned baby on her knees. The children were fascinated but we couldn't afford more than two pieces. So we obtained a catalog and each autumn we select one new piece and send away for it.

Whatever your religion, there are special holidays with deep significance. Make the most of these with your children. See that they understand the historical background of that holiday and the present-day celebration of it. Because our schools are now including more than the Christian tradition in holidays, our children have come to appreciate Hanukkah, Buddha Day and the Swedish Saint Lucia's Day. While teaching our children a better understanding of our chosen religion, we must also teach them to understand those who are equally committed to *their* chosen religion.

Teaching religion to your child gives him an anchor in turbulent times. It gives him a faith to rely on when human aids fail. Any system that has saved and comforted as many people as the belief in God has should not be ignored in the character-building of our children. A thorough background in religious beliefs would make unnecessary any other character training for our children!

Your Week Two Check List

Here's where you begin character building:

Review this list of child traits and check off those you feel need the most reinforcement at this time. Then re-read the sections on those you've checked off. (The number in parentheses indicates the chapter you'll want to re-read.)

	Today's date	6 weeks from now	6 months from now
Good (6)			
Happy (6)			
Affectionate (7)			
Truthful (8)			
Poised (9)			
Considerate of possessions (10)			
Unselfish (11)			
Polite, appreciative (12)			
Obedient to authority (13)			
Able to admit mistakes (14)			
Amusing (15)			
Able to solve disagreements (16)			
Able to organize time (17)			
Content when alone (18)			
A good listener (19)			
Able to revolt intelligently (20)			
Flexible, spontaneous (21)			
Optimistic (22)			
Diligent, determined (23)			
Learning about his religion (24)			

Start to work with these ideas. Character building takes time, so return to this check list again to see how you're doing.

Now, onward to Week Three!

Week
Three

3
3
3
3
3
3
3
3
3
3
3
3
3

Can Order
And Helpfulness
Be Fun?

Many parents don't have their children help around the house because they find the jobs have not been done satisfactorily. However, helping is a learning experience as well as a delegating one and parents who set about to teach their children orderliness and helpfulness must be prepared to explain and show and explain and show again.

Orderliness and helpfulness are stressed in school but these useful habits are primarily learned in the home. Teaching our children how to act in a civilized way at home can be fun for both parent and child.

First, remember that helpfulness in a *learning* experience may not be perfect the first time, and it may *never* be. Second, remember that the child cannot work under the fear of punishment. Order and helpfulness are taught in a most lasting way when the child realizes that he is learning to do what will bring him the greatest happiness. Don't expect him to perform like a trained dog. So relax, sit back and enjoy the progress of the child.

25
How To Teach
The Importance Of
Order And Helpfulness

One spring the circular flower bed in front of our house was especially beautiful. Several hundred daffodils had come into bloom in one week. This sea of yellow signified all the promise of spring after a snowy winter. Wendy was five and eager to be the "big girl" in front of the younger children. While they were having a long nap one day, she and I went out to look closely at these interesting flowers. We picked three for a simple arrangement in the front hall where all could enjoy it. She was fascinated and I told her that I would help her make an arrangement for the supper table when the soon-to-bloom iris were ready. A few days later when I was in the windowless laundry room, she stuck her head in the door and asked how much longer I would be folding. I said about fifteen minutes. She asked that I call before I came out because she was working on a surprise. It was quite a surprise. I was taken by the hand and lead from room to room to see all the flower "derangements" of daffodils she had made in pails. She had carefully cut the circular flower bed right down to the nubs!

I didn't know whether to laugh or cry. I had to admit that her motive to be helpful and bring spring into the house was great. Then we turned it into a fun project and made arrangements —not in pails— for each room of the house. There were STILL flowers, so we made small bouquets which Wendy took to the other five houses on the street. In return our neighbors gave her conversation, cookies and compliments for her thoughtfulness. Later we did have a private chat on cutting only some of the flowers, leaving some to be enjoyed outside.

Yes, it takes extra patience and extra time to teach and supervise child-helpers. But in the long run their aid will save you time, give them an appreciation for a cooperative family unit and make them more responsible as adults and future parents.

110

You know the 3 R's; now you can practice the 3 P's: Purpose, Procedure, Praise — essential to teaching order and helpfulness.

PURPOSE

Often a child wants to know why he should do a certain task. Although there are times when he should quickly be obedient, usually we have the time to give a simple reason. And keep it simple. Avoid the habit of giving a big sales talk before getting cooperation. Any one of these is a sufficient purpose: that the parent needs some help; that it is something everyone learns to do; that it will give the parent time to read a story later; that it will make the child happy; that it will make the parent happy; that it shows responsibility; that it will increase the child's abilities. Sometimes you can turn the question "Why?" back to the child: "I wonder if you can figure out why I want you to set the table tonight?" Some tasks are simply done as a fair share of the homemaking.

PROCEDURE

You may know which is a Phillips screwdriver, how much soap to put in the dishwasher, the way to start the record player or how to fold a diaper. Your young helper may not. So with each task give simple instructions, including safety precautions. With some jobs, the child may watch the first time, help the second time, do it as you watch the third time and do it himself the fourth time. Even then it may not be quite right. Be patient, show again and praise for the part that was done right. Soon you may hear those welcome words, "Let me try it" or "Let me do it by myself."

Teaching tasks this way means they'll be done close to your specifications. And don't be surprised if the child is able to do some tasks better than you! Be open to suggestions on how to do some jobs a better way.

PRAISE

The frosting on the cake of helpfulness is praise. Use lots! Maybe teaching and redoing took as much time as if you'd done the job yourself. Try again. In the long run, you'll be saving time and giving the kids invaluable knowledge. Reinforce the right procedure when you praise. For example, say to a child:

"Did you notice that Kent put the fork here on the left and the knife and spoon here on the right? Maybe you'd like to do it tomorrow."

"That was great that you fed the dog. Tomorrow remember that along with the food he'll want a fresh bowl of water."

"Look at all these pages of trading stamps, pasted in so neatly. What do you think we should buy with them? Before bed, let's look through the catalog together."

Let the good words flow, phrases like "Thanks a lot," "I really appreciated that," "You did a good job," "That really saved time," "It was a kind thing to do." Letting words of praise be part of YOUR conversation, you may even hear them coming back to you for something you've done.

26
Helpful Things
A Child
Can Do

Our children are able to do much more than we give them credit for. Too often we give them tasks that don't tax their abilities. As children measure up to certain tasks, we should be alert to issue more difficult assignments.

The helpful things a child can do fall into three categories:
1. Daily tasks they do routinely.
2. Special tasks they do over the weekend or after school.
3. Tasks they are able to do on request.

Though far from complete, the following list will lead you to tasks that fall into each of the three categories.

AGES 2-3
Dress self
Tidy room
Scrub fingernails
Wash face and be checked
Brush teeth and be checked
Smooth bottom sheet on bed and fluff pillow
Pick up toys
Open curtains
Bring in the newspaper
Wash doll clothes
Help sort laundry
Stack prefolded diapers
Run errands around the house
Empty wastebaskets
Help set the table
Pick up leaves
Fetch tools and learn their names and locations

Naturally you won't have a toddler doing all these jobs simultaneously. If so, parents could just retire! However, it is well to inspire very young children with the desire to be helpful. With a little training none of these jobs is beyond the ability of toddlers and they will find joy in the doing.

AGES 4-5-6

During these years when children enjoy being considered bigger and want to try more difficult jobs, a safe, lightweight step stool is helpful.

Wash self
Wash own hair
Brush teeth
Make bed
Fix own hair
Remove dishwasher contents to counter
Sweep floor
Wipe countertops
Deliver laundry
Run can opener
Bring in mail
Start to learn home repairs
Put up flag outside house
Paste in trading stamps
Feed pets
Make flower arrangements
Run record player
Put name labels into books
Entertain baby
Conduct family meeting
Draw pictures for thank-you letters
Help pack own belongings for family moving day
Weed garden

There are two special tasks this age group can do. At our house, they are called "outside pick up" and "inside pick up." When the call, "Supper in ten minutes" is given, the child assigned to outside pick up makes a circuit of the yard and brings in the jackets, balls and toys. This doesn't mean the other children are entitled to leave all their toys outside. Each is responsible for his own things; however, the outside pick up person can also shut gates, make sure all doors are closed, and guarantee that precious bicycles are not left out in the rain.

The inside pick up person is responsible for seeing that what we call the "public areas" of the house are tidy before the dinner hour. The public areas are living room, dining room, porch, stairs and hallways. Thus, should the doorbell ring late in the day, no one would be embarrassed to find his school books, apple cores, galoshes or underwear on display. Toys are removed from those areas that are for general family use, cushions are put back, newspapers are picked up off the floor and we are ready for a leisurely evening without having to legislate tidying. Playrooms and bedrooms can be as messy as their occupants wish at this time of day.

We use our record player a great deal and our inside pick up person is responsible on Fridays for collecting all the records that have been used and left out of their jackets, dusting them and filing them back where they belong.

AGES 7-8-9

Any of the foregoing tasks, of course, can be done by older children. It is well, however, to add new tasks as children become older and to release them from some of the simpler jobs. You may have to assume these yourself if there is no younger child! The 7-8-9-year-old child can read and has learned to follow directions at school. So at this age, before much homework sets in, there are many things that these interesting youngsters can do.

Wash the car
Take over breakfast or lunch-making on the weekend
Rake leaves
Fold laundry
Deliver laundry
Clean bathtub
Clean lavatories
Run sprinklers
Make home repairs, with some supervision
Learn to bake
Water house plants
Dust
Replace bathroom and facial tissue
Write own thank-you notes
Make own phone calls
Run vacuum cleaner
Put chemicals in swimming pool
Paint fences
Aid in putting up storm windows and screens
Help dress younger children
Plan own parties
Plan menus
Stamp and post mail
Answer telephone and take messages
Polish silver
Sew, with supervision
Load dishwasher
Change lightbulbs
Shovel snow
Help with grocery shopping
Serve as baby sitter while parents nap or bathe

Walk baby in stroller or carriage
Run errands on bicycle
Do own homework
Do own Sunday school assignments
Wash piano keys
Wash mirrors and picture frames
Build —but not light without parental okay —fire in fireplace
Build fire in barbecue
Select records to be played
Select television programs
Read reviews and recommend movies to attend
Read story to younger child
Test younger child on spelling words

You can see from this list that many of the helpful things this age child can do involve decision-making and planning abilities —assets at any age.

AGES 10-11-12

Now you're preparing for teen years and greater freedom. This may be your last chance to establish the helpfulness habit.

Make supper on own
Clean own room
Wash windows
Clean up kitchen after a party
Defrost, wash and reload refrigerator or freezer
Empty cupboards, wipe and replace shelf paper (parents to put contents back)
Polish own shoes
Copy recipes
Sew and mend
Iron
Shop alone
Babysit at age twelve
Change or bathe baby
Make own charts and rules
Serve guests at parties
Address envelopes for bill-paying
Keep family scrapbook
Scrub floors
Cut grass

Again, you wouldn't present this entire list to 10-11-12-year-olds! However, at this age it's easy for the child to see that these things have to be done and that spreading the work also spreads the time for fun.

Starting at age seven or eight you can give children a choice of jobs and take over those that are left. But, don't be afraid to change the jobs on a monthly basis, so that sooner or later the children are exposed to all of them.

27
Methods
Of Getting
The Job Done

Now that you are excited over all the useful things your children can do, the question is how to assure accomplishment — not just the first day but on a regular basis, week after week. This is where creative thought comes in. Forgetfulness is your biggest enemy.

Children may tell you they don't have time to be helpful. When one of our children says that, I sit down with him and total his estimates of how long the daily helps take. With four children, the work load is spread so that no child spends more than 20 to 45 minutes a day in carrying out his tasks. Multiply this by the number of your children and you can see how much extra time you'll gain.

THE GOOD AND HAPPY BOOK

My first attempt at writing some basic rules for behavior and helpfulness came when Mark was born and Kent and Karen were still small. On a whim one afternoon I created for them what has been called *The Good and Happy Book.* I felt that with two pre-school children, one baby and one fairly efficient grade schooler, we needed a set of rules that the pre-schoolers could understand and remember so that I wouldn't have to be reminding them all the time. On about 30 sheets of 8½ x 11 paper I wrote two-line jingles, really corny poems but ones the children could remember. I wrote them at the bottom of each page. Then flipping through magazines, I found funny ads and pictures to use as illustrations. I did not illustrate all the points, so when the book was given with great fanfare to the two toddlers, they saw that they could hunt for pictures to illustrate the other rules.

The Good and Happy Book became a most beloved volume. The very last page of it was a blank sheet on which the child could write his name in any way he chose after he had pasted in a picture. Today the book is dirty, spilled-on and torn, pages are falling out, and the back signature page is scribbled all over; however, many of the lines of the book we still

117

smilingly say to each other.

The dedication of the book took several pages. On the first page I wrote: "This is a book for a big, little boy named Kent." On this page I pasted a magazine picture of a swim-suited four-year-old jumping into the pool. I took a photograph of Kent's head and pasted it over the head of the boy in the picture. I did the same for the other members of the family, parents included. The dedication lines continue, "We love you very much and want you to be good and happy. That is why this book is called *The Good and Happy Book*." The next page is almost blank and says, "Let's read *The Good and Happy Book*. The what? *The Good and Happy Book*." It starts, then, with the basic rules I wanted the children to learn.

You could easily copy the idea of this book and your children would enjoy reading and illustrating it. You won't wish to copy our family rules but here are some of the captions from our book to give you an idea of what to include. I'm sure you can improve on my rhymes!

1. When Mom or Dad calls my name,
   I come as fast as a speedy jet plane.
2. Once in a while I see TV
   If the program's good for me.
3. When having fun or doing a chore,
   I remember to shut the kitchen door.
4. When someone hits me or is naughty or sad,
   I tell them what's right so they won't be bad.
5. "Please" and "thank you" are easy to say.
   How many times have you said them today?
6. When someone says, "How are you, dear?"
   I answer, "Fine," loud and clear.
7. When I get hungry and want a treat,
   I ask permission before I eat.
8. I wipe my feet when I come in the door.
   That helps me keep mud off the floor.
9. When crossing the street, a hand I hold.
   That's the rule 'til I'm five years old.
10. I never get into a car, you know,
    Unless I've asked if I may go.
11. In the car there is just one way to be:
    Seated and belted so that I can see.
12. When I am told to go to bed,
    I don't argue or shake my head.
13. My clothing never goes on the floor,
    Just in the wash or in my drawer.
14. Before I go to bed at night,
    There are three things I do right:
    Go to the bathroom

Wash my hands
Have a little drink
15. When I've been tucked into my bed,
    I shut my eyes and rest my head.
    I don't get out of bed and play.
    I think about the fun today.
16. When I go to sleep, I say my prayer.
    I know that God is with me there.

Children like to know what is expected of them. That's why a set of basic rules is helpful. The familiar line from *The Good and Happy Book*, "When someone calls my name, I come as fast as a speedy jet plane," is probably the most memorable for our children. When they hear their names called or when they hear the family whistle or the dinner bell, there is no one who shouts, "What?' There is nothing more exasperating than to want a child to come and to call, only to have him shout back, "What?" When you are called, you appear! By the way, we use a familiar tune as a "family whistle" to call one another in crowded places. Anyone hearing it knows he must come at once. It's saved us much time and concern. The whistle is quite distinctive but the whole family knows and can whistle it.

Every parent needs to inform his children of certain basics expected of them and these can easily be taught to the toddler. Our children had *The Good and Happy Book* memorized long before they could read. We were able to build on these basics and then teach the children new things.

FAMILY HEADQUARTERS

A corkboard in the breakfast area has proved to be a most effective information center for us. On this board can be pinned party invitations, job assignments, family calendars and other reminders. Permanently posted on the board are a list of important telephone numbers and the rules for baby sitters. The bulletin board must be a living, changing thing in order to get any attention. Once a month everything on the bulletin board comes down and new things go up. Depending on the size of your board, you can be festive or factual. Ours happens to be a big one so we can put up photographs and clippings, seasonal items and decorations. This is not necessary and if your bulletin board can merely take a few sheets of paper for the rules, the monthly task assignments and calendar, that's all you really need. Teach all family members that there is one place to look for important notes. Perhaps you want all messages put next to one particular phone or tacked up on the family bulletin board or written on the chalkboard.

THE MONTHLY CALENDAR

An essential to organization is the monthly calendar. The next month's calendar is revealed and reviewed on the last night of the month. I use one of those inexpensive jumbo calendars with plenty of space to write with colored pens. I write in everything that concerns the family: school, church, Campfire and Scout events, birthday parties, nights when parents are going out, entertaining at home, parent's business travel, family trips, dental appointments, arrival of relatives, date of book reports, etc. This gives everyone at the first of the month a bird's-eye view of what the next 30 days hold. Special party days, school holidays, arrival dates for relatives are ringed with special colors so we can look forward to them along with the routine. Children are welcome to put onto this calendar dates when important school or service projects are due.

This calendar is separate from my own daily calendar which shows the things that I must accomplish each day. The family calendar outlines what the children must do, what the family will do together and what the parents are doing that affects the children. When it is all written down in one place, you can then adjust or eliminate some activities to avoid rushed times. On the other hand, you may look over the month and find that you have some inactive time. Here, then, you can plan a major project or excursion that you have been waiting to do — a picnic, an afternoon with friends or a children's overnight. We once scheduled "Painting Saturday." Everything that needed to be painted was taken care of on that day.

The monthly calendar lets you keep things in balance. It also gives the children a sense of order and direction because they can see what lies ahead.

THE HELPS LIST

The final element of my bulletin board is the work assignment sheet, introduced the last day of each month. Some families call them tasks or chores; we happen to call them "helps." I've experimented with switching helps on a daily, weekly or monthly basis and find for greatest efficiency and ease of remembering it is best to change jobs once a month. When assigning a help for less than a month, I found that the child rarely reached top efficiency; however, if the help is assigned for more than a month the child begins to get bored with it. You may test this with your own children and come up with a different schedule.

Assignment to a brand new job shows the child he is becoming more mature and responsible. However, introduce only one *new* help at a time to a child. If his major new assignment is to fold and deliver the laundry, then go a little easy on him and give him other helps with which he is familiar and successful.

One of the hardest helps is to be "After-supper kitchen chief." I feel that whoever has to make the dinner is entitled to sit down afterwards to chat with spouse or read the paper. Four sturdy children can, within ten minutes time, put the dining room and kitchen back to rights! At our house the after-supper chores are divided this way:

1. Clearing the table and putting food away
2. Wiping counters
3. Sweeping the floor
4. Loading the dishwasher

However, with several children working simultaneously, there needs to be a "chief," so one doubles as chief and is responsible for the whole crew. Thus, the job of being kitchen chief is considered a very responsible one around our house. If you are kitchen chief, your other tasks during the month are easier.

Children should be given some tasks that require teamwork. It's good training to let them use their winning ways to get their peers to complete the task and do it right. They should also be given certain jobs that enable them to show what they can do completely on their own initiative, independent of brothers and sisters. Some children work well as a team; others do best on their own.

HOW MANY HELPS?

Just how much help you should require around the house is an individual question. If you have no household help, you will require more child-help. In the summer, children can double their help-time. During the school year, each of our children spends 20 to 40 minutes a day on about three tasks apiece. Special tasks on Saturday bring the total to about 90 minutes. With more children there is more work to do but more people to divide it among. A pre-school child can do about 20 minutes work with ease and enthusiasm.

GIMMICKS

I use all sorts of gimmicks, charts and incentives to see that the daily, weekly and monthly helps get done. The children also have a system to accomplish the necessary civilized morning tasks. I find incentive and reward far better than punishment. As the four children have grown, I have used a variety of charts for letting the children daily register their successes and also so that I don't have to be constantly reminding them of what to do or wondering if they've done it. You will find that after awhile certain things get done automatically and thus can be dropped from the chart. Eventually you can eliminate the chart.

Certain charts work with certain temperaments while other charts are a complete failure. Don't use a chart all the time. At times I have gone three or four months without any chart. Here are some ideas on how to chart jobs around the house.

CHARTS FOR LITTLE CHILDREN

1. **The Picture Chart.** Your first chart will be for a child who cannot yet read. The picture chart introduces helps to be done for the first time. You can draw simple stick outlines (or cut pictures out of magazines) to represent the five or six things you want your child to do each day. A little face means wash your face. A toothbrush means brush your teeth. A bed means make your bed. A picture of a truck or doll means pick up your toys. A little piece of newspaper pasted down reminds him that it is his job to bring in the newspaper. A drawing of an overflowing wastebasket reminds him that his job is to empty them. The first assignments for your young child should be easy for him to do in fifteen to twenty-five minutes a day.

After going over the meanings of the pictures, you will find him eager to perform the first few days. Be sure to acknowledge that he has done his work. Perhaps after supper is a good time to look at the little pictures and congratulate him on what he has accomplished.

In a few months he can mark when he has done that job for the day. Ruled notebook paper has sufficient lines for each of the days of the month. Paste or draw your pictures across the top of the page and rule lines downward so that he can put a little x on his chart when he does that job each day.

2. **Stars.** Some parents like to carry over from school the idea of putting a star on the chart for a day when the child has done his assigned tasks. One mother I know lets the child put the stars up himself; one star for each of the tasks he does during the day, using different colored stars. Then the mother rewards with a gold star any day when every help is done. She uses large gold stars for a perfect week.

3. **Building Blocks.** This chart is fine for parents who aren't too good at drawing, cutting or pasting. Just cut a number of one-inch squar s from colored paper and put them in an envelope. Any day that the child is successful in getting his assigned helps done, he has the right to take one of the blocks out of the envelope and paste it on his piece of paper on the board or on the refrigerator. The object is to see how tall a stack of blocks he can make. Perhaps a reward would be offered for making a stack 25 blocks tall.

4. **Little Pictures.** This chart is similar to the building block except you cut out inch-square pictures from magazines and put them in the envelope. Any day the child is successful at getting his helps done, he can take a picture and paste it on a blank sheet of paper. By the end of the month, he has made a unique collage. A variation for an older child: take one large magazine picture and cut it up like a puzzle. Each day he receives one piece of the puzzle for having done his helps. He puts these on the bulletin board to make the puzzle picture piece by piece, using

thumb tacks to hold them in place until he is sure of the position.

5. Decorate the Christmas Tree. This seasonal chart is adaptable for a family with one child or many. Cut out a simple green paper Christmas tree for each child. Make it at least twelve inches high. In an envelope put a lot of round, diamond-shaped and rectangular pieces of glossy paper, little trimmings, stars and other miscellany you find around the house. Any day that a child successfully finishes his helps, he may choose an ornament from the envelope and trim his tree. By Christmas some of them are decorative if the helps have been done! Children will compete to see whose tree is best decorated.

6. The Easter Bunny. Cut out a big Easter bunny and provide ears for the bunny for those who do their helps each day. A child who has done his helps is blind-folded and given a paper ear so he can "pin the ear on the bunny." The bunny must be large enough to have dozens of pink ears sticking out of him by the end of the month.

7. A Space Chart. With so many big pictures of space travel available, cut one into about 25 horizontal strips. Number the strips from top to bottom. Give out a strip any day that the tasks are properly done so the picture will build from bottom to top. Label it "Mark's Blast-Off" or "Karen's Countdown."

8. Spring Flowers. One year I cut out simple little flower heads in four different colors. Any day a child did his daily helps, he took his own color flower and pasted it over that date on the calendar.

9. Cooperative Charts. As the children get older, introduce teamwork. This is especially helpful when you have some go-getters and some laggards. There is nothing like peer pressure to help the slower or disinterested child get going on his duties.

You can use many of these first charts as team charts. The star, the flower, the Christmas tree decoration are rewarded only when each member of the team has been successful in completing his helps. One month you may want to assign the helps to two children as a group. See how they insist on a fair division of work! It may be noisy at times, but the valuable lesson of cooperation is too good to miss. When children work together they see the need to help the slower one or fall short of the goal. The slower one observes how the faster one gets things done. Rarely does the slow child take advantage of the fast one and let him do all the work.

10. The Bell Ringer. I happen to collect bells and one my husband ordered from the Sears Farm Catalog was so big it had to be put on a post outside. It can be heard for blocks around. The honor of pulling the big rope and making the bell ring is given out on special occasions. The bell is rung by each child on any day when all four have finished their helps. On those days when the bell is not rung, the one or two children responsible for its silence are resoundingly reminded by their peers to do their part next day!

11. The Secret Pal Chart. To teach our children the fun of quietly and inconspicuously helping another, I made a chart with a bonus column for those who did something for another person. Karen and Wendy found it easy to earn these extra points since all they had to do was go into Kent's room and put away his shoes or hang up his pajamas! Kent's room improved but he soon learned that he could count on the girls to do his work. Rather than stopping their help, they increased it. In another week, Kent realized that if he tidied his room, the girls would have to go elsewhere to do good deeds. He was exulted the day Wendy forgot to feed the fish and he could magnanimously do it for her.

12. Be Your Brother's Keeper. A chaotic chart that provided fun for one month, this one isn't something that you would want to do often, perhaps best for summer use. Aside from the regular assignments, each child had three things he did daily for another child. For example, each child made a different one's bed. Mark cleaned somebody's washbowl and hung up the towel. Each cleared someone else's place at the table and put that person's chair and napkin where it belonged. The first few days were confusing, since everyone forgot who he was helping. However, by the end of the first week, it settled down and the children began to learn from the experience. Wendy noted that Kent always left his chair pushed back and his napkin on the floor. She pointed this out to him and I didn't have to do it. It helped her remember not to do the same thing. Karen complained about Mark's inability to make her bed. She considered making his bed in an equally sloppy way. We pointed out that he was younger and couldn't do as good a job and that in return for a poor job we still do our very best work to set an example.

This chart also gave the children opportunities to spend time in one another's rooms and to get acquainted with the possessions of the other child. Often one child came in to make another's bed and got sidetracked into an hour of happy play. Karen, in her officious way, even felt that Mark's furniture should be rearranged so that her fine bedmaking could be more readily seen from the hall. There was much talk about the great things they were doing for each other, but aside from all the noise and complaints, it was a good experience.

CHARTS FOR OLDER CHILDREN

As soon as a child can read, your charts can be more sophisticated and contain incentives to get the job done. If you spend time on a strong incentive program to achieve order and helpfulness, you won't need a strong punishment program.

13. Follow the Dots. This was a poster I made by putting dots on a piece of paper and numbering them. The dots formed the outline of a picture such as a house or child. Each day those who had completed their tasks got to connect two dots with a straight line. Eventually, it revealed the entire picture as the helps were done. There was a reward if all the dots were connected by the end of the month.

14. **The Reveal-A-Word Chart.** This was an incentive for the children to complete their helps regularly over the course of a month. I typed out what the reward was: dinner at a new restaurant nearby, but I described it in great detail and revealed the name of the restaurant at the end. I numbered each word and cut them apart. Each day a child who had done his tasks could draw out the next word and paste it up. Thus the story of the reward was constructed bit by bit.

15. **The Tape Machine.** This one takes more than the 30 minutes I allow myself each month to set up duties, calendars and charts, but the response was so great that we have repeated this gimmick. I created what was called "The Tape Machine." We planned that summer to take an extensive trip with the children through the West. Rather than just tell them about it, I had them *earn* the information. I typed out the day-by-day trip adventures, never revealing what was to happen next. My saga began: "On Monday, June 30, we will take a jet plane and land in California at 9 p.m." Then I typed three asterisks and continued: "The following morning we will rise early and take a helicopter to Disneyland," etc., etc. When I had finished the story, which was helpful to us in planning, I cut the typed sheet into separate lines and with pieces of scotch tape, joined the whole story together in one ten-foot-long, half-inch-wide strip like ticker tape. I rolled this onto the old scotch tape holder upside down so the wording wouldn't show. I could then pull out a piece of the story up to the asterisks, and tear it off on the cutter.

The tape machine was kept in the center of the dining room table and sparked much interest. Each night if his helps had been successfully completed, a child could pull off a section of the tape and read it aloud. It thrilled them to have the story of their vacation revealed bit by bit in this way. The events sank in and increased their anticipation. You can imagine the groans when someone had failed to do his helps. "But we want to know what happens next," the others would insist. "Then do your helps tomorrow."

16. **Racing with the Clock.** This is good for children who are becoming bored with their daily tasks. Ask the child to figure how long it takes to make a bed, feed the dog, raise the flag, etc. Twenty-five minutes? Out of generosity add five minutes to this total. Then, at a designated time, start a kitchen timer to click off the 30 minutes. When the bell rings, he has to stop and check in. For the child who beats the clock the most mornings, our funny prize was a new, loud wake-up alarm.

17. **Achievement Rewards.** One mother I know has a little daughter who loves to have her hair curled in a time-consuming way. Usually the mother does this only for Sunday. But if her daughter is helpful and thus

gives her mother extra time, the mother uses part of that time to curl her daughter's hair on other days.

The Dad at our house realized that our children loved to play chess and card games after supper, so he offered to play with the first person who finished his tasks. This speeded the completion of the daily helps and especially the loading of the dishwasher.

18. **The Monthly Dinner.** The children had done extremely well on their assigned helps and so I planned an elaborate supper the last night of the month, complete with cloth napkins and candlelight. This dinner became known as the Goal-of-the-Month Dinner. It honored those children who had set and achieved certain goals for themselves. Getting into the spirit, Wendy made a paper mortar board with gold tassels for Mom or Dad to wear while announcing the names of those who had done a good job of being part of the family that month. Although the hat is now collapsed, it is a nostalgic part of our scrapbook.

The monthly dinner continues, sometimes elaborate, sometimes simple. This is the night we also look over our long-term goals to see if we are moving toward them. At this meal the new monthly calendar is revealed and if there is to be an incentive chart, it is also shown. New tasks are announced and even though the children have been used to our work assignments for many years, they still find it intriguing to see what their next duties will be.

During the second year of the Goal-of-the-Month Dinner, we created certificates of merit. With fancy marking pen writing, elaborate big words, an expired notary seal, some ribbon and old picture frames, these awards looked very official. The four awards were for "supreme excellence," "excellence," "cooperativeness" and "effort." With twelve blank lines on each of the awards, they could be awarded monthly for a year. The person receiving the award for the month had his name inscribed on it.

At the end of the month we parents tallied up the helps completed and inscribed the awards. The fourth award was not considered a bad one. It was presented first with great applause and hopes for more success the next month. Then the other awards were given with humorous speeches by either parent. I really didn't know what the children's reactions would be to these awards, but all were displayed proudly in their bedrooms. The day of the next Goal-of-the-Month Dinner, the certificates were collected and re-inscribed. During the year everybody had the first place award at least once. After a year, when this idea was ready to be retired, the awards were permanently given to the person who had held that award most often. Karen made off with the "supreme excellence" award and although several years have passed, it still stands on the top shelf of her bookcase as an example of past glories.

19. **The Envelope Game.** Perhaps our most exciting chart was "The Envelope Game." Each of the four children has four things to do each day.

The chart enabled each to put an X each day in the square under his name for that task. Thus a perfect day would be 16 X's, a perfect month, 480. Few children achieve perfection, so I set up three goals. The first would be for having 200 to 299 X's; the second for 300 to 399; and the third, 400 to 480. For each of these three goals, I made a sealed envelope and in it listed a surprise that the family would enjoy if they achieved it.

The children were anxious to total out each day to see how near to 16 they got and how their grand total was going toward those goals. Some shouting among themselves took place if they found one child falling down. I noted that they would occasionally cover for each other and do one another's tasks to up that day's total to 16. In the three months we used this system, they received the middle award the first month, the third award the second month, but came back smashingly the third month to get first prize.

The prizes included a family trip to a fabulous ice cream shop, hamburgers and a movie, and a toy that everyone wanted. You can imagine their disappointment the first month when they found out what they had missed in the first envelope and how they felt the second month when they got the third award and I wouldn't tell them the first and second awards. That was why they worked so hard the third month!

I also did this on an individual basis with each child reaching for a numerical goal I had set, higher for some children than others. This, of course, is easiest for the orderly child and more difficult for the forgetful child. But I prefer the chart that combines all their efforts, for, in this, they see that their successes are in some ways dependent on other's achieving.

EVENTUALLY, NO CHARTS

Most children respond positively to the chart and reward system for getting helps done. By using new ideas monthly, omitting charts for awhile, making the rules firm so that you're not taken advantage of, you'll find this system most successful. As a child gets older, he can register his successes himself and you don't need to keep a daily record. These systems set up what you expect, relieve you of constant reminding, and leave it to the child to do it or not. Charts give him a visual reminder. They heighten his spirit of competition and his desire to achieve.

Many parents don't ask their children to be helpful because they think the child will forget and it's too hard to be constantly reminding. As your children become older, you should have to remind less and less until they need no reminding. The choice to help is theirs; thus monthly rewards are theirs also.

If a child has been especially good at getting all his helps done, declare him "off the chart" for one month. Now he has complete freedom and responsibility to do as he chooses for one month without supervision.

This, of course, means that certain tasks may be left undone but with the exception of feeding the dog, there are few things that will cause disaster if a child forgets to do them. But if the charts and rewards have been well-used, the child will want to be responsible, orderly and pleasant because that course leads to maximum happiness.

28
Let The Correction Fit The Deed

Childhood is a learning experience. If our children could do all things correctly the first time, they wouldn't need parents. We must be sure that mistakes and forgotten items are not over-stressed. Every wrong need not be punished. The purpose of punishment is to see that the mistake is not committed often or again. Sometimes the mere expression of our disappointment or disapproval is sufficient.

In selecting ways to punish a child for wrong doing, mistakes or forgetfulness, take into consideration his age and nature. When Mark was small, a spanking meant very little to him. He was of a sturdy constitution and not only was the spank over quickly but so was the remembrance of its cause. On the other hand, a spank for Karen was a great emotional experience and after it was over, if you asked her why she was spanked she was so upset she could hardly remember. Perhaps this is why physical punishment went low on my list of options.

When punishing children, be absolutely certain that they know *why* they are being punished. You may wish to talk to them both before and after the punishment to point out that this is being done to help them remember to do the right thing the next time.

The punishment should not be so severe that it drives all thought out of the child's head or makes him resentful. Certainly it should not be physically damaging. Children need to be reminded regularly that we correct them because we love them.

The child should be aware in advance of certain sure punishments. Having a pool, our children have been warned never to swim without an adult's permission. They know that if they break this rule, they will be refused the use of the pool for a month. These automatic punishments help the child to weigh his decision to do wrong or right.

Never announce a punishment you don't intend to carry out. Don't say it if you don't mean it or would find it difficult to follow through. Some parents avoid punishing from a misdirected sense of love. Also they may find that the punishment, say the cancellation of an outing, punishes themselves, too, and so they renege. When you have said it, stick to it.

On the other hand, when the punishment is over, that should be the end of the matter. The child should not be punished again nor continually reminded of the wrong. The punishment should be sufficient.

As much as possible, the punishment should fit the misdeed and in some way make amends for it. A punishment that impresses the child with the correct action is far better than the punishment that leaves him hurt, sullen, beat down or confused. Punishments fall into several categories.

PHYSICAL PUNISHMENTS

When we think of punishing children, often the first thing that comes to mind is spanking. But let's go back to the purpose of punishment. It is applied to correct a child, to bring about better behavior, to save him from doing something dangerous, illegal or foolish. We have to choose the punishment that achieves this, not the one that merely assuages our own anger or disappointment. It's easy to spank or shout at a child. It is difficult to use a more memorable form of punishment, but it usually achieves our purpose. Physical punishment IS remembered by the child, but what he remembers is the hurt of resentment, which usually has a negative effect.

With small children who don't have a highly developed sense of reason, a firm pat on the bottom may be the best way to express our disapproval. But we can also indicate our disapproval through a serious, firm tone of voice, facial expression and attitude.

If you are letting a toddler help cook, he may reach out to put his hand on a hot burner. A slap on his hand may remind him that this is wrong until he is of the age that you can explain or demonstrate the danger. However, one of the first words a baby should learn is "no." If you use "no" when you really mean it, it will often save you from having to use physical punishment. There are better means of making your point than spanking a child.

Many parents have used the old "wash-out-the-mouth-with-soap" routine in response to sassy language. Soap manufacturers may say this does no harm, but a child old enough to use bad language is old enough to understand that there are better ways to speak emphatically. So help the child to express his strong feeling in acceptable ways. Give him strong, acceptable alternate words. "Heck," "darn" and "drat" may sound silly to you, but will satisfy a child. When Kent was about five, he liked strong words and we suggested "thunderation!" which he found impressive to strangers.

130

UNDOING WHAT YOU'VE DONE

Often a child may require correction for a careless act. He has spilled a box of 1,000 toothpicks on the kitchen floor. He has dumped over a paint can. He has taken out six decks of cards, mixed them all together and left them in the living room. He has knocked over a vase and broken it.

The best punishment is that he remedy the wrong. Little children may need help, but it is wise to let a child of any age attempt to right the wrong by himself even though it may be a struggle. This impresses him with the amount of damage or work he has caused. To have to pick up every single toothpick and put it back in the box is time-consuming and boring but may remind the child to be more careful or not fool with things that are not his. This is far better than the parent's striking the child and then cleaning up while the child merely watches.

By the age of five, children can usually clean up their own messes and we should not deprive them of this important lesson. It may take a child 30 minutes to re-sort the decks of cards, a job that we could do in five, but good discipline requires that he stick with it until he has the satisfaction of *our* satisfaction.

As children get older, instruct them in household repairs so they can mend their broken toys. To have to take play-time to repair broken toys or household items teaches conservation and care as no lecture can.

VERBAL CORRECTION

To talk to a child about his wrong-doing is the best form of correction when you believe that the child erred because he didn't completely understand. This is an opportunity for you to express patience and understanding without wrath or sarcasm. It is impressive to a misbehaving child to be singled out from the group and taken into a quiet room with the door shut to listen to a firm but compassionate explanation of why we do not hog the train engine, or why we do not play with matches or why we do not pinch our baby sister. This calm reasoning, showing the child why his behavior is unacceptable, is one of the best forms of correction.

You may think you are letting the child off easy but in talking with our children about past punishments, we have found that this sort of quiet discussion has been most effective.

DEPRIVATION

For a child who has done something naughty and knows it, for a child who has repeatedly "forgotten" something, or for a child who has purposely been mean, deprivation is an effective form of punishment. He has chosen to do wrong; thus, he will be deprived of some of the pleasures of life. You can point out to a young child that this parallels the laws of our land. If we as adults choose to do wrong, we are deprived of certain rights. If a child steals candy, continually comes home later than the assigned time, chooses to play rather than cut the lawn or fight rather than fairly decide an issue, he can expect to be deprived of certain pleasures.

To deprive a child of company works well with some children. With Kent, however, being isolated is a great joy. Until I realized this, he spent his lonely hour in his room having a happy and inventive time. To deprive him of candy for a week appeared to be effective. Contrariwise, to tell Karen that she was to have no candy for a week would mean nothing to her. So we have to be sure we deprive the child of something he values.

In this age, "money talks" and to deprive a child of his allowance may be effective. An allowance is never given in return for work done; it's given in return to being a cooperative part of the family. If he fails to act in this way, there is nothing wrong in depriving him of his funds.

A child can be deprived of outside play for a week. Sometimes to tell a child that he may not have friends in the house for a certain length of time is effective, especially if the trouble involves playing with friends. Many children are so devoted to television that to deprive them of TV for a week works well.

While the child is being deprived, he must be kept busy. He should be given some special project to work on, perhaps his homework, a special school project or some craft so that his time is not wasted. Nor should his being deprived of friends or television affect the rest of the family.

WORKING IT OFF

A child's naughtiness will often cause us extra work. Then we can assign extra work to him to make up for our inconvenience. For example, Kent insisted on leaving toys and papers in pants pockets. This caused me additional laundry time and repairs. After repeated requests and threats, I told him that he would have to help me fold the clean laundry if he caused me extra time in the laundry room. He did not heed my threat and so one Saturday while everyone else was out swimming, he and I folded laundry for 45 minutes. This happened once more but that was the end of it.

One child weeded for 30 minutes each day for a week to pay back a debt that he owed us for leaving a faucet on and causing a flood.

THOUGHTFUL PUNISHMENTS

Often what a child has done shows us where he needs help. Here a thoughtful punishment is the answer. When our swimming pool was new, the children were told never to go inside the gate without us; however, Wendy could not resist showing it to a baby sitter — and she fell off the diving board into the pool. When we came home, Kent was quick to report what had happened. I felt that Wendy needed a lesson in responsibility and so she devoted 30 minutes each night for a week to a theme on responsibility. She was to look up the topic in many reference books. She was free to interview anyone, including brothers, sisters and parents, concerning responsibility. She also used citations from the Bible. This was probably the most effective punishment I ever meted out. Another time Kent wrote a needed paper on honesty. Research into positive character traits may be time-consuming, but it gives the child an opportunity to think on the qualities we hope he will express.

ISOLATION

Sometimes it is sufficient punishment merely to remove the offender from the situation. Children who are easily excited or tend toward temper tantrums should be swiftly taken from the unpleasant, dangerous or exciting situations they are creating. An argumentative child can be quickly removed from all other people and thus have no opportunity to argue with anyone but himself. A vengeful child can be removed from the objects of his vengeance and put in a quiet place. However, isolation has to have some purpose. Tell the child that the reason he is sitting in a corner is to give him time to think over what he has done and to come up with a more desirable way of accomplishing his aim. Tell the child that as soon as he can solve the problem, he will be welcomed back into society. You will be amazed how quickly an arguing child will find a workable solution to the problem and go back to play happily with his friends.

DISCIPLINE IN PUBLIC

The moment we take our toddlers into the world, we should make clear to them the type of behavior that is acceptable. A child who runs through the store and handles everything, who constantly tugs at parents and says, "I want this, I want that," who at a party stomps his foot and says, "I won't do it," who tries all his tricks to stay up when guests are on hand — this child should be dealt with quickly and firmly. As soon as the child can understand the words, tell him that pleading and begging for favors or purchases in public is a sure way to get a "no" answer. Then stick by your admonition.

We are embarrassed in public by a crying or nagging child and hope the din will soon diminish. Such public scenes can usually be avoided by proper training at home or in the car en route. Teach children that punishment is swift when in public, that there are no second or third chances. That old threat, "Just wait until we get home," is no good if when you get home you have lost your resolve and let the child go free.

Children at movies, stores, churches, parties, sometimes have to be taken aside and reasoned with firmly. Give the child an option: Be helpful, quiet, good (whatever your aim) or be noisy, nagging, crying. If noisy, nagging, crying, he will spoil the event for you and you will give him that unpleasant work project to do immediately when you get home.

Sometimes you can eliminate punishable behavior by having the child help you to choose things at the store, to open the hymnal to the right number, to be in charge of popcorn, etc. Later chapters will give you more ideas.

For years I had four young children on the weekly grocery trip. At first their complaints about each other made it hectic. So I cut out for each one a little ticket showing a picture of a sad, crying face and a picture of a hand. At the end of each aisle, I punched their tickets with my pencil: a punch after the hand for a helpful attitude, a punch after the bad face for disruptive behavior. When we finished shopping, the one with the best ticket chose a "munchie" to be eaten on the way home by the group, excluding the trouble-maker. After a few trips, all were enjoying bananas or crackers en route home.

When the punishment is over, remember to reassure the child that it was his behavior that you did not like, not *him,* and that your affection for him is the very reason he was punished.

Your Week Three Check List

You have three big assignments this week, but they're fun!

1. Look over the list of things children can do and select helps appropriate to the age of your child. Choose a number of possible helps and then let the child pick two or three to do daily and two or three for Saturday. Be sure you take time to give him a good start at helping by using the 3 P's:
   Purpose
   Procedure
   Praise
2. Choose one of the suggested charts — or think up one of your own. Set up the chart to accomplish the helps you want done. Keep it fun and interesting.
3. Create your family headquarters — a tack board on the kitchen wall, a poster board in the family room, the front of the refrigerator. Make it as simple or elaborate as you like, but see that it includes:
   ☐ Basic family rules and information
   ☐ Monthly calendar
   ☐ Helps list
   ☐ The monthly chart

Now, onward to Week Four!

Week
Four

4
4
4
4
4
4
4
4
4
4
4

The Important Mess Of "Do It Myself"

If our children are to be loosed from paint-by-number kits, vicarious fun via television and other forms of canned entertainment, we must encourage them to be creative and to make much of their own fun. Making fun makes a mess. Once parents understand this and see the value of the mess, they can look at a child's creativity in a more relaxed way.

Here are some basic rules to make creative fun palatable.

1. **Have only one mess going at a time.** If a child is to paint, he'll bring out paper, bottles of paint and the easel or plastic table cloth. Soon there will be paintings set around to dry. He is NOT to follow the painting mess with the construction of a large block city until the painting is put away. If you aren't firm, you'll have blocks in the wet paint and the city builders stepping back to admire their work and onto their own masterpieces.

One big project at a time will also encourage the child to develop longer attention spans and not flit from one activity to another.

2. **Invest time in introducing a project.** If your child says that he and a friend are going to bake cookies, make sure they know how the first time they bake. Showing them where the kitchen tools are and how to measure will take time that first day; but once the project is explained, you can expect them to put things back where they belong and to be more independent the second time.

3. **See that the equipment works.** Nothing is more discouraging to a child than to be working creatively with faulty equipment, whether it be the cord for the sewing machine, the bent mixer beater or the dead batteries. Have a quick equipment test before starting a project.

4. **Check occasionally to see how it's going.** When a child becomes deeply engrossed in a great masterwork, we may heave a sigh of relief and feel we have the next hour to ourselves. But if you don't check, he may have run out of painting paper and be starting on the walls!

5. **Carry one creative project over into another.** If you are stressing

137

art and music, play joyful music in the background while the child paints. In encouraging a child to read, point out the importance of a book's illustrations. If drama is the creative event of the day, suggest painting the scenery. A scientifically-inclined child will enjoy mixing paint or cookie dough. Tie creative activities together and you maximize the learning.

6. **Make use of the child's creativity.** Don't let your kindergartener find his great painting in the wastebasket! It has value for him as a symbol of achievement, and while it may not be your favorite colors, it deserves appreciation. Give him a place to show off his creativity. Let him hang a picture on the kitchen door so all who enter may see it. Display a clay piece in the living room along with your fine art objects. These artistic creations needn't be with you forever, but they do deserve a time in the spotlight. Shelves, bulletin boards and easels show off a youngster's artistic work.

7. **Don't mention the mess.** Learn to keep your eye on the goal: to teach the child to have fun, to be creative, to use color, to enjoy music or to experiment. When you have made a luscious three-layer cake, you don't moan over the dirty dishes. You clean up and think of the elegant cake. So teach a child to clean up after himself and to do it speedily —when he has finished a project, not the next day or the day after.

Be pleased with your child's creative efforts and don't look for perfection. His eagerness and interest are far better than a neat, precise little picture that lacks spontaneity. Express your appreciation. Kent painted a cooking oil bottle for me one year but it was in such unusual colors that after its first use as a vase I put it in the back of the cupboard. In our next house the wallpaper near my dressing table was in similar exotic colors and I found that the bottle-vase was perfect for a single flower. When I placed it there with a gladiolus in it, Kent was so happy that I realized he had been aware that the gift had not been used. I explained the reasons and how pleased I was that I could now find regular service for it. He kept me supplied with one single flower for that vase for many weeks.

Be prepared for highs and lows in your child's creativity. What you are doing is exposing him to the arts and giving him a little knowledge in many areas so that he has a broad background. Where he shows real talent, experts are available to take over his training. But above all, don't be afraid of the paraphernalia of creativity —instruments, books, baseballs, clay, dough, paint pots. The mess is worthwhile!

29
Music
In The Home

When Wendy was about four, an aunt sent her a music box that played a beautiful classical melody. She was delighted with it but confided to me that the tune was misplayed. Sure enough, when I listened carefully, one note was wrong. How did a four-year-old know this? We had sung this tune to her since she was a baby and her educated young ear had caught it.

When we think of music in the home, unfortunately our first picture is of a short-legged child perched on a piano bench while he plays his scales over and over again and strives almost tearfully for perfection. In too many cases, this is what most children think music is. Until recently, it usually meant the enforcement of daily piano practice with its accompanying threats and tears.

Music has been liberated in the last 25 years and our children can now enjoy the creativity of music even if they are nearly tone deaf. When a child is very young, encourage the music and rhythm in him by giving him a sturdy musical or rhythm instrument. As soon as you have more than one child, you can encourage them to make music together. Simple musical instruments are not an extravagance. Even with four children beating on them, our wood sticks, drums, tambourines and bells are still useable. Children will use these simple musical instruments to create pleasing sounds and rhythms without any instruction from you. Let them experiment but also supply them with some music or recordings that will encourage them to develop their talents further.

A small child can be content with peppy radio music. To an older child, the ownership of his own record player is very important. Teach him how to operate a simple record player and care for his records.

There are excellent recordings of rhythm bands, marches and other music for children. From these the child can grow into more classical music.

LESSON-TIME

A child may graduate from simple instruments to harmonicas, uke-

139

leles or guitars. Usually around age seven or eight, parents feel that it's time for their child to study seriously some musical instrument. The instrument they select is often the piano or violin. This is where the child who has loved music may begin to hate it.

Before beginning lessons, expose the child to the varieties of instruments available, either through recordings and pictures or through trips to see the instruments in an orchestra or band or in a large music store. Find out what instruments interest the child. Beginning in third or fourth grade, some schools have programs to acquaint youngsters with instruments.

Friends with six children have refused to buy instruments due to the high cost of child rearing. They are presently renting a piano, a harp, a guitar and two violins for their children. They find this a great economy. And, if the lessons don't "take," they don't own an unused instrument.

We decided some years ago that our children were all of an age when they should be exposed to formal music instruction. After discussing the merits of many different instruments, the children decided that they would most like to have a piano in the house. Since we already owned an electronic organ, we decided to rent an upright piano until we were sure we had a virtuoso.

The children understood that it was a one-year project and that everyone would take lessons. Only those who really enjoyed the piano would study beyond the one-year point. They understood that they were to practice for a half hour, six days a week. With four children using one piano, we set up a simple schedule, the two younger children having the early morning practice time and the two older children the before-supper hour.

To keep our sanity, we agreed that each one would simply take part in the experiment to the best of his ability. We also agreed to be on call to help the child with new assignments and that we would come to all recitals and applaud.

THREE IDEAS

Once we got rolling on the project, I found three systems that helped me to keep my poise. The first came with the realization that it is hard for a student to "crack" a new subject. Thus, the day after each piano lesson I sat at the piano for ten minutes with each child to help him read and play his pieces. In this way the new material wasn't ignored until the end of the week. After he had played it once, it didn't seem so strange and formidable. Rarely did I have to state on piano-lesson day, "You mean you haven't yet tackled your new piece?"

Second, to avoid last minute panic, I had a small recital given me once a week by each pupil the day before his lesson. I got to hear what he had accomplished during the week. I sewed or scanned the newspaper but was aware of what rough areas needed to be practiced that day.

The third idea came shortly after the novelty of the lessons wore off and practice started to be a bit of a chore. Mark would come to me half a dozen times during his 30 minute practice to ask me if his time was up. He spent more time walking than practicing. Finally, I put an old kitchen timer on the piano. It wasn't beautiful but it did the trick —each child set it for 30 minutes and kept practicing until it rang.

After the year experiment, we knew we had no future Van Cliburns in the household. Wendy had previously had organ lessons and has continued to play. The others opted to end their piano experience but not without benefits. All the children are able to read music, appreciate the piano and sing much better.

If you intend to conduct an experiment like this, let the child choose his own instrument. Agree beforehand as to the practice time and its duration. But learning to play music is not the essence of music appreciation. Few of our children will become professional musicians but all may enjoy music. Piano training gives a child a good classical repertoire, but at the same time he should learn to accompany those who want to sing popular songs. While studying classical guitar, the child can learn to play today's popular folk songs. Music lessons should be fun. If they become work, children may cut themselves off from the joy of music for many years.

CLASSICAL MUSIC

A child's musical experience starts when he's a baby, usually with the lullaby sung by father or mother or played on a music box. After this the child plays with musical toys and then makes music himself. However, the music you play in your home can be an important part of your child's music training. Children hear contemporary music via TV, radio and records. What about classical music? At first, a child may feel that classical music is boring and meaningless. Select his first encounters with classical works with great care. *Peter and the Wolf, The Sorcerer's Apprentice* and *Pictures at an Exhibition* introduce him gently to light but serious music.

Help the child enjoy classical music by giving him an understanding of the structure of the various music forms. Look up "symphony" or "concerto" in the encyclopedia and educate the family to the various segments of a classical piece. Read jackets of phonograph records and familiarize yourself with the music's highlights.

Select classical music that has a story line or imagery. We've enjoyed Debussy's *Afternoon of a Faun* and Richard Strauss' *Alpine Symphony.* Having been to Switzerland with the children, we asked them to listen to the music and tell us what they saw in their mind's eye. (If your children are familiar with the West, you could try Grofe's *Grand Canyon Suite.*)

We didn't require that they sit quietly during the playing of the symphony. In fact, chess games and reading went on while the music was played, but everyone freely talked about the pictures the music suggested. After that, whenever the *Alpine Symphony* was played, Mark proudly announced he knew what it was.

Playing recorded music in the home can fit into the regular family schedule. Getting-up music; cleaning the garage music; music during the dinner hour; music as a background for craft or homework time; or mood-setting music when entertaining.

Rarely do we listen to music at home without doing something else. But one warm evening we all stretched out on the lawn, looked up at a star-filled sky, and listened to the recording of Richard Strauss' *Also Sprach Zarathustra,* the theme from the movie, *2001: A Space Odyssey.* The mental pictures of the future it conjured up dispelled beliefs that classical music is old-fashioned, although that music was written in 1896.

Because our music system plays throughout the house, we've taught the children how to operate it and also how the phonograph records are cleaned and filed. All have permission to put on records of their own choice. One child specializes in musical comedies, another prefers ballet music, another likes synthesizer music and the oldest gives us a steady diet of movie themes.

Include the children in the selection of music to be played in the home. You willingly listen to the child's music and in turn you ask that he listen to yours. Play a record when it's time for the children to go to sleep and when you say goodnight, tell them the name of the music that is being played.

Our children have become so music conscious that even at their own parties they want background music, usually something like *Switched on Bach*. Include a variety of music in your record library so your child becomes familiar with music of all countries, talk records, operas and sacred music. Many public libraries have rental record collections which can broaden the range of music in your home.

In the summer when everyone has more time, we have a weekly "music appreciation night." From 6:30 to 7:30 we listen to and talk about music. Each member of the family has one night that is totally his. One year I did the life and music of George Gershwin. Sounds lovely, doesn't it! But, the next week Kent played painfully loud rock music and explained why he enjoyed it. The following week Karen played ballet music and told about Russian ballet defectors. These summer sessions have been broadening for all of us. Wonder of wonders, our collegians actually *requested* that we have these evenings together again. It may be years before you realize that your training has some impact on the cultural lives of your children.

LIVE MUSIC

Don't overlook the importance of live music in the home. Children throughout the world are taking music lessons and parents throughout the world are paying dearly for those lessons. How rarely, though, do these children have an opportunity to play before an audience. I don't mean that we should have to listen to our neighbor's six-year-old play his basic pieces! But once a year we can gather three or four families with children who are taking music lessons for an hour recital. The children enjoy this when they are all in it together and it gives parents an idea of how their children are progressing. In fact, they may feel that their children are not as bad as they thought they were!

Let's not forget the possibilities of more-professional entertainers in our home. Many people think nothing of spending $50 for special refreshments or alcoholic beverages at a party when for the same price they can hire a musician to provide an hour of live music. After reading a newspaper article about the importance of contributing to the poise and finances of college-age musicians, we contacted our local university music department for names of some of their better students. That spring we had monthly dinner parties to which we invited one of these promising young musicians for the after-dinner entertainment. These young people played for the fee of $40 and we enjoyed the talents of a vocalist, a violinist and a harpist. The harpist was the most thrilling to our children. She was near enough to their age to understand their curiosity when she brought her harp over the afternoon of the event. She let everyone investigate it and pluck a few strings. Since for many of our guests as well as for our children this was the first time they had been close to a harp, this turned out to be one of our more successful parties.

One night at a Junior Achievement dinner we heard a young guitarist play music that was contemporary and appealing. I asked how much he charged and found it was only $20 for an hour of music. I mentally recorded that information and used his talents at a special teenage party in our home.

GO TO WHERE THE MUSIC IS

Perhaps the budget does not stretch enough to bring live music into the home. Don't despair. The next best thing is to go to where the live music is, whether it be the free Sunday band concert in the park or the Tuesday evening performance of the local symphony. Many cities also have youth orchestras which can inspire young listeners with the possibility of achieving similar success. The public is invited without cost. Schools have special excursions to musical events and sometimes one number is a musical story with a popular local figure as narrator.

Encourage your child to sample all kinds of music: symphonic, oper-

143

atic, musical comedy and the current fads. If we take our child to a baseball game, we don't expect him to enjoy it if he has no advance knowledge of the rules. In the same way we should not take a child to a symphony performance absolutely cold. Prepare him in advance. Books such as Milton Cross' *Complete Stories of Great Operas* or the *Encyclopedia of Concert Music* can be borrowed from the library or purchased. Use them to prepare the child for what he is to hear. Give him something to look forward to by telling him to expect a great crash from the timpani at the beginning of the second movement or a repetition of the same theme by various sections of the orchestra.

If we want our youngsters to be as comfortable listening to classical music as they are listening to popular songs, we should make music a part of the day. Encourage them to use music creatively at home, to choose a record to set a mood, to use it for dancing or rhythm play. After you have encouraged them to have fun with musical instruments, be ready to listen to the great six-piece band made up of neighborhood children!

Sometimes a child will compose a tune he likes. Write it down for him so he can preserve his own creation. Wendy writes simple music and for awhile everyone who visited our home was given a copy of her short farewell song.

Aside from its cultural value, music can help us perform many tasks around the home. Washing dishes or doing homework goes better with music in the background. I have long let it be known that I make beds best with John Philip Sousa band music playing in the background; so it was not at all surprising one day when Kent, assigned to fold a great quantity of laundry, announced he wanted my "bed-making music" in the background because it helped him sort sox faster!

30
Art
From The
Heart

There may not be any Michelangelos hiding out in our home, but we will never know until we have encouraged our children to be artistic and creative through handicrafts. We cannot do this if we wish our children to have clean fingernails and unspotted clothing. Where there is art there is spilled paint, stiff brushes, scraps on the floor, dried pieces of clay, short tempers due to faulty color-mixing, broken crayons and missing needles.

For some reason we discriminate against art in favor of music. We insist that our children have music lessons but ignore their art development. Granted, there are fewer art teachers in most areas but almost every art museum offers instruction. Lessons in art can be a pleasant summer change for a child.

At home a variety of artistic pursuits is available. A generation ago it was mainly crayon, chalk and paint. Today children are exposed to oil, tempera, chalk, water color, collage, ceramics, clay, plastics, copper and needle craft. Art and craft materials make excellent gifts for a child. To start, choose inexpensive needlework sets, painting kits, ceramic sets including small kilns, copper or leather craft kits. Great satisfaction awaits the child who has made his own leather wallet, a copper wall decoration or a large paper mural for the wall of his bedroom. In selecting kits for children, avoid the highly structured types that are merely exercises in following numbers and putting the right color in the right square. These rarely teach anything but neatness and obedience and leave the child no lasting feeling of creative accomplishment. Some of the large mosaic kits with pre-cut pieces and prescribed pictures are acceptable but eventually the child should be encouraged to design his own.

In introducing an art project, remember these points:

1. **Allow ample time.** At the beginning allow twice as much time as you think the project will take. Don't start a large painting project ten minutes before dinner.

2. **See that the child has needed equipment.** This means the right size

brushes; an apron, towel or sheet to cover his clothing; ample newspapers to cover floor, counter or table, and a selection of pots, jars, etc.

3. Make sure he understands the basic techniques involved. Stay with him until he has begun to master these techniques. For example, if he is pounding nails into copper to make a pattern, make sure he is pounding with sufficient strength before you leave him on his own. If he is molding a clay animal, be certain he understands that to have the animal stand up, the legs must have a sturdy dimension. Try to foresee where he may become frustrated or disappointed and guide him to meet these challenges. Let him experiment but stay nearby him until he has a feeling of success.

4. Give him a place to show off his work. Appreciate the artistic pursuits of your child. When he brings home a clay piece or painting, you may have difficulty finding something complimentary to say. But you *can* appreciate its vivid colors, free-form nature and the fine job of getting paint over every surface.

When Mark carried in his first clay piece from kindergarten, Kent, who is fairly artistic, was disgusted with his younger brother's endeavor. Kent knew, however, that I would not be pleased with any "knocks" about his brother's art. When Mark proudly displayed his masterpiece, Kent put his hands on his hips, looked at it and said, "Well, I can think of something good about this. I have a brother who is certainly not ashamed of what he does!"

Sometimes the most enjoyable art projects come about spontaneously. A crystal bowl, a gift, arrived packed in little styrofoam donuts about half an inch in diameter. We found that with paints, string and toothpicks these donuts could be turned into fanciful jewelry, decorations and free-form sculptures.

Keep your eyes open for scraps of fabric, yarn, colored paper, pictures and other items useful in art projects. The most popular art material in school one year was egg cartons. Your local wallpaper store will be glad to have you relieve them of obsolete sample books. These make excellent materials for collages, book covers and paper doll dresses. Obsolete fabric samples from decorator studios can be used in collage and needlework projects.

Along with creating art, don't forget art appreciation. Our homes should display pictures and art objects that please us. When shopping for these on trips or at home, take one child along and let him express his taste.

Remember that once a picture is hung in a room, it need not be there forever. The artistic touches in our home need revitalization as much as our wardrobes and menus. An interior decorator friend shared this idea with me: Twice a year remove every vase, candle and picture from every room of the house; put them on one end of the dining room table. Next, from your cupboards and drawers, bring out all your stored decorative items and place them on the other end of the dining room table. Now you are ready to "shop" from this collection for new accents for each room. When I do this, I include the children in the selecting. In the child's own room, of course, he should have the pictures, posters and art objects that mean the most to him. Along with his dirt-bike posters, let him select for his room a favorite graphic or watercolor from the family collection.

THE ART MUSEUM

A trip to an art museum needn't be a dismal experience! Start with a brief visit. With young children don't insist on seeing every gallery on each visit. Sometimes it's fun just to stop for a fifteen-minute visit to one particular area — a nice break in a shopping trip.

Knowing that it is not going to be a long hike or a boring experience, a child gets into the mood of the event, especially if you challenge him by saying, "If you were a millionaire and could purchase just one painting or piece of sculpture in this gallery, show me the one." Children will quickly begin to look at pictures with a view toward discovering the reasons they like or dislike them.

Our museum made a wonderful new purchase several years ago and we made a special trip just to see that single new painting. In advance, we read about the artist and his works that were familiar to us. This one-purpose excursion impressed the children with the importance of the new acquisition.

Many areas have annual art fairs or Saturday art marts where local artists display their wares. These are fun to wander through with the children, and they learn to appreciate art and develop their tastes. It was at an art fair that Mark purchased his first oil painting. He was so intent on having a painting of a sailboat as his very own that he withdrew funds from his savings account. We had to agree that such a permanent purchase was a good use for savings.

A child cannot be expected to appreciate art when it is a foreign field to him. Three excellent books by Alice Elizabeth Chase can give youngsters an excellent introduction to art. The first is called, *Famous Paintings*. This book, published by Platt and Munk and available in most libraries, has beautiful full-color plates of all the familiar pictures that will make us, as parents, feel we know more about art than we thought. It discusses those well-loved paintings of George Washington, Mona Lisa, Blue Boy, The Child with a Watering Can, and others that have hung in print form on the walls of school classrooms for many decades. The brief, peppy descriptions of each picture are excellent to read even to a pre-schooler who looks at the pictures. The second book, *Famous Artists of the Past*, considers about 20 prominent artists and what made them well-known.

A more advanced book than the other one, it can be rewarding if you will take time to study it with your children. The third is currently at your bookstore and is one you might want to buy. It is called *Looking at Art* and is a good introductory book.

Open such a book as this to one of the full-color plates. Put it on a counter where your children are painting or drawing and ask them to create a picture with the same feeling or colors or to interpret in their own style what the artist was saying.

One Christmas we were given a beautiful book of color prints. But it was so big and heavy that it was difficult to hold and far too much to consume at a sitting. To make the best use of it, we put it on the hall table and opened it to the first print. The next day someone turned to the next page. Over several months we daily appreciated a different print in the book. The exposure was not forced, nor was it unusual to find one of the children reading the text opposite the print.

A HOME ART COURSE

Because we felt that our art education had been poor, my husband and I enrolled in a by-mail course provided by the Metropolitan Museum of Art. Each month we received a large portfolio of color prints and accompanying text to study. After we had been through the twelve-volume course ourselves, we still felt we had not fully assimilated it. By this time the children were interested in art and so we decided we would teach the course to them. This would mean that we ourselves would have to understand the text well enough to describe it to children from pre-school age to pre-teens.

We took prints from the volume and taped them on the wall by the breakfast table without any advance information. The children's speculations about what the artist was trying to depict included subtle points that impressed us with what they were seeing. After they had become familiar with the paintings, we then explained the color, perspective and technique involved. After a few months, the children were able to recognize unfamiliar paintings by now familiar artists and really enjoyed trips to the art museum. You can imagine their joy when they first saw the originals of some of these masterpieces in museums. (Your bookstore or art museum can provide prints and information similar to this.)

Because I saw the benefits of teaching art appreciation to very young children, I developed this system into an art course for first graders. They were exposed to 60 masterpieces during a series of art lectures. I used the masterpieces to teach the children how to arrange objects within their own pictures, how to use color and perspective and generally, how to improve their art. Learning from the great masters was not beyond these young children and their regular teacher was impressed by their progress.

In our family room is a large cork display wall. One Christmas Wendy and I thumbed through all the art books with an eye to depicting our family's year through these prints. A painting of a child holding a watering can represented the digging of our new vegetable garden. A gallant man on horseback represented Kent's summer pursuits at camp. The girls in a ballet class represented Karen's dance recital. Thinking over the year, we found 30 exciting family happenings. With great glee, Wendy and I found pictures to depict them all. We then hung them on the cork wall and on three by five cards described each event in proper chronology. The family enjoyed looking at our art show and zany comments as did our friends.

I tell this incident to stress the importance of including good art as part of the family way of life and not relegating it solely to a museum trip. Let art become a natural part of your family life. By providing the time and place for art *creation,* you'll enhance your own efforts at art *appreciation.* To some, everything in the world has to have practical value. Today we see that beauty and creativity DO have practical value to make us happy and responsive to the world around us. Art is known to have great therapeutic value.

Certainly beauty is in the eye of the beholder. There is no such thing as an ugly clay piece — if *your* child made it!

31
Literature Versus Trash

Books have been called a child's window to the world. Have you thought of what your child is seeing through that window? Is it the comics, Nancy Drew, Dear Abby and *Mad Magazine?* Each of these has its purpose, but the parents' job is to see that their child has a desire for and interest in good literature. This starts with reading to the very young child and teaching him how to care for books. It then carries over into establishing reading habits, for as he gets older, the child has the opportunity to choose reading material for himself. Some choose not to read at all!

If reading is used as punishment or forced upon a child, literature will become distasteful to him and he will read only the required school books. If reading is pictured to him as a living adventure, books will become his companions by choice when he has had his fill of more active pastimes. You'll know you've achieved your purpose when you find your youngster reading of his own volition when he could be looking at television. With so much reading material available, there is no excuse for a child's saying that he can't find anything interesting to read. It's up to us to stimulate his interest by helping him find good books. We can keep current on children's books either by scanning the book section of the newspaper or by visiting the library where new books and old classics are displayed.

A CHILD'S BOOKSHELF

At home, start with a current reading bookshelf in the family room or in the child's own room. This is different from a child's own private bookshelf which holds the familiar books that he has read and doesn't wish to part with. The current reading shelf includes books he intends to read soon. But most important, this bookshelf has the books he can read and enjoy right now. Enlist an older child's help in sorting his books once a year to pass on to a younger one books enjoyed and outgrown. The older child will stir the interest of the younger by saying, "This is a really great book; you're going to enjoy it."

150

Be sure your home offers attractive places to read —comfortable chairs with good light, an outside bench or swing, a soft rug by the fireplace or a night table light so that children can read in bed. Kent likes to stretch out on the grass to read in the early evening.

Encourage children to use what they have read by making a skit about a book, by sharing favorite illustrations with the family or by reading or telling the story to a younger sister or brother. Sometimes in dinner table conversation family members can share what they are reading.

THE LIBRARY

For most families, the reading of good books is tied closely to library trips. Once a child gets the reading habit, parents can't keep up financially with his desire for more and more books and so his going to the library, either with the family or on his own bicycle, should be encouraged. A librarian friend of mine says that since children rarely ask for suggestions, libraries give careful attention to new book displays. Acquaint your children with these displays and with their friendly librarian.

When relatives want to know what to give the children for birthdays or Christmas, suggest books on a subject of interest to the child. Too much money is spent on gifts that have little or no value, but a good book, especially a children's classic, makes a welcome and lasting gift.

At your library, you can obtain a list of books recommended for children in elementary school, books of current interest and also classics such as *"Heidi," "The Jungle Book"* and *"Little Women."*

MAGAZINES

If possible, let your child have a magazine subscription of his very own. Children love to get mail and look forward to the monthly magazine. They should be encouraged to make full use of the magazine, not just by reading the stories but by following up on the many other projects, crossword puzzles and suggestions that these worthwhile magazines contain. Some that you might want to consider are: *Cricket, Ebony Jr., Ranger Rick's Nature Magazine, The Kindergartener, Child Life, Jack and Jill, Trails,* or *Wee Wisdom.* Today's children have been trained to use and enjoy magazines and newsletters in school, so the monthly magazine subscription is one that even five- and six-year-olds will eagerly anticipate.

Don't rush your child in his magazine tastes. Let *Mad Magazine* and *Seventeen* wait for the teen years. Kent, however, can hardly wait for *National Geographic* and *National Wildlife* to arrive. While *National Geographic* has an appeal for a much older reader, it has meaning to younger children with a strong outdoor bent. Kent "read" *National Geographic* long before he could read —by intently looking at each and every picture. Don't hesitate to supply your child with *Popular Mechanics,*

Newsweek, or *Hot Rod Magazine* if these will reinforce his interests.

BOOKS AS COMPANIONS

Most people who enjoy reading relish an entire evening of it. Sometimes the whole family may be found reading around the fireplace in the living room on a snowy night. But our busy lives usually necessitate snatching reading time when we can get it: 30 minutes before bedtime; fifteen minutes at lunch; in the bathtub; or on a rainy day while on a vacation. Encourage your child to make books his companions. Let him have one on his night table, another to read on the bus, train, or whenever there may be waiting time such as before dental appointments or on family shopping trips.

When traveling with your child, you will find a book is a far better pacifier than a game or a doll. When children go to camp, tuck in a few good paperbacks, for after the day's strenuous activity, a book is relaxing.

Summer is an excellent reading time. Without school, a child faces an additional seven or eight hours during the day. Almost every summer we create our own private book club. Each child lists the books as he reads them. On the list I indicate a reward after three books, ten books, 20 books, etc. Perhaps after reading three books you might buy him a copy of his favorite magazine; after ten books, a new book of his choice. One summer when Kent read 20 books, I ordered for him simple book plates which he has continued to use to ensure the return of loaned books. Your library may have a book club with numerical goals for the children.

Mark went over to visit a chum and came home with a whole collection of books he enjoyed reading. Rather than going to the expense of buying more and more books for your child, you might try a book exchange among friends and relatives.

As your child grows older, encourage him to read the stories he has enjoyed in movie or television adaptations. The joy of hearing or reading them again is strong among children and they gain more the second time. I'm not recommending that a child often re-read books, but some do enjoy reliving certain episodes. After listening many times to the recording of *The Man of La Mancha,* Wendy found the reading of *Don Quixote* far more interesting than she had earlier.

Characters in books often become part of our lives so that we can refer to and benefit from their personalities. Characters become friends, part of our daily conversation. The children in *Harriet the Spy* are very much alive to Karen, and for many years Mark was equally confident that *The Cat in the Hat* really existed.

COMIC BOOKS

Many parents ask, "How can I keep my youngsters from a steady diet of comics and cheap books?" Simple, don't pay for any! If a ten-year-old has been permitted only this literary fare, it will be difficult to wean him at this point. To teach appreciation for good literature, start with your toddler and keep at it! Boys and girls can find greater adventure in *Kon Tiki, The Wizard of Oz* or *Black Beauty* than they will in comic books.

Karen visited friends with me one day and sat on the floor by their magazine-filled coffee table. On the way home she said, "The magazines were DUSTY—and some were from last year!" Don't underestimate parental example in literature. If a parent's highest reading is the *National Enquirer,* there's small literary encouragement for the children. If your children actually see you reading—in bed, in the sun, on the plane, in the living room—they are likely to join you. Have good books on shelves and tables. Leave some open. Talk about past and present authors so that your young people become familiar with writers they may never read.

Our happiest experience in family reading began one cold winter when we read aloud *The Snow Bird.* Each evening for fifteen minutes we read this compelling classic tale that held everyone's attention. Certain classics do not lend themselves to oral reading. Books heavy on description and light on action and conversation are difficult to read aloud.

Since parents eat more quickly than children, supper hour is an ideal time for reading. After conversation and when supper is nearly concluded, ten or fifteen minutes of oral reading around the dining table can be enjoyable. Choose a book that will interest all your children, perhaps a mystery or adventure story so that the youngsters will be eager to have the next installment read each night. Reading ten or fifteen minutes each evening is a slow process, so it's well to choose shorter books for this project. As the children become smooth readers, they too can take part in the reading.

GIFTS TO SCHOOL LIBRARIES

Several of our grade school libraries have adopted a unique system for increasing the number of books on their shelves. At the beginning of the year, the librarian circulates to parents a list of books that the library would like to own and can buy through its suppliers at advantageous prices, usually from about $2.50 to $5.00. To honor a child's birthday, rather than sending cupcakes or candy to school, the parent and child select for purchase one of the books from the list and inform the librarian. On the birthday, the librarian has already received the book from her source and presents it on behalf of the child to the school library in a short ceremony in the classroom. The child's classroom then has first chance to read the book. Children are proud to have in the school library books whose plates indicate that the books were given on the occasion of their birthdays.

Although reading should never be a punishment, a child needs some-

153

thing quiet to do when he's overexcited or obstreperous. Sometimes merely suggesting that he separate himself from his current project and find a quiet place to curl up and read is sufficient. When life's disappointments overwhelm or when we are dissatisfied with the way things are going, there is great solace and enjoyment in retiring into the world of books and to our good friends there. Children, too, can early learn that literature stretches the mind, rests the body and brings excitement, joy and fun into ordinary hours.

32
Drama
In Everyday
Experiences

A play is nothing more than literature made visible and audible. This powerful, dramatic method of teaching is used early in school experiences from puppet shows, which subtly carry the message to brush one's teeth, to more elaborate stage productions that teach racial harmony.

We can broaden our children's enjoyment of drama by taking them to suitable youth plays and as they grow older to our community or legitimate theaters. Proper preparation enhances the experience. This was brought home to us one year when we planned to be in New York where our children could see the musical *1776*. The story would have meant nothing to them, especially the younger ones, if they hadn't had some briefing. In our art course we found a painting of the signing of the Declaration of Independence and this became the centerpiece on the month's bulletin board. We also played the recording of the musical, since the hearing of the familiar heightens anticipation and enjoyment for children as well as adults. Since we parents had seen the play once before, we explained to the children where the various songs fit it. One evening at supper we read the story of the signing of the Declaration of Independence and Wendy briefed the younger children as to what had been going on in American history just prior to this time. The Boston Tea Party and Paul Revere's ride became familiar episodes to the children. By the time we went to see *1776*, Karen could sing most of the songs and the children were excitedly anticipating each event in the play. They were thrilled when things turned out to be as they had imagined them, and equally excited when things were different than they had pictured them. Karen wept when John Adams pleaded with his fellow legislators to care about the future of a young country. There was a sober stillness as the young soldier from George Washington's army told exactly what the war was like. They found the humor of Benjamin Franklin interesting enough to look up his sayings after the play. This, of course, became a total experience, one that the children absorbed before, during and after the actual performance.

Not every play takes on this importance, but you will find that a child who has seen a play in school will be excited about relating it to you in your afternoon snack-and-tell time. If he has some dramatic ability, he will tell it to you as a character in the play. Encourage this.

PLAYS AT HOME

Since most children have access to a phonograph, let them listen to plays and musicals and then tell their peers these stories.

The next step in encouraging drama is the reading aloud of plays. We had never encouraged our children to do this until our adult social group decided to give a play reading of Jean Kerr's *Mary, Mary.* They heard us rehearsing and found it so funny that they found some suitable plays at the library to read with their friends.

This led to the next step of presenting a play at home. It takes only three or four children to produce a simple home play and even those without dramatic ability can be put to good use in making scenery from shelf paper and cardboard boxes. We have productions several times each year, some commemorating holidays but often just for the fun of doing it.

Kent and Karen have two friends of like ages who also enjoy acting. One year, along with two younger twin boys, we had a spectacular production of *Snow White and the Seven Dwarfs.* In fact the twins and Mark played all seven dwarfs!

Putting on a play needn't be complicated. If the scenery sets the mood, that is adequate. Children are quick to improvise. Elaborate costumes are unnecessary. Once Karen's aunt gave her a special gift: a costume kit which included twelve simple tunics in various colors. These tunics were lengths of fabric sewn up to arm slits, with a hole cut for the head and various belts and ties. A long one in a leopard-print fabric made an ideal animal. One fashioned of pale blue chiffon remnants of someone's prom dress, tied with a gold belt, clothed a princess. These tunics provided sufficient costumes for almost any play the children wanted to do.

Some of the better toy stores such as F. A.O. Schwarz in New York supply kits of simple plays for children with ample copies of the script and list of props. But children are soon beyond these and are ready to improvise. Your child may be creative enough to write his own plays, and with a few pieces of carbon paper, you can type a simple play very quickly.

Of course, a play is no fun if there isn't an audience — an appreciative audience. So, moms and dads have to be quick to come and watch these short performances and applaud loudly.

If your children enjoy creative dramatics, encourage them to set aside a summer afternoon and invite the neighborhood children to their latest production. You can volunteer to supply cookies and juice to everyone after the play.

Most children love to act and have ample opportunities to do so in school. Simple charades and pantomimes will loosen them up and give them opportunities to use their bodies in actively dramatic ways. Encourage the actors to do more than speak to us, for if there is no action, no interplay between the characters other than the spoken word, we could well shut our eyes and simply listen to the play.

Children love the simple embellishment of play acting such as fake fights, villainous characters, sleeping princesses and comic relief. Help them prepare a few polished phrases to introduce their production. Show them how to bow when the audience applauds. As they progress, you'll find them adding props, music and programs. They'll enjoy setting up chairs for an audience and acting as ushers before dashing behind the sheet curtain to open the play.

Encouraging children to use drama as a form of play expands their literary horizons, uses up their surplus energy and teaches them to speak with poise and to use gestures, effective in future public speaking assignments.

PUBLIC PLAYS

There is no substitute for seeing a live play. Parents may spend a good portion of the family entertainment budget in taking children to movies, but even a less professional production of a play for children is generally an improvement over movies. The schools provide some live entertainment, but parents should still take their youngsters to live theater and teach them the protocol and good manners of theater attendance.

While I would not recommend taking children to plays such as *Who's Afraid of Virginia Wolf,* they can enjoy plays that are somewhat beyond their age level. Musicals, historical plays, mysteries are often interesting and acceptable for youngsters. If there is a youth theater with inexpensive tickets, taking children to their productions makes an enjoyable birthday party.

IMPROMPTU FUN

A spontaneous, unstructured production is often fun for children. With no script, no one knows in advance what the other characters are going to do. This keeps the players mentally alert to react and respond to their fellow actors. You might set the scene by saying, "The action begins in a dark woods. There is a space ship on the left with a robot behind it. Two characters singing a song enter from the right." At this point the children take over. You will be amazed what they will do with this simple setting.

For additional fun let each child act out the same setting in his own way. Dramas can also be used to harmonize experiences that children find intimidating. We can have an impromptu "play" about the first day at school, going on an airplane or attending a party. Valuable do's and don't's can be easily emphasized this way.

As mentioned in the chapter on music, few of our children will become great concert pianists, but we want them to be able to carry a tune and read music. The same goes for drama. There is seldom a Katherine Hepburn or Meryl Streep hidden in our family circle, but it is almost impossible to go through life without having to stand and speak with intelligence, conviction and clarity. Home theater also lets the child use his imagination and energy to create.

33
Sports —
Even If You're Not Sporty

After sitting in school all day, most children need an hour of sport activity. Usually it doesn't take much to get a child outside to play. Depending on the climate, he will quickly get up a game of ball or biking, swimming or sledding. Still, a child's view of the field of sports is too narrow. With a small investment in equipment, there are many sports and games which a child can enjoy.

For some sports, an investment in equipment is essential, but you can also make do with very little. A volleyball game can be had with a ball and a piece of string between two trees. We used scrap lumber to make a ping-pong table and have ping-pong tournaments with only $6.99 invested in the paddles, ball and net. A large ball purchased for under $5.00 can suffice for water sports, dodge ball, volleyball, basketball and throw-and-catch practice. If price is no object, it's great to have the best equipment but young children will be as happy with a simple hoop as a basketball goal.

Parents who are not particularly sporty must make a real effort to encourage sports if their child isn't so inclined. You can begin by taking your child to watch his friends play. A professional baseball game is a special treat. Make it a family outing for the girls and boys to see the local high school play football. Watching the baby sitter run in school track events will also increase the child's interest in sports.

A FAMILY SPORTS DAY

During nice weather, invite another family or two with similar age children to join in a day of sports. Along with a potluck picnic lunch, set aside times for active and passive sports. Two or three families can be divided into two volleyball teams and even five- and six-year-olds can play. Grade school children enjoy games such as red rover and dodge ball. Entire families can take part in croquet if there are an equal number of adults and children on each team. Water sports such as keep-away can be great with two generations playing. Tetherball is good for a twosome.

159

Hide-and-seek, long considered a child's game, takes on new adventure when parents and children play it together.

As children grow older, scrub football can be a family game for 30 minutes after supper with as few as three or four children. Later touch football can be added. Mothers shouldn't hesitate to throw themselves into these games! With pools becoming more common in communities and backyards, water sports have become popular. Boating is an expensive but favorite family activity along with skiing and snowmobiling. Sledding and roller skating continue to be less costly alternatives.

One active sport that even the most unsporty can enjoy is bicycling. Safe bike seats enable toddlers to be taken along on mother's or dad's bike and thus the whole family can enjoy this sport. Besides the fun of riding around the neighborhood, this sport can be extended to include longer excursions. Try an evening bike picnic. Divide the components of a supper and let each family member carry part on his bike to a destination 30 minutes away.

When teaching the elements of sports to your children, include good sportsmanship. Stress the activity, the team spirit, the skills developed, the concentration, the fun, rather than the question of winner or loser. It seems natural for little children to be poor losers; remedy this by quickly and profusely praising the losers for not sulking, never laughing at or about the losers. Then make a big thing of congratulating the winners: applaud, shake hands, shout hoorays. Give a hooray for the losers since they made it possible for the other side to win!

When starting a new sport, show the child the proper care and use of the equipment, as well as any safety precautions. Although children are anxious to get going on a sport, whether it be archery or sailing, we will have greater confidence in their expertise and safety if we carefully teach them how the sport is to be performed.

For those living near water, certain basic rules should never be broken. Living near a beach, we ruled that children had to go in two's for beachcombing or rowing. And if they were ever caught on the boat without wearing a life preserver, that privilege would be withdrawn for a month. The wearing of a life preserver became second nature and as soon as we enforced this rule, we noted that other beach families did likewise.

Perhaps the greatest sports training we can give little children is an early ability to throw and catch. Even the youngest child can play roll and catch. The old game of *Teacher*, in which one is at the head of the row until he drops the ball, seldom gets boring. The ability to throw, catch and aim well will help our youngsters in sports from tennis to billiards.

ORGANIZED SPORTS

In many communities, young children are encouraged to become involved in organized team sports — soccer and baseball primarily. Little

League and other such team organizations become a big part of life with fund-raising for uniforms and trips, regular practice sessions and attendance at games taking up much of the family time.

Your child's joining such a team should depend on how it is organized in your area. Before letting your child sign up, go as a family to some of the games and find out how the players are rotated into the games or used on the basis of skill. Get to know the coaches. See how they handle defeat, victory, individual mistakes and inabilities. Find out if all the players have an opportunity to play. If you feel your son or daughter would benefit by this highly competitive play, be prepared for this to become a major activity of the family during the season. Parent help is required. This will mean late suppers and busy Saturdays.

INDOOR SPORTS

Don't overlook table games for the cold and rainy days. Little children are often surfeited with box games that involve merely rolling dice and moving markers over a variety of courses. These have their place in teaching them to take turns and to be graceful winners and losers, but children can quickly graduate to more sophisticated games that require greater intelligence.

Card games such as hearts, pinochle and bridge teach numbers and tactics and are not beyond the comprehension of children eight to twelve years old. *Monopoly* makes a good family game for one long or several short evenings. *Pit* is a good old standby; and, for the more thoughtful members of the family try checkers, chess and *Scrabble*, which strengthens spelling and vocabulary.

We once set up a chess game in the dining room because we had to walk through that room to get anywhere else in the house. We never sat down to play the game. As each participant walked through the dining room, he made his move, then put underneath the piece played a 50 cent piece we used as a marker. When the next player came through, he could see where the preceeding one had moved, make his move and put the marker under his man. Whole chess games were played for months on end without any of the participants seeing each other in action!

Another good sit-down sport that taxes the mind is putting puzzles together. This can be a family or solo game. We usually have one of the more complicated ones under construction on our game table.

On a recent three-day weekend, I gave every family member a score card listing six sports, two each day. Anyone was welcome to practice in advance. Points would be given for winning, losing, being on a winning team or just for participating. On Friday morning we had the volleyball tournament and Friday afternoon the ping pong elimination. Saturday it was water relays and a chess competition at night. Sunday was basketball in the afternoon and baseball after supper. With a variety of sports, everyone excelled in at least one. This gave younger children opportunities to win when they were teamed with older children or adults. We totaled our tallies at the end of the weekend and the losers had the task of making fancy fudge and strawberry sundaes for the winners —and for themselves, too!

When winning, losing, competing and participating become an integral part of family life, sports are enjoyed for the skill. The wins and losses take on their proper perspective. Simple forms of wrestling, hide-and-seek and indoor games are good for rainy days and there are plenty of outdoor sports you can enjoy with your children without being a phys-ed major.

34
Scientific
Experiments
At Home

The inquisitive child can be a joy or a pest. Sometimes a child asks us "why" just to keep the conversation going. Others find it's a good way to "get our goat." Most often, the inquisitiveness of children should be encouraged. A child's scientific bent can be discerned early in life. He will find new uses for conventional toys — new ways to put them together and play with them. Since the manufacturers of toys and games do not always achieve the ultimate in creativity, let your child experiment.

Be alert to a child's interests — especially when his talents don't coincide with your own. Eight- to ten-year-olds with scientific leanings should be supplied with simple equipment to carry on safe scientific experiments at home. Chemistry sets can be costly but they are as important as music lessons. We realized a few years ago that Kent had no interest in music although we were willing to spend money on his lessons. However, he had a great interest in science. It dawned on us that this would be just as good an investment, so we alloted a monthly sum for the purchase of tools and equipment to encourage his experimental nature.

Without much expense, young children can do simple experiments in the home with equipment on hand. As with any craft, you want to be on the scene at the beginning and to check several times to see what is going on.

To satisfy the inquisitive nature of very young children it is not necessary to buy prepared kits. When Mark was little, he watched me use food coloring to give white frosting a sunnier look. He was quite fascinated with how one small drop could do so much. So began my finding of simple experiments for our pre-schoolers.

1. **Food coloring.** Children love to mix things together. Let them experiment with your food colors. Give them small jars to show off the greens, browns, and purples they learn to make. In season, let them pick flowers to put into the jars.

163

2. Colored cookies. Using a simple cookie recipe, let the children add a few drops of food coloring to the dough and after rolling it out, turn them loose with animal cookie cutters. If the animals are missing ears and legs, remember it's the fun of making them that's important. The more grotesque the color combinations, the more rapidly they are eaten. If you don't have a good quick recipe, try this one:

Cream one cup of margarine with ¼ cup confectioners sugar. Add two cups of sifted flour to the mixture and work together with your hands until it's a soft dough. Add color. Let the children help pat it out on a pastry cloth or between two pieces of waxed paper and then roll it until about ⅛ inch thick. Cut into shapes. Put the finished product on ungreased cookie sheets. Bake about 20 minutes in a 325 degree oven; makes about 36 animals.

3. Bread. While you are in the kitchen, don't forget simple bread dough. Using yeast and seeing bread rise is fun for children from three on up. By encouraging this kitchen experiment, I now have a teen-age bread maker who will happily turn out half a dozen loaves when requested.

4. Gelatin. Give the children a package of clear gelatin and some juice to see how the gelatin solidifies the liquid. Heat and refrigerate so later they can eat their project.

5. Salt. Put some hot water into a small saucepan and dump in a few spoonfuls of salt. Let the child stir until the salt is dissolved. Put the pan aside until the water has evaporated and you'll have square salt crystals left. Look at them through a magnifying glass.

6. Seeds. Select seeds that germinate quickly, such as morning glory. Soak them in water until they split a little. This gives the children something to watch. Help them plant the seeds in a pot, box or flat. Put them in a sunny window with strings up to the curtain rod. Have each child choose his own seedling to see which morning glory reaches the rod first. These will bloom in a sunny location.

7. Paste. Give the child a cup of water and either flour or starch to mix gradually until he has paste of the proper stickiness. Continue with paper craft projects using the paste.

8. Magnifying glass. An inexpensive magnifying glass will keep a curious youngster happy for a long time. First let him look at his own feet with it; then various objects around the house. Widen his horizons by giving him fabrics so he can see the size of the various weaves; leaves and flowers so he can study their veins; and newspaper photographs so he can look at the dots comprising the picture. Finally, have him put some ants or other small bugs in a box to observe these through his magnifying glass.

9. Mirrors. Inexpensive small mirrors are fun for young children to play with when they are beyond the age of hurting themselves on broken glass. Show them how to play with them in front of a large bathroom mirror to make multiple reflections. With three or four small mirrors they can encircle an object for all-around viewing.

10. **Pulleys.** With string and empty thread spools, children can make simple pulleys for hoisting small toys.

11. **Inclined plane.** With cardboard or pieces of wood, show your child how to make an inclined plane. Roll cars down it to see how steep the plane can be tilted before the car will tumble off. Or invert a paper cup, put a marble underneath and let it glide down the plane. Racing two cars or two cups adds to the fun.

With only a few minutes of your time, these simple ideas can start a child experimenting. They are good for children under the age of eight. As older children become interested in more sophisticated experiments, you may wish to purchase chemistry and plastic kits, radio crystal sets, magic kits. You can save money, however, by letting children experiment with old wheels, wires, and parts of radios and phonographs.

When you see that your child has a proclivity toward one branch of science, you will want to purchase the necessary equipment to reinforce this interest. If the subject is beyond you or other family members, find the needed guidance at school or among friends. Safety precautions should be covered to instill respect, though not fear, in the child.

When a toddler first asks HOW and WHY, take the time to show him how things work. Gradually you'll find he is able to answer the questions more often himself, and ultimately you'll find opportunities to ask HIM how things work—an important step in his maturity and self-appreciation.

35
Enjoying
The
Outdoors

Whether he grows up in the city, suburb or country, a child needs to be taught to appreciate the world outside the walls of home and school.

ON LAND

Young children often think that everything under foot is merely dirt, cement or grass. Even two- and three-year-olds can learn to observe the life and formations of the ground itself. Let the child place a garbage can cover on the lawn for 48 hours. When he lifts the cover, he will find that worms and other insects have chosen to reside in this dark, cool place. This gives the youngster some idea of what he may find when he turns over rocks on a nature hike.

What youngster doesn't collect interesting rocks! Most bookstores have a simple handbook that will help parents explain the characteristics of rock formations. There is no sense letting a child collect a bushel of rocks if he learns nothing from the experience!

A child of eight or nine will appreciate using your field glasses to observe birds and small animals up close. A hike for the sake of exercise alone is certainly one way to enjoy the outdoors. But after the novelty of hiking has worn off, it's well to alert a child to the possibilities of new discoveries. If you have several children, stir their competitive natures to see who can spot the most birds or find the most interesting item on the ground: rocks, decaying leaves, insects, plants. Sit quietly during a rest time on your hike and listen to the sounds. You'll be surprised at the number of different sounds in a quiet woods or even in town.

Since most of us aren't naturalists, rely on rangers in state or national parks to enlarge the child's — and your — factual information.

With older children, vary the hike by starting half the group, usually with one adult, ten minutes ahead of the second group, the first leaving clues as to where they are going. See if group two can follow the clues and reach the same destination. Have some pre-agreed meeting place should your tracking not be particularly adept.

Learning the names of growing things is fun for some children, but others may find that leaf collecting and tree identification is too much like school. Most children, however, are proud to know the names of ten or twelve common trees and few rebel if you introduce one or two new trees on each hike. After identifying a tree by its bark, leaf formation, flower and fruit, you can then reinforce this information on the remainder of the hike by seeing who can find the same tree the most number of times. Picking leaves and wild flowers is forbidden in some places but where it is not, children often enjoy gathering them to press at home.

Encourage young children to hold small animals without fear. An ant crawling up a finger, a woolly caterpillar climbing across the palm, a wiggling land crab in his hand, all these are exciting experiences for a young child and tend to play down fears of other small creatures such as spiders and harmless snakes.

BY WATER

Vacations by lakes, streams or oceans open another world to your youngster. After a basic discussion of water safety and water sports, young children can be happy for hours discovering life in lakes and streams. Again, turning rocks over, looking closely at water plants, digging down into the mud or overturning a shovel of sand will uncover new adventures. Make sure your young explorers are armed with pails, nets and plastic bags for their collected items. Children should learn to respect the lives of fish and small animals. If they decide to take them away from their natural habitats, they should be reminded to provide proper living conditions for them or to return them to their original surroundings at the end of the day. Such collecting should be done only if the species is not endangered and if plenty of specimens are seen on location.

When your children are hiking or beach walking with you, a rest stop lets everyone stretch out on stomachs to take an eye-to-eye look at moss or sand crabs. Close observation of small fish in the tide pools can fascinate children for a long time. Books that identify fish or shells make the outdoor experience more worthwhile.

BRINGING NATURE INSIDE

Encourage your child to bring the outdoors inside. A sculptural piece of driftwood, a shell collection, a rock with an intriguing contour can make an attractive table decoration, a unique item on the sideboard or a valued possession in the child's own room. I noticed that when Kent packed for a trip, he took along his favorite rock!

One Sunday afternoon while traveling, we saw people walking in the country and gathering armloads of field flowers. Having been contained in the car sightseeing for many hours, our children, boys and girls alike, were happy to be liberated for 45 minutes of running through fields and collecting flowers to take back to the hotel. We had brought on the trip a roll of plastic bags, so when we checked out of the hotel we conveniently carried our flowers with us to our next destination.

THE HEAVENS

The third area of the outdoors is the sky. Don't introduce this study by insisting that everyone memorize the constellations! You'll stimulate interest better by starting with the moon. With a calendar that shows the phases of the moon, take a moment before bedtime to check outside to see if it's doing just what the calendar said.

Ask which star looks brightest and then identify it. That's far more memorable to the child than pointing out to him that Venus is that bright planet over yonder. He'll remember it better and locate it himself if he has a part in its discovery. To children under five, point out the North Star and simple constellations such as Orion and the Dippers. When children are of school age, visit a planetarium and introduce them to more sophisticated star-finding.

Most bookstores sell good star-finding books along with local charts so you can determine where the stars will be at a certain hour in the evening. Some newspapers publish this information. Lying on a blanket on the lawn to look at the stars can be a peaceful and family-bonding experience right before bedtime. Children like to "stay up a little later," so make that time memorable!

With so many man-made satellites in the heavens, it's not unusual today to see one traversing the night sky. Don't forget to include a knowledge of these essential objects.

Since man's first walk on the moon, its place names, like the Sea of Tranquility, have become part of our vocabulary. A child with this interest will enjoy moon maps or a moon globe which identify these geographic areas and the touch-down spots of the astronauts. The exploration of our planetary system will make Saturn's rings and Jupiter's moons familiar even to second-graders.

The better informed our young people are about nature and the outdoors the more apt they are to be supportive and knowledgeable in the areas of pollution and ecology. An appreciation and respect for the outdoors and for plant and animal life is certainly part of home education and can help our children to make the intelligent choices the next century will demand.

PETS

The question as to when to let a child have his first pet certainly depends on the responsibility of the child and the nature of the pet he wants. Although the complete care of a pet rightfully should be the child's, parents need to monitor that care in the interest of the pet's welfare.

Prior to pet ownership, rules for its care and enjoyment should be worked out with your child so that he fully understands that a pet is not his merely to enjoy or ignore as he chooses. Make it clear that its care should not fall on parental shoulders. If he realizes that he will have to mop up after the new puppy, clean the mouse cage or wash the turtle bowl, he will take the care and enjoyment of his pet more seriously. Point out, too, that animals, like people, require more than food and shelter. Love, attention, exercise, even conversation may be part of the responsibility of owning a pet. When buying a pet, consider the commitment you are making for the lifetime of that animal.

Children from two to five enjoy pets such as fish and turtles, insects like the popular ant farm, and the increasingly popular gerbil, one of the cleaner rodents.

Children from five to eight can train and enjoy birds, white mice, hamsters and guinea pigs. Following these, of course, come dogs and cats. Nowadays ownership of more exotic pets, such as possums, raccoons and monkeys, is discouraged and often prohibited.

Sometimes parents encourage a child to want a pet long before the child is ready to handle that responsibility. Facing it honestly, it's the parent who wants the animal! So if you want a fluffy poodle for your own enjoyment, level with yourself. Don't say that this animal is the child's when the child would much prefer a nondescript dog that will follow him to the baseball field.

Exploring the world of plants and animals, your child learns a two-fold lesson: it increases his unselfishness and responsibility and, at the same time, it gives him a better understanding of the magnitude and wonders of creation.

36
Creativity
In The
Car

Do you cringe when you have to go someplace with a load of children in your car? If you do, the problem may be that you have not insisted on certain basic rules of car safety nor have you creatively planned riding time to make it pleasant.

Starting with a toddler, teach the child that the car does not go anywhere unless he is seated, strapped-in and the door is locked. When I drove a carpool with seven or more children on a regular basis, they knew that my car slowed down and stopped when the noise level reached a shout. A car is not a park or a restaurant or a playroom. It's a modern convenience that enables us to get from one place to another. Still, it should not be a source of boredom or time-wasting. Sometimes turning on the radio will be sufficient entertainment to make the trip harmonious. But the ingenious parent can use short car trips as creative adventures.

RUNNING ERRANDS

When two or more children are with a parent, the children concern themselves with each other. For this reason when running short errands, try to take only one child with you. This uses the ten-minute drive to the best advantage since it gives you that unique opportunity, often missed during the day, to have a one-to-one chat with a child. If at all possible, never go anywhere alone. Single out one child with whom you haven't had a good chat lately and take him along. Don't use these excursions as occasions to reprimand a child for mistakes or work poorly done but rather use them as listening experiences to find out more about the child's thoughts and interests. Discuss *his* topics, not *yours*.

CARPOOLS

A little humor helps a lot if you're part of the carpool circuit. There are the children who have forgotten their lunch money and those who are rarely at the appointed place at the appointed time. By encouraging team spirit, however, and by insisting on safety and noise level rules, you can make this an enjoyable experience. On the morning run to school, it's the driver's responsibility to send the children off in a cheerful and optimistic frame of mind. Singing, telling funny stories, pointing out interesting things along the way will help bring this about when the children don't have too much in common.

A carpool I drove daily passed a boy sitting on the curb while waiting for his high school bus. We decided that he looked so glum that it would be fun to wave to him each day. It got to be such a game that soon my rather conservative group of carpool children would roll down the windows, wave and throw kisses to the surprised young man.

As we turned into one residential area, a certain mountain came into view and we would always check to see if a cloud was sitting on it. This gave us an indication as to whether it would rain that day. When the carpool was picked up in the afternoon, we assessed our weather forecasting.

Parting comments are one of the carpool driver's jobs. "Have a good day," "Remember, I love you," "Do you have everything with you?" will help to send the group off merrily. I was considered the corniest mother in our carpool since each week I tried to think of a new parting line such as: "Everyone who can write his name may get out now" or "If you are wearing stripes today you must get out last." This made *me* feel good as I carried on this daily chore!

THE FAMILY SONG BOOK

For ten years we had the same 30-minute round trip to church every week. The scenery along the way was not spectacular, so to use this time creatively, we hit upon an idea that Karen originated. She had learned a song she wanted Kent and Mark to sing with her. I typed the words. She put them in a folder and thus began our family song book.

After dutifully learning her song, everyone else had one he wanted to teach. Gradually we included words from popular musicals, folk songs and patriotic anthems. With six of these folders of perhaps twelve or fifteen pages each, we now have a selection of songs the whole family enjoys singing. On car trips we distribute the song books and tune up as we go along. We even take them in our suitcases on long trips. We made quite a sensation on our first European jaunt when we taught our guide songs such as *I've Been Working on the Railroad, God Bless America* and *Yellow Bird.* Our repertoire includes *Seventy-Six Trombones, Try to Remember, Food — Glorious Food,* and *I Love to Go A-Wandering.* Once or twice a year we add a new page to our book.

WORD GAMES

If you're not musically inclined, try word games. Start with these:

1. With tiny children, alert them to call out words they can read along the roadside and see if they can achieve certain numerical goals.

2. There's the old game of "I'm going to Indianapolis and I am going to take along my apple, bike, cougar, etc." This can be made into a more sophisticated game for older children if you limit the words to be selected for each letter of the alphabet to ones in a certain category such as animals, birds, food, toys, etc.

3. When I have a load of Campfire girls in my car, they like to find the alphabet, in proper order, on signs along the roadside.

4. Someone calls out a word and the next person responds with a word starting with the last letter of the preceding word. For example: zoo, ostrich, ham, mustache. This game is easy at the beginning and harder the longer you play since repeats aren't allowed.

5. Games like *Third of a Ghost, Twenty Questions* and *Password* will keep a group of youngsters busy and happy on a long trip.

6. Play automobile lotto with preprinted forms you can purchase. They picture stop signs, gas stations, churches, schools, etc. Children who cannot read enjoy putting an X through the item as they see it; whoever gets five in a row is the winner.

7. Word associations can be played with younger children. One says a word and another tells the first thing that pops into his mind. It can be hilarious!

8. One person makes up a first line for a poem; the next person follows with a rhyming line. Some examples:

The bird will chirp
But I will burp.

I want to stop,
'Cause there's a cop.

Sit on my knee,
Unless you're a bee.

Later in this book we'll take up travel as an educational parental responsibility and consider what we can do to make longer trips in the car more enjoyable.

Long trip or short, don't under-utilize the hours in your car. You may make only one or two short trips a day, but these can give you time to speak appreciatively to each child at least once a week. This in iteself is a plus value.

37
Visiting
Can Be Fun

Rare is the child who shouts "Hurrah!" when parents announce a necessary visit to an older friend. When we visit friends who have children the ages of ours, there's no problem. But, when a child is taken to visit adults, he may, if not prepared in advance to appreciate this occasion, consider visiting one of the more boring events of his lifetime. Let's examine three aspects of going visiting:

1. When to visit
2. Preparation in advance
3. What to say and do

WHEN TO VISIT

A child's visit to your maiden aunt, a school chum, a shut-in or any person of a different generation from the child should be made only at a time when the child is rested and calm. For young children who nap in the afternoon, visiting time is best first thing in the morning or an hour after nap time. Don't wake a child from a nap to take him visiting. Most children require time to become their peppy, happy selves again after their naps. Also, it's well to give a child a little exercise after his nap. A placid visit will be too much like the nap unless you vary the activity. Late night visiting should be avoided until children are old enough to be more flexible in their visiting times.

PREPARATION IN ADVANCE

Before you go, tell your child the purpose of the visit: that he is going to see Aunt Nellie since she hasn't seen him for six months; that he is taking a casserole supper to Mr. Jones who has no one to cook for him; that he is going to cheer up Mrs. Smith who is in bed; or that he is going to see the neighbor's new poodle puppies. Next, enlist the child's help in accomplishing the purpose of the visit. If the visit is merely for you to chit-chat with the adults, either leave the child at home or take some

173

alternate activity such as a puzzle, game or book.

WHAT TO SAY AND DO

Prior to the visit, reiterate the proper manners. When your child arrives, is he expected to kiss or hug the person? Should he shake hands? If he's offered food, should he accept or decline? If he needs to use the bathroom, what does he say? If he's told he may go to another room and play, should he accept? What happens if he knocks over the candy dish? What does he say when leaving?

We once visited friends who had a new house. We told our four children that the purpose of the trip was to see their home and we reminded them they were to comment on something they especially enjoyed about it. This was not difficult since it was a handsome house and showed a happy family life. Wendy commented on the beautiful blue and green carpet in the living room. Kent was quick to notice that the new lawn was absolutely weed free. Karen remarked about the wonderful storage space in the children's closets. Mark being the youngest, however, forgot his compliment until it was time to leave. During the 45-minute ride to the home I had said in jest that I would be grim about anyone who did not make a pleasant, polite and honest comment on the home. We were saying our good-byes at the door when it struck Mark that he had said nothing nice to the hostess. His look of dismay was quickly replaced with a smile as he spied the shiny new front doorknob right at his eye level. He beamed, looked up at her and said, "You certainly have the most beautiful doorknobs!"

Sometimes it helps a child to take something to the person being visited: a newspaper picture he would like to share, a little batch of cookies, a bone for the dog or a game to play with the person.

Many children want to know just what you "do" during a visit. Visiting is good practice for children in listening, asking questions, observing and unselfishly making others feel good. If they are told that this is *not* an opportunity for them to show off, sing or do tricks, then we must fill this void with suggestions as to what they may do. Should they sit on the floor or on a chair? Should they enter into the conversation? Is it polite to ask questions? May they look at the bric-a-brac Aunt Nellie keeps in the cupboard?

The major part of a visit is conversation. Here we should help children in knowing what to say. They would not *intentionally* ask embarrassing questions, so our advance education should emphasize the type of things they should say rather than a list of "thou shalt nots." If Mr. Jones does not wish to speak about his deceased cat, you should make this known to the children. If it would be unwise to ask about the health of the person being visited, they should know this, too. There may be private things about our own family life that our children should be alerted not to

174

mention. In making conversation, this is one of the basics we teach our children: what is for general publication and what is to be kept within the family.

It helps the child if we clue him in on something interesting concerning the host. Is he a war veteran? Did she needlepoint all the seat cushions in the dining room? Did she make the bread in the tea sandwiches? Did he build the new room by himself?

One evening our family was asked to dinner by a woman the children didn't know well. We knew, however, that she was living in Honolulu the day Pearl Harbor was bombed. This seemed like a wonderful topic to our children. Since they knew something of the events surrounding Pearl Harbor, they asked questions and learned much. Our hostess felt honored to relate stories about that exciting day. Conversation never lagged and Mark still refers to her as "A hero of Pearl Harbor."

Everyone has some specialty or event in his life that he'd like to be asked about. Let the child ask a question or two to get the conversation going.

Usually it isn't necessary that our child give a long monologue on his own activities, but he should be prepared to say more than "yes" and "no" when the host or hostess graciously asks him a question. Visits should be kept brief. Thirty minutes is ideal.

When home again, assess the effect of the visit. The child can easily tell if the purpose was achieved and will be quick to tell you if he helped bring it about. The satisfaction of a cheering visit with someone who is lonely, sad or ill is an essential part of a child's growing up. In their winsome ways, children can enhance these visits.

Too often we blame children for being pigish or clumsy at simple social events when the fault is ours for not showing them in advance what is expected. Many children are not familiar with matters of etiquette. We should not blindly lead them into discouraging or embarrassing situations.

When a child sees the pleasure of "going visiting," he'll suggest someone to visit: a school friend who is recuperating, a friend's mother and new baby, or a neighbor whose dog had puppies.

38
Shopping
Can Be Fun

Do you groan at the thought of shopping with the children? Many parents enjoy the quiet privacy of shopping by themselves, that rare occasion when the trip isn't rushed and they can browse and find new items. These occasions, however, are the exception rather than the rule for most of us. More than likely we have our little helpers with us on our shopping expeditions. Shopping with help can be a time saver for you as well as a learning experience for the child. It can increase his sense of value, his mathematical aptitude and his ability to make decisions on style and appearance.

But before we take a child into the stores, there has to be this basic understanding between parent and child: a playground is where we play, a store is where we shop. While both can be happy experiences, stores were not created for the amusement of children but for supplying needs and luxuries. Thus a child's behavior in a store differs from his behavior on a playground. This one simple ground rule is all you need to get across in order to shop with peace-of-mind. By using creative thinking to let the child really take part in the shopping trip, you'll both look forward to the adventure.

GROCERY SHOPPING

With the advent of the infant chair and the body sling, even small babies nowadays go on shopping trips. A trip to the grocery store for the new mother with the young baby in his safe little chair can be an enjoyable break in the routine of bottles and diapers. Armed with a plastic bottle of juice or milk so that the baby's voice will not echo through the store, even the newest mother — or father — can have the confidence to get essential shopping done.

As junior gets older, a little rattle can be taken along, later a small book or toy, preferably tied to the infant chair so it won't fall to the floor. When Wendy was small she was never particularly noisy until we got

176

into grocery stores. I made a deal with my favorite check-out person that I would pick up a little box of animal cookies when I came into the store and although they might be partly eaten by the time I left, she knew I would pay for them. When Wendy began to squirm and exude joyous but ear-piercing sounds, I would open the box of cookies and hand them out one at a time. This got us through six months of shopping trips until she could take a personal interest in the procedure.

As soon as a child is old enough to walk alone, he likes to get out of the cart and push it. This is fine until he pushes it into the posterior of another shopper. To forestall this, teach your toddler to sit in the child's chair above the basket and organize the purchases as you toss them in. Let him be the custodian of list and pencil so that you can cross off the items. Don't turn him loose yet!

Beware of toddlers such as Kent who sat in the cart and methodically removed the paper labels from about 20 cans of fruits and vegetables before I realized what he was doing buried under all the groceries!

Grocery shopping can be a vocabulary builder. As soon as your child begins to speak and understand, you can point out the fruit, crackers, bread, juice, cereal and his other favorites. By age five he is a good help in pushing the wagon and putting things on the bottom rack.

Your kindergartener can graduate to being an errand runner for you. You keep the master list and the children report back to you for assignments. A good memory tickler is to give each child three assignments and then see who can get back safely first, no running permitted in the store.

After a year of having your child work on the "Get three items and return" system, he's old enough to read well and can be entrusted with his own short written list which you've copied from your master list. Now he really becomes a time-saver for you and you note his behavior in the store is excellent since he has the responsibility of collecting about 20 items.

If your shopping list is long, you may wish to have each child use his own cart. I cut shopping time by about a third to a half this way. If we let our children help put groceries away and cook, they become familiar with what brands and sizes we want.

Ultimately the aim is to have the child so proficient at shopping at age eleven or twelve that you can send him off alone with a fairly difficult list.

When children are helping with the grocery shopping, point out prices. Your young mathematicians will quickly figure out the best buy. You can counsel them when the cheaper item is consistent with its use or quality.

As a reward for helping on the grocery trip, I usually let each child select one surprise food item to hide in his basket. We get so routine in our selection of groceries that it is good to introduce new ideas. Some of the unique foods that have been legally "smuggled" home have turned out to be family favorites.

If your child takes a sack lunch, let him collect all the items for it so there can be no complaints. Any child who won't eat the lunch offered at school should be willing to make his own. This is a service that parents need not provide. The child, however, should be able to select at the store the balanced lunch that he will eat.

When Wendy and Kent started school and Karen became my sole grocery companion, I found she always ate best on grocery shopping day. I let this small eater pick out foods she especially liked, and she always had a good appetite that lunch time. Occasionally we had a "walking lunch." As we ran errands after grocery shopping, she would lunch en route on the bananas, crackers and cheeses she had chosen. A glass of milk at home was all she needed before her afternoon nap.

Probably the most boring moment for a child on a grocery shopping trip is check-out time. A child of seven or eight can be liberated then to go to the car and prepare the area for the grocery bags, to run other errands or to do a little shopping on his own.

CLOTHING SHOPPING

In shopping for clothing for yourself, you'll enjoy it far more without any help. If, however, you have to take a child along, see that he is well armed with a book or coloring book and a strict set of rules of behavior (especially in dressing room areas). Promise a special treat when the ordeal is over.

I once had to buy a formal dress for a wedding and was in a small dressing room with about twelve gowns to try on. My constant adviser was not one of my own children but the child of someone in the next dressing room. This child had not been schooled in proper shopping procedure and had stretched himself out on the floor with most of his body in his mother's dressing room but his head in mine. He was cheerful and pleasant, commented on each gown and let me know which one he preferred. However, had I wanted juvenile advice, I had a few like him at home that I would have brought along.

When shopping each autumn for everyone's new school shoes, all children can go together. But when selecting new slacks or skirts and blouses, the one-at-a-time procedure is best, or at most two of the same sex.

The question is, what do you do with the others if you don't have a convenient friend or free baby-sitter or time to shop when your spouse can keep an eye on them? Depending on the ages of your children, those left behind can enjoy an afternoon at the park, if old enough to be left without supervision, or a Saturday matinee at some trusty movie house.

In clothing shopping trips a child can exercise his own taste and desires. If you want him to like the clothing selected, be sure to choose what is acceptable to his peers. On the other hand, we need not kowtow to styles we find abhorrent or at variance with our principles.

Sometimes a child refuses to take an interest in deciding about his clothing. We really must work with this child to help him make up his mind. The best way to interest a child in clothing decisions is to look over the selection and show him five or six that you would find acceptable. In the dressing room let him pick from this limited number. Whatever he chooses will already have our blessing.

Now is the time to give a child hints on colors that go together, patterns and designs that mix well. A well-dressed child is not a matter of budget but of careful selection. Until a child learns what shirts and trousers, blouses and skirts pair well, you may wish to hang suitable combinations together in the closet to speed learning.

Don't hesitate to point out the economics of shopping. If there are two outfits that Karen likes equally well and one is $16.00 and the other is $24.00, it's my duty to point out that if she chooses the $24.00 one it had better be worth the additional money. If children feel that money is no object, they will take little interest in the price of clothing. This leads quickly to a teenager with expensive tastes and a fickle attitude toward previous purchases. Children should understand that if they have been consulted on an outfit, they should wear it.

A nine- or ten-year-old can be trusted to purchase small items on his own, such as socks and underwear. By eleven or twelve he can be loosed to purchase pajamas, sweaters and blouses on his own. When you start these solo purchases, it's a good idea to be shopping in the same store, perhaps with another child. Stay with the one that is finalizing his purchases and let the other go to the proper department and select for your approval several garments that interest him. This way he gets used to dealing with sales clerks, asking intelligent questions and making basic decisions himself.

At home, my shoppers like to put on a small style show or display their purchases for all to see.

GIFTS AND TOYS

When the birthday invitation comes home in Mark's hand, we know it's time to head for the store and pick out another gift and card. During the ages of six through ten we seem to go through this on the average of once a week! Gift buying, of course, is exciting for a child. It gives him an opportunity to look at all the toys in the store.

Often children find choosing one gift a hard decision. It's made easier if parents give a few guidelines at the beginning, especially concerning the price. While you are shopping for new running shoes, the child can be in the toy department lining up two or three possible presents, with modest price tags on them.

A child of six or seven can learn to read prices and this should be taught early. Older children can learn percentages by letting them figure the tax.

Remind him of these good manners in the toy department:

1. He may look. While he may pick up certain items, he should not appear to be playing with the toys or taking them apart.
2. He should not open boxes or turn on the mechanical toys unless he has permission from the salesclerk.
3. He should not carry toys around the department. Looked-at toys should go back in the same place.

A toy section salesclerk in a large department store talked with me one afternoon. I had sent two children on ahead since they both had birthday presents to purchase. When I had done my shopping and caught up with them, they had each selected two or three items from which I was to help them choose. The clerk said that she was always happy to have well-behaved children in the toy department since it made the department come alive and it gave adult shoppers ideas of what toys really interested children. We *can* teach our children to fully enjoy the toy department without taking it apart.

In deciding what toy to buy as a gift for another child, the question, "Which would you enjoy?" is probably the most pertinent. By age eight or nine the child can make these gift purchases by himself.

Teach a child to be able to walk through a toy section without having to buy. Constant buying and wanting and spending does not instill self-control or economy. While we certainly don't put strings on a child's allowance, we do want to teach him the value of saving for a big purchase. Help him to budget his allowance for present and future wants.

How sad a sight is a child screaming in a toy department, "I want this!" Not that a child doesn't deserve treats and little gifts on special occasions, but these are what we give because we *wish* to, not because he demands. Aside from such gift-receiving occasions as birthdays, Christmas and Hanukkah, a child's purchase of toys should come out of his own allowance. When the child understands this, the little gifts we bring him "just because" become even more exciting.

When you take your child toy shopping for himself, let him consider in advance the *type* of toy that interests him. Some children feel that because they don't find the toy they want, they *must* spend their money on something else. Good counsel at such a time will often save them from an unfortunate purchase and their savings will be useful another day.

Children have occasions during the year when they need to buy gifts for sisters, brothers or parents. The purchase of these gifts, budgeted in their allowances, comes out of their own money. I still remember buying a perfume bottle in a dime store when I was seven years old. It was a Christmas present for my mother. It was a frosted glass bottle with a

180

stopper. I paid fifteen cents for it. When wrapping it, I discovered to my deep disappointment that the bottle was empty! My wise mother knew how much it meant to me to have made this purchase by myself and she filled it with cologne. Now, decades later, this same little bottle stands on her dressing table.

The selection of a gift, no matter what the price, is exciting for a child. Sometimes though, our children do not have sufficient funds to make a useful purchase. With prices rising rapidly, I have helped the younger children in two ways.

First, I provide matching funds. In other words, I subsidize the child in an amount equal to what he has for the gift.

Second, I run "Mother's Little Store." This idea originated one Christmas when Kent, Karen and Mark were between the ages of three and seven, and Wendy was eleven. I realized that with their small savings and long list of much-wanted gifts, they would not be able to purchase for one another any of the desired items. Thus "Mother's Little Store" was invented. It has become a popular December tradition ever since.

MOTHER'S LITTLE STORE

Through the year as family members mention items they would like for Christmas, I note these in the back of my date book. As Christmas approaches, the children shop with me for gifts for brothers, sisters and father. These are hidden until all shopping is done. Then for one day our bedroom is closed off and becomes Mother's Little Store. I unpack the gift closet. On the bed are gifts for each child. On the dresser are gifts for father. On the night table is a selection of wrappings and ribbons. Since Mother's Little Store is a discount store, all gifts are "marked down" to half price or below, depending on the children's budgets.

It's a very exciting day since the door is closed for a long time while I get everything attractively spread out. Then each child, piggy bank in hand, comes separately to the store where he is given a shopping bag for his purchases. (Gifts that have been purchased for him have been covered with a sheet so all that is exposed are the gifts for other family members.) Each child looks at the various gifts, totals the discounted prices, makes his choices, pays up, chooses some free wrappings and ribbons, and with everything packed into his bag returns to his room to secretly wrap his gifts.

The children draw numbers to see who comes first. When one is finished shopping, the next comes in and the procedure is repeated. It's interesting to see them figure that if they spend a dollar or two on one gift they'll have to be more careful on another. When the children have finished shopping, what is left are the gifts that mother and father give.

Some might say that "Mother's Little Store" gives children an improper sense of values, but I've always made the retail prices clear to the children so that they appreciated the fine prices in my boutique! It was a great day when Wendy announced that she was old enough to forego "Mother's Little Store" and ready to shop alone with her own funds.

But who selects gifts for mother? Most dads take the children out for the selections: often many *little* things, some useful, some necessary, some pretty, some personal.

SHOPPING FOR FURNITURE, HOUSES, CARS AND OTHER MAJOR ITEMS

When making a big purchase, try not to have small children along, but if it can't be avoided, go armed with an interesting book or toy to keep the child busy. In shopping for furniture, a child may have opinions and while you will follow your own taste, you certainly can ask which colors and styles appeal to him.

As soon as a child can write clearly, he can be the notetaker on the trip and record the name of the store where a certain chair was found and its cost. Later he can note a similar chair in another store and give you the difference between the prices and qualities of the two.

Too often we underestimate the abilities and interests of our children. I realized this when we moved into a larger house and needed several new pieces of furniture. I thought the pursuit of this furniture would bore the children but found that they were attentive to details of design, style and workmanship, many of which I had overlooked.

SHOPPING ALONE

At about age eight a child can go to a neighborhood store on his own to make a purchase. This becomes a smooth and progressive step if these six precautions are observed:

1. Ask your child to take a limited sum of money with him. He shouldn't take all of his savings or his entire bank, just a little more than he plans to spend.
2. Urge him to ask himself, "Is this what I really want?" "Is it worth it?" before he decides to make the purchase.
3. Teach him to ask for a receipt or cash register tape.
4. Remind him to count his change. You can alert your child to this on other shopping trips. If you are paying for $35.40 worth of groceries and you give two twenty dollar bills, ask your child how much change you'll get back. In this way, he won't be easily confused money-wise.
5. Remind him to walk or bicycle safely and not to talk with strangers en route.
6. When he gets home, ask him to account for his money either to himself or to you.
7. Most important, compliment him on his adventure, on the fact he

has made a purchase all on his own.

Trading stamps have a value like money only after they are pasted into books! At our house, stamp licking is often an assigned monthly task. I have little difficulty in getting them pasted in since one out of every five books completed can be kept by the paster for a personal item.

A large portion of our free time is used in spending money. It's up to us to make the best use of these hours, either as an occasion for togetherness with our children or for teaching them the importance of economics.

39
Having Friends Over — Are You A Keen Parent?

Friends are an important part of growing up. Parents can teach a child to be likeable and pleasant company for his peers, but parents can also do much to create a home atmosphere that is attractive to a child's friends.

Statistics show that where the home is desirable for play and entertaining, children are less apt to go out and get into illegal activities. When a child wishes to be sociable, to have friends over, to play in his own yard, to have a friend stay for supper, be grateful. He is complimenting the home, and the time spent on making it a happy place is well invested. Something is definitely lacking in the home that is only a place to eat and sleep!

Learning to be a friend starts when a child is small. A friend of mine had her first child at the same time Kent was born. When the boys were six months old, she could no longer contain her desire to have our young sons become friends since their fathers had grown up together.

So one afternoon after nap time, she brought her baby over. Kent, already in his playpen, was busy firing one toy after another over the rail. She planted her son in the opposite corner and we sat down across the room to watch our young sons become friends. Nothing happened. Kent continued to throw the toys out of the playpen as if there were nothing alive near him. His young chum leaned against the railing and didn't even watch the fun. When all the toys had been fired out of the playpen, each child slid down into his respective corner and sat there watching us. Absolutely no interplay took place between the two babies.

My friend was dejected at this first try, but a year later the boys had a good time taking our electric train apart.

Usually at about eighteen months children begin to play *with* each other rather than merely fighting for possession of toys. By this time, many children have gotten used to their peers and are ready for friendship.

At the toddler age, children playing together provide a social outlet for the parents who supervise and chat. Sometimes one parent will watch both children so the other can have a few free hours to shop or work. Or two parents will watch children of four families. It gives an opportunity for parents to talk, a welcome diversion to those who spend much of their time with small children. For children under five, the parent in charge needs to be alert and available, not necessarily in the same room but certainly within earshot.

Playing as a gang comes as children grow older and arrangements to play together become less formal. Children naturally know who's available to play. In some areas no plans are made at all. Everyone simply turns out on the streets and sidewalks after school.

When a child is kindergarten age, he enjoys asking friends over after school. Freer as he now is, we still find it helpful and wise to ask him what he intends to do and until he's about seven, check on him occasionally to be sure he's playing safely.

When a child has friends over, parental duties fall into three areas. The first is to be responsible for the safety of the visiting child. The second is to give some guidance to the play when necessary. The third is to provide a snack. Food may be trivial to you but it isn't to kids. During snack time you can get to know the friend. Parents shouldn't intrude on play but are welcome to intrude when serving the snack. Food and talk go together naturally. This chat should be friendly and not inquisitional.

Learn the names of your child's friends for this in itself is a compliment to both children. Kent once had a friend over to play and during the afternoon the friend and I evidently had a short conversation. A week later he told Kent he was coming to play again and added, "I'll be sure to wear my leather tool belt since your mother thought it was so neat." How easy to make a pleasant impression and let the visitor feel welcome.

When friends come over, your child should make it clear that they'll be expected to follow the safety and house rules. They should be shown the location of the bathroom and the sink where their used glasses and plates go. If your child doesn't use glue in the living room, neither should his friends. If your child is not allowed to throw darts in the house or put scotch tape on the walls, it's up to him to see that his friends don't.

Your own child should be aware of his host responsibilities. A friend is to play with, not ignore. Nothing is more disconcerting than to find that a friend has been abandoned and is wandering about your home. When play time is over, your child should see his friend out the gate with a good-bye and not simply leave him to find his way out.

Often guest children will ask you to remind them to go home at a particular time. We set a timer bell for the departure hour.

Parents should avoid entering into the play of children, being obtrusive or trying to settle disagreements. Short of bloodshed, they should stay out of arguments and avoid partiality. Learning to get along with others, to make choices and to compromise are the precious blessings of having friends. We would not wish to rob our children of these experiences. If one child is continually bullying or beating up on another, then step in and offer suggestions as to a settlement.

Here is a good neighborhood rule, one that all children seem to like: when playtime is to end at five p.m., parents give a fifteen-minute advance notice. This allows the youngsters the opportunity to do one last bicycle trick or play one final round of a game and still have time to put away games or equipment they've brought out.

Mark had a new friend over one day. They had played with many games and left all the pieces of money and cards and markers scattered about. When five o'clock came, the friend went home and Mark was left with a huge mess. He said, "I'll never have a friend over again." Since this was the first time it had happened, we all pitched in to help him unscramble the games. Now Mark remembers to take out only one game at a time. He is also keen on having his friends help pick up toys before they go home.

GOING TO FRIENDS

As soon as your child can manage his trike, he's ready to strike out on the sidewalk and call for his best pal three houses up the street. As he gets older, he goes farther afield on foot and on bicycle. Start early to let your child know that he is not tied to his home base but needs only to tell you where he is going and when he will return. If he is going to a new home, he's to give you the phone number. To avoid worries, have the child check in after school, change to play clothes, and have his snack and chat before going on to another child's home.

SOME SPECIAL IDEAS FOR POPULAR PARENTS

1. Remember the line, "That's okay." Small accidents do happen. Juice glasses are dumped, paint is spilled, baseballs knock over gladioli. Parents must learn not to fret. In such cases, there are no more comforting words than, "That's okay, let's clean it up!" While we may not enjoy what has happened, we have no desire to make it into a major offense.

2. Learn to laugh with the children. Often young children and their friends want to tell you something funny that has just happened in their play. The good parent is a listener and learns to laugh with them over these experiences.

3. Avoid reprimanding your child in the presence of his friends. If you note that his room is messy or that he has gotten a bad grade in

spelling, this is not the time to mention it. If your child is being nasty or unfair in his play, give the critical comment in private. How easy it is to say "Mark, I'd like to chat with you for just a moment," and alone with him quietly suggest a better way to act.

4. Be ready with suggestions when the youngsters are bored with their play. Kent and a friend were restless one afternoon and went from one activity to another. I had just finished cleaning the linen cupboard and had come up with two worn sheets. I asked the boys if they could use them. In short order a tree outside was turned into a fantastic tent. Since then we've kept a collection of what we call "play sheets," good for putting over tables, hanging in trees, or throwing on the floor when we are working on a project. With large stitching of yarn through the corner of each, they're never mixed up with the bed sheets.

One day Wendy wanted some activity. Since it was Saturday, I suggested she call a friend who lived several miles away, that they each pack a picnic lunch and see who could first arrive at the park halfway between the two houses. After a quick telephone conversation, the girls decided to include one more girl and to take a game to play in the park.

Sometimes we need only to give our youngsters the kernel of an idea and they'll take it from there to turn it into something great on their own. Remember that it is not material possessions that make our homes attractive to our child's friends. All the fancy games and sporting equipment in the world will not take the place of genuine interest, warmth and love. We can't fret over fingerprints on the walls or worn patches in the lawn. The home belongs to the children as well as the parents. Those whose children have gone off to college remind us that the quietude and neatness of a house without children comes all too soon.

40
Children's Clubs And You

Each June the leaders of most children's groups shed their young charges and retire for a summer without organization. Yet come September, child and leader are eager again for these experiences.

Many children grow up happily without any organized group activities. Some get enough social experience at school. Many children's groups, however, offer experiences that go beyond school activities; but those groups are only as good as the leadership. It doesn't usually matter what group your child joins, for it's the creativity of the person in charge that makes the difference.

Group experiences have these advantages: first, they put the child in contact with another adult. A child knows his school teachers as symbols of authority. The adult leader of a child's group, however, is a happy composite of friend and authority.

Second, a children's club gives the child a circle of friends, a ready-made group. This is especially important if you are new in town or if your child is an only child or is shy.

Third, it gives the child an opportunity to observe and take part in democracy in action. A child in a group learns the importance of voting, of winning and losing elections and of functioning as part of a whole. It is, in essence, a miniature society.

Fourth and most important, a child's club gives him a different learning experience. You may be talented in selling or sewing, computers or cooking, but you may not have the time or interest to become expert in crafts or outdoor sports. Planned programs open new windows for your child and expose him to activities he might not choose for himself.

Starting at second or third grade, there are groups available under the leadership of the Scout movement, Campfire Girls, Indian Guides and YMCA as well as those organized by local churches. Before signing up your child, scrutinize the type of activities the group offers, as well as the character and temperament of its local leader. A child who enjoys competition fits well into a program where achievements are rewarded by badges or beads. Other children find this too much like school and quickly become disenchanted. They need a more loosely structured program. A club is an optional activity and should be fun!

PARENTS' PLACE IN CHILDREN'S CLUBS

When your child joins a club, you find that in some ways you've joined, too. Unfortunately many parents view a child's group as an inexpensive way to get baby-sitting for their child one afternoon a week. But your child's membership in a group brings you certain responsibilities.

1. **Weekly reminders.** The group will probably require dues, equipment or supplies and a special uniform. While you may hand these responsibilities to your child, it is your duty to the leadership of the group to see that your child is not a constant offender in forgetting the basic requirements.

2. **Support on special occasions.** Parents should expect to be called upon occasionally to supply food, chaperonage, transportation or a house for a meeting. Parents should help the child achieve the group's main goals (such as selling cookies to make money for an overnight trip) and give encouragement when the achievement is difficult.

3. **To be present when other parents are present.** Parents are periodically expected to attend a meeting of the group. The reason is two-fold: to let you know what your child is doing and to let your child know of your interest in his activities. If work makes it impossible for either parent to attend, a neighbor, relative or good friend can take your place. Several years ago when I was a leader of a group of little girls, it came time for their final awards meeting. The parents of one girl had been absent all year and were the only ones missing at the final event. As each girl received her award, one parent stepped up with a small pin and a kiss for the daughter. Realizing that this child had no family on hand, I stepped in and said quietly, "I'm sorry your parents couldn't do this for you. I'm sure they wanted to be here." The child very tensely answered, "Oh, that's okay. I'd rather have you do it anyway." This made me feel that the hours spent with the group had filled a real need for at least one of the children.

4. **Taking leadership when needed.** Don't be afraid to accept the leadership of a group. Too many groups disintegrate because no one is willing to take the responsibility. When we've had a child in one of these groups and seen how much he's gained from the companionship and happy events, we have felt that our leadership time was well spent.

If the job of leadership comes to you, these ideas will help you to cope:
1. Let children know right away that while you are their friend and buddy, you are in charge and expect cooperation. By making this clear at your first encounter, you'll find your life much smoother the rest of the club year.

189

2. Don't take everything too seriously. This is a group organized for fun and education.
3. Remember that you are working with *children*. Don't give them assignments beyond their abilities and don't be distressed when they fail.
4. Don't forget that it is involvement, not necessarily perfect results, that's important. Our group was weaving place mats for a retirement home. I had given them a sample of what I expected the finished mats to look like. As they continued to turn out place mat after place mat, with the goal of 50, I realized that none of them resembled my sample. However, they were done with flair and creativity and fulfilled the object of the project, to give service.
5. Have paper and pencil handy. Nothing frustrates a leader more than forgetful children. If you want them to remember something for seven days, have them write it down and take it home. You have a better chance of getting through in writing than verbally.
6. Preserve your sense of humor and repeat certain jokes with the group. If they had a funny experience two weeks ago, mention it again. Stress the positive and the joyful.
7. Finally and most important, appreciate their efforts and love them for their youthful spontaneity. And remember that next year will be somebody's else's turn to be leader!

41
Party Time—
Not Panic Time

His birthday or party day is a time of wild excitement for any child. Parents often work themselves into a frenzy over "running" a three-hour party while the child sails through the event as if in a dream.

New parents are anxious to have that first party but by the time children finish high school, parents are glad to see the end of party time. With some basic organization and creative thought, party day can be just as enjoyable for the parents as it is for the child.

WHEN TO START

When should you have the first party? Many parents like to have parties to honor a child's first or second birthday. Such parties are mainly for parents and their friends. If the honoree is involved at all, it is usually just for a short appearance to show him off before an admiring audience.

By age three, some children may be ready for a party with their peers, but age four is a more usual time.

THE DATE OF THE PARTY

The party needn't be on the birth date. Many of today's parents permit a special party each year for each child. If a child's birthday comes at Christmas, let him choose a party day at another season if he wishes. This stresses the festivity of the occasion, allows you to emphasize other holidays and plays down the importance of "how old."

HOW MANY GUESTS

A simple guide for how many friends to invite is one friend for each year of age. Thus, a three-year-old can enjoy a party with three of his peers, while a child of eight will revel in a larger circle of friends. Twelve is a good maximum number for most homes and yards. In selecting those to be invited, try to hold to a two-year age span. Even numbers are desirable for relay and partner games. Of course, older or younger sisters

191

and brothers of the party-giver are always welcome. If their ages vary, perhaps they can carry out a special assignment at the party.

THE LENGTH OF THE PARTY

A snappy party filled with plenty of activities plus a little free time provides the ideal combination of organization and spontaneity. For children four and under, a party of an hour to an hour-and-a-half is plenty. They are not as interested in the social amenities of eating, cutting the cake and opening packages. These elements will fly quickly and the entertainment of toddlers is more strenuous. By the time children reach kindergarten age, they are ready for a party of an hour-and-a-half to two hours. At age seven or eight, they should be able to cope with parties of two to two-and-a-half hours. The maximum time for any party should be three hours, and this privilege is extended to those who are eleven and older.

THE TIME SCHEDULE

Although a child's party rarely sticks to a rigid schedule, let's look at a typical party plan to get some idea of time alloted to various events. Let's say eleven-year-old Karen has invited eight friends to a party on Saturday from noon to 3 p.m. The schedule worked out in advance might look like this:

12:00 — Arrivals. Karen sees that gifts are put on the gift table and mom or dad takes pictures of the guests as they arrive. Most children come on time so you can figure that all children will be present by 12:15.

12:15 — Lunch. Since Karen has helped decorate the table, she won't want this event over too quickly. Let's allow 30 minutes at the table. Most children, however, will eat in about fifteen minutes so we have to provide additional merriment at the table — hats, or a simple table game. We'll talk about these later.

12:45 — Free time. Lunch is over and while parents tidy up, Karen takes her friends to wash the jam off their hands and to see what's new in her room.

1:00 — Everybody outside for games.

1:10 — Game #1.

1:20 — Game #2.

1:30 — Game #3.

1:40 — Game #4.

1:50 — Awarding of game prizes.

2:00 — Free time.

2:15 — Open packages.

2:30 — Cake.

2:45 — Karen gives favors to friends. Free play time.

3:00 — Take guests home.

The game time can be replaced with swimming and water activities, sledding and snow games, a two-team hike, a home movie or puppet show, depending on your child's interests and the season.

TYPES OF PARTIES

This basic schedule can be adjusted to the type of party your child wants. It may be games, it may be a sports party with baseball or football. It may be a party with a definite theme.

Girls under age seven may enjoy a doll party to which they bring their favorite doll also dressed for the party. The table is set for girls and their dolls. Imaginative, doll-loving little girls enjoy pretending to be mothers. You'd be surprised how many sandwiches and cookies dolls can eat!

The highlight of Kent's cowboy party was an item we found at a surplus store — small army knapsacks at 50 cents apiece. These became the containers for each child's lunch and take-home favors. The party centered around cowboys and horses and included "Pin the Tail on the Bronco." Excitement peaked when each received his knapsack, packed with a picnic lunch. Led by their fearless Indian guide (who just happened to be Dad), the eight boys crept through the underbrush of our overgrown lot to a secret place where they encamped, opened their knapsacks and ate. (This party theme was used another year for girls just as successfully.)

Mark's birthday is in March so his party often has an Easter theme. One year the lunches were packed in small Easter baskets which each child took home. Games centered around the Easter theme with a bunny-hop relay race. The highlight of the party was the egg hunt and the visit by the Easter bunny — Kent in costume.

The library has books on parties for children which give many ideas on party themes and how to carry them out. But don't exhaust yourself working out an elaborate party theme. Most children under twelve won't appreciate it.

THE DAY OF THE PARTY

Although the party lasts only a few hours, for most children the entire day is a big event. Some families observe special traditions on the party day. We excuse the honoree from all helps for the day and the other children pick up his work. The party-giver gets extra time to make his room orderly and to choose something special to wear. Balloons are tied on the front door and to his chair at the table. The American and state flags are raised in honor of his party and he is encouraged to sleep later that morning, if possible.

THE ARRIVAL OF GUESTS

The party-giver should be trained to receive his guests at the door, to show them in and take care of any outdoor clothing they have worn. A separate table in the living room or dining room holds the gifts. This protects them until the exciting package-opening. Give each arriving guest a lunch bag and crayons so he can label it with his name and decorate it. This fills the waiting time and gives each a bag in which to put his place card, favor, candy and prize so that when it's time to go home he has everything in one place.

PRIZES AND FAVORS

Everyone loves to be a winner, which means prizes for every game, inexpensive but plentiful so that everyone wins at least once. Award one prize for each game and have many games, or award two or three prizes for each game. You may want to rule that nobody can receive an additional first prize until everyone's received one. If you do this, make sure you give proper honor to the winner, even though he receives no prize.

Since the prizes are awarded *during* the party, have an inexpensive favor for everyone to take home at the *end* of the party. Make this a gift that can be enjoyed the free fifteen minutes before departure. One year Karen gave plastic balloon kits and we had great fun blowing them out in the yard just before the guests left. Kent had an automotive party one year and the favors were tiny cars. With nine little boys racing their cars simultaneously, this final event became the highlight of the party.

Finding inexpensive prizes and favors is not easy, especially with inflation. Diligent searching, however, will uncover good 25- to 50-cent items. Depending on your budget, you may wish to hold your *game* prizes to 25 cents and make your take-home favors more elaborate. Favors that cost 75 cents to a dollar are fairly easy to find. Colorful tablets of paper, ball point pens, felt markers, balls, magazines, all make good favors. In this case you can use candy bars or small boxes of raisins as game prizes.

PARTY FOOD

Refreshments may be *your* major concern, but most children don't remember next day what they ate at the party. So for the sub-teens keep party foods simple and portions small.

One year I made an elaborate array of finger sandwiches — shrimp, tuna, egg salad, ham and cheese, peanut butter and jelly. The peanut butter and jelly went first and the shrimp sandwiches fed the family for the next three days! Three items are sufficient: sandwich, jello and potato chips go over well. Hamburgers, tacos and hot dogs are more expensive but children love them.

Serve the food where clean-up is easy. If your dining room has a carpet, set the party table on the porch or in a decorated basement where spills can be easily mopped up. I know one family who lets the child set up the party table in his own bedroom! If the weather is nice, eating outside is an adventure. With eight or ten children present, the odds favor

194

someone dumping his chocolate milk.

If only one adult family member will be home during the party, select food that can be prepared well in advance and merely set out at eating time. Avoid hamburgers and grilled cheese sandwiches in this case.

As for the cake, I like to serve it late in the party. Children are sometimes too full after lunch to eat cake. The cake-cutting event in the afternoon gives the cake more prominence. Many families like to buy elaborately decorated cakes from the bakery. A large sheet cake made from a mix can be decorated as simply or elaborately as your talents dictate. Every child likes to see his name on the cake! Tiny plastic cars, dolls or other toys placed on the cake can make it festive. Candles are essential and those that re-light are good for laughs. We use one sparkler on the cake plus a candle for every year plus one for each guest, plus one to "grow on."

Let the child choose the kind of cake he wants, both as to flavor and frosting. After cutting the first piece, he may be willing to relinquish this job to mom or dad. It's tradition in our house that the last piece of cake belongs to the party-giver to eat the next day. If candy is placed on the table, the tiniest nut cups filled with chocolate bits, candy corn or peanuts will suffice.

GAMES

The organized activities and games fill most of the party time. But allow one or two free times as breathers. You don't need to be a social director during the entire party. As a rule, avoid paper games which seem too much like school.

Active games that work off steam and can be played indoors or out, depending on the weather, are best.

1. Races. Relay races with team prizes or races against the clock are always popular. An egg balanced on a spoon, a raisin on a toothpick, pushing a ball with the nose, wheelbarrow and piggyback relays and blindfold races are especially fun. With a stopwatch or sweep second hand, time each child as he puts on a costume or threads a needle and sews on a button.

2. Hunts. Searching for specified items is fun. After the hunt, count up who found the most toothpicks or wrapped pieces of candy or small Easter eggs. Give each child a sack for collecting.

3. The Obstacle Course. If you have a large playroom, a long hall or a good-sized yard, lay out an obstacle course with things to climb under, over or through. Walk around the course with the children to be sure they understand what to do. Then, at a given signal, one child runs the obstacle race. If he makes it all the way through and back in a minute and 20 seconds, the next child will try to beat it. Sometimes children will want to try this again and again and there is no harm in letting them improve

their times.

4. Balloon Games. Every child blows up a balloon. The first one to burst his balloon by blowing is the winner. Play balloon volleyball sitting on the floor, two teams foot to foot. Time each child to see how fast he can break a balloon by sitting on it. Have participants form a circle holding hands. Start the balloon in the center, with children blowing. When it touches a child he's out of the game and it continues with a smaller circle.

5. Outdoor Games. Tag, hide-and-seek and red rover are always popular.

Games should be varied and quick. Before the game begins, every child should understand just how it goes. By giving several prizes and by reassuring the children that everybody's going to be a winner, we take the anxiety out of the games and children settle down to have a truly enjoyable time.

GIFTS

The opening of birthday party gifts may be the big moment for the honoree but it is *not* the most exciting part of the party for the other children. So the party-giver must make it fun by expressing genuine and personalized appreciation.

Teach a child early the three parts to opening any gift:
1. Opening the card and acknowledging who it's from.
2. Opening the package and expressing interest in the contents.
3. Verbally thanking the giver.

Before any birthday, review these three steps so that the honoree has them down pat. Let the children attending help by presenting the next gift to be opened. Let them all look at the gifts by passing them around the circle. Let one child be in charge of folding up the paper or collecting all the ribbons. Since few children write thank-you notes for birthday party presents when the giver was on hand, it's essential that they remember the three steps. Sometimes the child opens a package and has no idea who it's from. This is why he should be taught to open the card and read it aloud. Then he can pass the card around as he opens the package. You can't do much to keep a child from ripping the wrappings off the package and it certainly shows his excitement. A child should rehearse in advance how to handle a situation when he receives duplicate gifts or a game he already owns.

Most birthday party gifts range from $2.50 to about $10.00 so their selection must be carefully made. When you advise your child on choosing a gift for a friend, consider the kind of life that friend lives. An outdoor child may not like a painting set. An only child may not enjoy a game that requires six people to play. For some little girls, dolls would be a waste of money.

Be alert to adult items that a child wants. The following are some good

gift ideas:
1. Bike speedometer
2. Large ball for kick ball
3. Set of felt pens
4. Label-making machine
5. Inexpensive transistor radio
6. Globe of the moon
7. Picture for the wall of the child's room
8. Book plate labels
9. Bag of plaster of Paris
10. Old-fashioned alarm clock
11. Box of batteries, wires, buzzers and bells
12. Clear plastic umbrella
13. Little plastic cabinet with many drawers.

Parents often give a child one gift, something especially memorable. Here are some ideas, but remember that these are extra special gifts usually given when parents are presenting only one gift for a birthday or for Christmas.

1. Sporting equipment: bike, wagon, surfboard, skis, sled, skates.
2. Doll equipment: doll house, large mechanical dolls, an outside play-house.
3. Musical equipment: musical instruments and record players, a piano and lessons.
4. Scientific equipment: telescopes, chemistry sets, erector sets.
5. Automotive toys: race track sets, electric trains, rockets.
6. Outdoor play equipment: swings, slides, tent.
7. Wrist watch, tape recorder, walkie-talkie.
8. Telephone extension, new bedroom furnishings.

When you decide to purchase one of these major gifts, be sure you are not buying in advance of the child's desires. Some parents buy for themselves, rather than the child. This usually happens with the first child who receives a doll carriage and a tricycle on his very first birthday when he is scarcely able to walk.

The longed-for gift, anticipated for months or even years, is doubly appreciated by the child. There should be times too when the child receives only necessary gifts. Don't spoil a child into thinking that a spectacular item awaits him on every party day. Remember that "little things mean a lot."

THE END OF THE PARTY

To make sure the guests leave and the party ends on schedule, note on the invitation that you will bring the children home. This can be fun. It saves everyone's gas, too. Five minutes before the end of the party, parent or young host tells everybody to gather his prizes, candy and favors and pile into the car. This gives a controlled atmosphere for farewells and an easy way for the honoree to remember thank you's as each guest climbs out of the car at his house. This time-saver spares you a straggling end to a party as children disappear one by one over a period of 30 minutes. If you don't take the guests home, plan a final game in the front yard as parents arrive to pick up their children.

When the party is over, paper plates, spilled juice, package wrappings and equipment must be tidied up. If a child wants a party, he should agree in advance to help clean up, not necessarily immediately but sometime before bedtime. A child old enough to entertain is old enough to throw away paper plates and cups and gather his gifts into his play area.

ALTERNATE IDEAS FOR PARTIES

Friends of ours let their grade school children have a party only every other year. For some families this is a wise idea, especially if there are many children. These friends are not holding back primarily for financial reasons. They feel that birthday time can be a precious family time and on alternate years they take their child out for supper with them alone.

A slumber party is a popular substitute for the conventional birthday party. Children under the age of nine or ten are usually not ready for this longer type of party. If your youngsters have a sleep-out in the yard or a slumber party, be sure to check them frequently during those giggling hours before they finally fall asleep.

Parents who feel unable to cope with a party in the home can plan a party-picnic at the zoo, a beach party, or a trip to a special sledding hill. Simple enough. But some alternates are costly: a baseball game, an extravaganza such as the ice show, a children's play or amusement park. While these are certainly pleasurable experiences for the children, they greatly increase the budget and confine the children more than home parties. More expensive doesn't always mean better. These events are best for children over the age of ten.

In planning parties with your children, remember that there are party occasions other than birthdays and that a party on a special holiday is refreshing.

REMEMBERING THE PARTY

Take pictures of the party if you can do so without impeding the action. Candid shots of games, gift-opening and the cake are records worth having and sharing with relatives. While slides are popular, snapshots are cheaper. Polaroid pictures taken of each guest at the party make nice take-home favors. If a child has "thank-you's" to write, he can enclose a photo with the letter.

Most important, make parties fun to prepare and have. This is your child's big day. Make it memorable for him.

42
What's
In A
Holiday?

With more holidays celebrated back-to-back with weekends, the real meaning of some holidays is being lost. We are raising a generation of children who know a holiday is coming but have little cognizance of its significance. Holidays are really occasions for building memories, sharing unique experiences and doing special things with family and friends. Let's go through the year and consider ways to make the various holidays more distinctive.

NEW YEAR'S DAY

Usually a sleep-late day, New Year's is a quiet family time of planning the year ahead and rejoicing over the past year. Our day often lacks vigorous projects and sports although we have friends who stage an annual New Year's Day sledding event. Others use the day for open house for neighbors and friends. We have the tradition of putting together the family scrapbook for the year gone by. I have a drawer where I put programs, report cards, poems written by the children, photographs and all the other paraphernalia that we collect during the year. On New Year's Day everyone helps sort it into twelve stacks, one for each month. Then with rubber cement, we quickly organize it into a scrapbook. After that I take a felt marking pen and scrawl comments concerning the items to help us recall each event. When this is done, we sit down together and look through the events of the past year. Putting together such a scrapbook is about a two-hour project that eliminates those tiresome boxes we're going to get to "some day." Everyone in the family seems to enjoy reminiscing over the year's exciting, amusing, sad or trying events. I leave the scrapbook on the table in the living room for several weeks so everyone can have an extra look.

We don't happen to make New Year's resolutions at our home. Instead we consider the year ahead in light of what goals we would like to achieve. It is well for the family to sit down together, look forward and make some realistic family goals. These might include a hoped-for trip, the raising of school grades, the completion of a project such as an attic or basement room or learning some new skill.

New Year's Day can be a quiet and introspective time, but never an unhappy or dreary day. We know a family who plans a New Year's Day supper and movie or play with another family with similar-aged children. Since New Year's Eve is an adult event, it's nice to keep New Year's Day festivities for the entire family.

VALENTINE'S DAY

School children find the exchange of valentines exciting. Several weeks before the holiday let your children pick out the cards they want to send or decide what sort of cards they are going to make. There are also kits for children who enjoy putting together their own cards. The nicest cards are the handmade ones.

The sending of valentines to grandparents, aunts and uncles should be voluntary but nonetheless encouraged, especially when grandparents and other close friends and relatives are separated by many miles. Simple and sincere messages from children are greatly appreciated.

We make our own valentine mailbox every year. One child volunteers to paint, crayon or decorate a box with paper lettering and doilies. This then becomes the center of our breakfast and lunch table and is a good reminder that Valentine's Day is coming. Into this box we put the cards that we've made or purchased for each other. We also toss in a few mystery cards, since it's always fun to get mail from a secret friend. Valentines that come in the mail are put in the box, too. Little candy gifts or other surprise items are secreted in the box. Then at Valentine's Day supper, the box is opened and the mail distributed. We all exclaim and appreciate the thought that went into the poems and cards made at home and at school.

One year we decided to have a red and white supper in honor of the day. The children planned a meal consisting of hot dogs with catsup, beets, cauliflower and red jello with whipped cream. It sounds rather ghastly in retrospect but at the time it was festive and was one of our more memorable Valentine's Day events!

PRESIDENT'S DAY

This is a holiday that gets lost in the shuffle. No one remembers any more the "old days" when we separately honored Washington and Lincoln as outstanding Presidents. Now the day honors our heritage and all those who have served as President, but for most school children, it merely means a day off from school.

One family we know invites a foreign student to come for supper that day and they have a healthy exchange of ideas on their two countries.

200

Other friends who have six children between the ages of seven and fifteen told each one that at dinner they were to speak only as if they were one of the Presidents of the United States. By the end of this enlightening dinner hour, everyone had finally recognized what President the others represented. One year we took the encyclopedia to supper and capsulized the lives of various Presidents. While this isn't one of the gayer holidays during the year, it is an opportunity to instill patriotism and learn about the highest office in our country.

EASTER

For many families Easter is an important religious holiday. However, Easter festivities now include children of all religions. Easter eggs, parades, new dresses and suits have long been part of the Easter season.

Since Easter often includes a feast, it's a good holiday to share with another family. The traditional ham or leg of lamb can be prepared by one family and vegetable and potato casserole can be brought by another.

Our Easter begins the week before when we draw names for the making of Easter eggs. We find that putting a small hole at each end of the egg and blowing the insides out gives us scrambled eggs for several days and eggshells we can keep. The elaborateness of the egg depends on the age of the maker. Some of ours have collars to sit on and are complete with ties and hats. Others are done with decoupage, some with decals and some with written messages that snake their way all over the eggs. If an egg breaks, that's an opportunity to put a larger hole in it and make a scene inside the egg as on a small stage. With fine pointed felt pens, everyone can write on and decorate his eggs. One year we made sketches of one another on the eggs. The eggs are then delivered anonymously to our places at the breakfast table for a humorous game of guess-the-artist.

When our family was young, my mother-in-law presented me with a heavy iron mold in the shape of a rabbit. (They also come in the shape of a lamb.) The day before Easter the rabbit-shaped cake is baked. One child volunteers to frost and decorate it with a cherry nose and coconut fur. When the mold is empty, half of it is used for a jello salad for our feast.

The highlight of every child's Easter day is the Easter egg hunt. At our house Dad is the expert at hiding eggs. Use the small *wrapped* chocolate ones and also hide one special large chocolate bunny for each child. In the interest of fairness, the youngest child is given a five or ten second head start, then the next child is started with a five or ten second advantage over the third one. Still, when the house is next cleaned, you'll probably discover a few eggs that no one has found.

We save our Easter baskets from year to year. Some of them are rather sad looking but no child would dream of parting with his. We leave them on the table for a week until the chocolates are slowly eaten and we've all had many looks at this year's hand-decorated eggs. Blown out eggs can be saved so that after a number of years you have quite a collection of spectacular eggs.

One year Kent put an egg from his school party in with the eggs that were to be saved. About a month later the house was filled with an odor that made me think something had died! By sniffing about, we finally tracked the smell down to the Easter egg bag and retrieved the offending *full* egg from all the hollow ones.

MAY DAY

May first is celebrated in many areas as a symbol of renewal or as a symbol of freedom and law. One place where we lived, it's not a holiday from school but is a special day when programs are presented on the lawns of every school. May Day has long been associated with spring and baskets of flowers. In Hawaii it's called Lei Day and everyone wears leis, flowers in the hair or flowered hat bands. Even the burliest men would not hesitate to wear flowers on Lei Day. A friend in Minnesota, where the ground is not yet ready for planting, buys herself a flat of pansies. She intends to plant them by the end of the month but on May Day she puts them in little containers for early blooms around the house.

MOTHER'S DAY

This is a very personal holiday and develops according to the desires of the children in the family. Father sometimes has to help set the Mother's Day events in motion. Some children like to buy mother a flower to wear. In many homes it's a strictly "no cooking, no work" day for mother and I'm sure none will object to that.

Every Mother's Day for many years my day has started with chocolate cake in bed. I'm not much of a breakfast fan but one thing I do love is chocolate cake. The children secretly bake and decorate a cake, I know not when. Around 7:30 on Sunday morning I'm awakened with a happy choir singing, "Happy Mother's Day to You." The fun and laughter is worth a certain amount of chocolate crumb's in one's bed!

Most schools have some craft project that results in a Mother's Day gift and many of us own pencil holders, recipe clamps and other useful items made by our children. After church on Sunday and after dinner, which is occasionally a surprise meal out, I get to search for my Mother's Day gifts by the hot-cold method. (Since we parents don't celebrate our birthdays, I get gifts on Mother's Day.) I'm sure you will recall from your youth the game in which you are turned loose in a room where a small item is hidden and everyone shouts "hot," "warm," "cool," "cold," depending on how close you are to it. My Mother's Day gifts consist of poems extolling mother's virtues, magazines, candy mints, flowering plants and many handmade items. Most mothers melt under such treatment!

MEMORIAL DAY

A generation ago on this day you solemnly accompanied your parents to the local cemetery, tidied up the plots of the deceased ancestors and planted new flowers on them. With the advent of perpetual care cemeteries, memorial parks of beautiful rolling lawns with simple markers, and cremation, cemetery trips are no longer popular. Few of us miss them. However, there are Memorial Day tributes that are worthy of attention.

At the larger military cemeteries there can be stirring ceremonies of re-dedication and appreciation for those who have gone on. In many smaller towns a Memorial Day parade features civic and youth groups marching with bands, baton twirlers and flags plus a local patriotic speaker.

In warmer areas this is the day parents enlist the work of many hands to set out flat after flat of small plants in anticipation of beautiful summer flowers. In many parts of the country Memorial Day signifies the return of outdoor living and is an ideal day for a hike or short motor trip.

You are fortunate, indeed, if you have among your family possessions old photograph albums, for these enable you to give a fitting memorial to relatives who have passed on. Point them out to the children and describe these fine people. With less stress on death as the years pass, this holiday seems to be losing its special meaning.

FATHER'S DAY

One of our best Father's Day events took place one year when we felt Dad needed to get away from it all. We rented a small cabin near the water about an hour's drive from home. Saturday noon before Father's Day, we went to his office and literally kidnapped him. We put the back seat of the station wagon down and with a pillow and a blindfold made sure that he was comfortable for his afternoon nap. He took it as a lark and thought we were just going on a short excursion. What he didn't know was that we had packed a change of clothes, a swim suit and food for three meals.

In midafternoon we arrived at our destination with Father bewildered but pleased at our ingenuity. A quiet one-day vacation in the country refreshed all of us. Along with water sports equipment, each child had brought a pad and crayons for sketching the scenery. In the evening we played box games and let Dad read his current book and magazines. The gifts each child had tucked into his small suitcase were presented on Father's Day morning. Kidnapping Dad is certainly something the children couldn't get away with twice but it is a spectacular memory.

SCHOOL'S OUT HOLIDAY

Since in our area the final day of school ends before noon, we have a "School's Out" party almost every year. This consists of a festive picnic lunch in some secluded spot or a trip to the local hamburger place with each child taking one friend as his guest. Or it may be a matinee at the local theater. Whether it is hot dogs or Disney, we make a lot of the end of school and the beginning of summer fun.

INDEPENDENCE DAY

The Fourth of July is one holiday that still has meaning for children. The story of how our country became independent is one with which they have great empathy today since it is a story of dissatisfaction, war, repression, revolt, riots, immortal speech-making and finally, the vote for independence. There is much to be admired in the staunch principles of our forebearers and our children never seem to tire of hearing the story and looking at the pictures. On this patriotic day, most areas have parades that can be a focal point of family activities. Your young Scouts or Camp Fire Girls may be involved. With warm weather, picnics, hikes and swims are popular. Although fireworks are prohibited in many areas, the public fireworks displays by community associations or civic groups have been a wise and colorful substitute. Support your local parade —and fireworks!

LABOR DAY

Another holiday losing its original meaning, Labor Day now signifies that autumn and cooler weather are coming and that school will soon resume. Thus Labor Day often has a sad connotation for children who are not looking forward to the change.

This year ask your children if they know the meaning of Labor Day. If they don't, look in your encyclopedia and read together how the holiday started.

We shared Labor Day with two other large families one year. One of the dads organized a junior olympics for all the children. Each was given a score card listing a dozen scheduled events. The children could enter as many or as few of the events as they desired. There were relay races, broad jump, 40 yard dash, 20 meter swim, etc. The competition was keen but friendly. Separate races were held for younger children so that everyone had an opportunity to win.

In many areas, school starts the day after Labor Day. Make sure that several days in advance each child has his notebook, crayons, pencils, tissues and other supplies ready. To make going back to school more appealing, let the child select something special to wear that first day. On Labor Day we set new bedtimes with the children and agree on what the new morning and afternoon routines will be. This is usually an early-to-bed night.

HALLOWEEN

Halloween has become the holiday for children who wish to collect as much candy as possible. In some cities children are transported by car into another residential area where it's known the give-aways are better. For this reason many parents are placing tighter control on children trooping from door to door on Halloween night. Neighborhood parties are becoming popular in an effort to discourage open begging or coercion. If your children go out, be sure an adult is along and that treats are checked for safety.

In some areas it is still possible for little children to go from door to door, show off their costumes and receive a small treat in return. Many older couples enjoy chatting with the children on the doorstep and giving them a special item. A single lady in our neighborhood annually makes 50 taffy apples to give the masked munchkins. This sort of individualized sharing and caring makes the holiday memorable.

What can you give other than miniature candy bars? Wrapped candy, of course, is preferred to unwrapped candy. Marshmallows in small plastic bags are a good alternate. One year we gave small donuts and another year, whistles. Most homes have 25 to 75 callers in the evening so it's sensible to keep the give-away inexpensive. A colored pencil, key chains, cookies, a small bag of potato chips, small tablets and balloons are other inexpensive treats. The most unique item Kent ever brought home was a baby food jar housing a live minnow.

Children up to about eight enjoy going out but as they grow older, they realize it's more fun to be on the giving end. The decoration of the front door area, even the preparing of a few surprises for those who ring the doorbell, suddenly become important.

A supervised six-year-old can handle a kitchen knife safely enough to carve his own pumpkin. The eyes may not be as symmetrical as you would like, but the child's satisfaction in carving his own jack-o-lantern is more important. We usually put our four candle-lighted pumpkins along the driveway leading to the front door. We have a flat roof over the front door and Kent likes to be stationed there with a few water balloons he can drop on special friends. Eerie sounds at the entrance or a front door opened slowly and followed by a blood-curdling shriek will soon be reported around the neighborhood so that your house becomes one of the favorite stops.

The most important aspect of Halloween is the costuming of the children. The easy way out is the inexpensive "canned" costume that can be bought at most discount stores. But if given a little advance reminder, most children prefer to make up their own costumes. Cardboard boxes and lengths of fabric can inspire a variety of animals, robots, witches, ballerinas and ethnic characters.

Sometimes children enjoy dressing as a group. One year Mark and his friends costumed themselves as three ferocious beasts from prehistoric times. Karen and two of her dancing class friends wore their ballet costumes one year and made quite a splash on neighborhood steps by doing fancy pirouettes and bows when the door was opened. Wendy and two friends went as a many-jointed horse. Their costume was comprised of a papier-maché horse's head and several old sheets dyed brown. Cardboard packing boxes and silver spray paint can turn into inexpensive astronaut outfits that are far more realistic than the purchased ones. If you're adept at sewing, you can help whip up costumes but they needn't be elaborate.

Halloween night is a good time for a party. The old-fashioned games of bobbing for apples and biting apples on a string are regaining popularity. Isn't it wonderful to go back into our own memories and find that our children like some of these good old games!

The spook tunnel is a favorite at our house. As guests arrive, they are blindfolded and then crawl through a "tunnel" made of about five card tables. Unpopped popcorn kernels on the floor make crawling difficult on bare knees! Various items are taped under the card tables above the crawlers: a feather, a rubber glove filled with dripping water, a cloth saturated with bad perfume, a bell...let your imagination run wild here. As soon as a guest is through and unblindfolded, he can take part in watching over a section of the tunnel and adding new "horrors" such as a wicked laugh, a harmless pinch, rain from a sprinkler bottle. Do this on a porch or patio or in a playroom since there will be some clean-up.

A pumpkin carving contest can be fun with children over eight. Get small pumpkins, sturdy knives and give good safety instruction.

Games of hide-and-seek in the dark, ghost stories around the fireplace or a candle add excitement. Rather than have everyone hide, switch the game around: turn out most lights and let one person hide. The others set out in different directions to find him — in a closet, bathtub, under a table or bed. When you find the hider, you hide with him — lots of fun and laughter. When the last person finds the hiding group, the game starts over. The hider this time is the one who was first to find the previous hider.

THANKSGIVING

Our schools do much to keep alive the purpose of this holiday and if we can only keep our merchandisers from steam-rollering Christmas right over Thanksgiving, I think we can enjoy Thanksgiving for what it is without confusing it with the big holiday that follows. This is an ideal holiday to share with your extended family and friends since it is probably the biggest cooking day of the year and who wouldn't mind help from all the feasters? We've had successful four-family dinners with the host-house doing the turkey, stuffing and gravy, while the salad, vegetables and pies are divided among the others.

No matter how many are coming for dinner, the setting of the table can be assigned to one child. A ten- or eleven-year-old can easily make the sweet potato casserole. Any child over six or seven is capable of peeling potatoes, picking over cranberries or helping to stuff the turkey. Not only does this save time, but the child who has helped appreciates the food and takes pride in what's being served.

Children can better enjoy a long feast if there are some interesting breaks in it. For this reason, we make a few Thanksgiving assignments several weeks in advance. One child is responsible for the grace at dinner, another with poetic tendencies can compose a verse in honor of this historic event, another might wish to sing a Thanksgiving song learned at school. We punctuate the dinner with these events.

The most notorious Thanksgiving happening at our home is the Thanksgiving Day pageant, an impromptu theatrical production. The child in charge of it has thought of a play that ties in with Thanksgiving and has gathered certain basic items of costuming and props. The invited guests are not informed until they arrive that they are to be part of the pageant. This makes for humor and a lack of anxiety. With cameras flashing and people laughing, we have sat through some hilarious retellings of the famous Thanksgiving Day feast between the Indians and the Pilgrims.

Several years ago we shared Thanksgiving with a family with two imaginative boys. One, assigned the important part of the turkey, made himself an elaborate tail. When someone inadvertently stepped on it during the pageant, he departed from the script with a loud "ouch" and this particular bit of business was then humorously repeated in each scene of the production.

CHRISTMAS

Of all the holidays, the one most anticipated is the season that includes Hanukkah and Christmas. Ours usually starts early in December with the bringing out of the box of decorations. We make or buy some new ones each year. This lets us throw away the more tattered pieces of decor. Decorations for the front and back doors, decorations a child can choose for his own bedroom, decorations for the stair railing, even decor for doorknobs, give the entire house a new and festive look. With garlands and mistletoe hung early in December, our family gets into the mood long before the Christmas tree is brought home.

We start cookie baking about the first of December and keep them out of reach by freezing many. Each child selects his favorite kind of cookie and becomes assistant baker for that one. Tree trimming night includes caroling and sampling cookies.

On gift wrapping night, everyone is entitled to complete secrecy in his bedroom until his packages are ready. Then he puts them under the tree unless he feels that their shape would tell all. It's fun to have a number of gifts under the tree, if you can trust children not to peek through the wrappings or pinch parcels in advance of the big moment.

Sometimes there are too many gifts for Christmas Day opening. Since we live far from relatives and many of our packages arrive by mail, we open these during the week before Christmas, one night for absent grandparents, another night for west coast or midwest cousins, etc. When children open a few in advance they can more easily remember who gave which gifts. Sometimes we save a round of gifts for Christmas night.

We try not to let Christmas get suffocated by so much preparation in the food and gift departments that we can't enjoy the spirit of the holiday. School and church programs, parties, music on radio and phonograph, television specials — all contribute to the festivity of our holiday season. We keep children's other activities as simple as possible, so that the youngsters are rested and able to enjoy all that is offered to them during the holiday season. This is why we stretch out the shopping and the package wrapping over a long period to avoid last minute pressure.

If we intend to entertain as a family or have a large gathering for Christmas caroling, we schedule this for seven to ten days before Christmas so that Christmas Eve and Christmas Day can be devoted to family pursuits.

Although our children have never believed in Santa Claus, we traditionally hang our stockings on Christmas Eve. Everyone buys or makes a regular Christmas present for every other member of the family and a few inexpensive items to tuck into the stockings. When I was a child, my father started the unusual tradition of rising early Christmas morning to bake one potato to put into the toe of my stocking. I have continued the tradition for my potato-loving children. We open the stockings as soon as everyone is awake on Christmas Day since Christmas breakfast consists of egg nog and packets of homemade cookies tucked into the stockings. No one needs cereal and eggs on this exciting day!

A few years ago we found that our children were merely ripping open packages without realizing who gave the gift. So we have tried a new idea that emphasizes giving. The gifts are stacked under the tree according to the *giver*, each child using a different pattern of wrapping paper. One at a time each of us distributes his gifts to the recipients. This way even the smallest child can keep track of what a sister or brother or parent has given him and everyone has a package to open. We admire the good taste of the giver and thank him, then move on to the next round of packages. We like Christmas to last as long as possible! If you just turn the children loose with a stack of presents, you'll find that your weeks of planning and selecting and your hours of gift wrapping are over in short order with little time for appreciation.

If a child receives an action toy, we stop to enjoy it. Bicycle riding takes place the minute the bicycle is discovered. If a doll walks, we watch her walk. If we receive a new necklace, we put it right on. How nice to have a day of no time schedules — just relaxed enjoyment of the gifts and one another.

We don't entertain on Christmas Day. We want to be with the family, not working in the kitchen! We let the grandparents stage the evening dinner. We feel that Christmas Day is best celebrated within our nuclear family.

Many little traditions make Christmas memorable, and you can invent more. For example:

1. We let each child purchase a new Christmas ornament every year.

2. On Christmas Eve we turn out the lamps in the living room, the better to admire the lighted tree, and sing Christmas carols in the dark while holding hands in a circle.

3. The last thing on Christmas Eve, everyone goes to his room where new pajamas are hidden, puts them on and reappears in the living room for a before-bed picture.

4. We display the Christmas cards we receive on the cork wall in our family room for a colorful and sentimental backdrop.

5. Each year we burn a special Christmas candle made by the children from the year's collection of candle stubs and colored by dropping a red crayon into the melting wax. A milk carton serves as a mold and a thin taper plunged into it provides a wick. The candle becomes the dining table centerpiece and is burned every night through Christmas.

6. Over the years the children have received many delightful Advent calendars, the kind with the many windows that are opened, one by one, each day. Since we don't like to throw these away, we carefully shut the little doors and windows again when the holiday season is over, and they are just as much fun to open the following Christmas. We tack them up in the kitchen on the bulletin board near the breakfast table. The first one through with his morning cereal has the right to open the window of his choice.

Some parents are anxious to clean up the colorful chaos of Christmas and get on with the new year. But for a child who has long looked forward to this holiday, it's important to sustain the close feeling. Unbend and let him have his toys and gifts scattered throughout the living room. All too soon the years of dolls and trains will be over and there will be ample opportunity for neat living rooms devoid of toys and tissue paper and for Christmas trees decorated with ornaments of one color.

NEW YEAR'S EVE

The last holiday of the year is usually an adult event. Some children are satisfied with staying up to watch TV until the midnight hour. Often it's a night when parents are at parties or large adult gatherings are going on in the home. But more and more New Year's Eve is becoming a family-oriented holiday. Since baby sitters are difficult to get, many families stay with their children to see the new year in.

A progressive supper with a course served for each major city currently welcoming the new year is one idea. For example, if you live in Denver, you have chowder at 10:00 in honor of midnight in New York, salad at 11:00 for Chicago, steak at midnight in Denver and lemon pie at 1:00 in honor of California's midnight..

One game is to write humorous resolutions for oneself and for others at the party. Someone reads them one at a time, and the others guess for whom they're intended. Another game is to write a resolution following this pattern: "I resolve to...because..." For example, "I resolve to feed the dog each morning because dog food is nutritious," or "I resolve to try new recipes because my husband hates leftovers." Then you cut these in half at the word "because" and put them in two piles. Each person takes a turn pulling out a first half and a second half and reading them together: "I resolve to try new recipes because dog food is nutritious!" Other happy party games can round out the night. But be sure the children get a nap that afternoon.

While these are the main holidays, you can invent a new holiday whenever you're in the mood. The musical, *Mame,* features a song that says, "We need a little Christmas right this very minute!" It is very true that we sometimes *need* a little holiday. We don't have to wait for a specific day to appear on the calendar to have a party, to make some special food, to give a little gift or to go on a special excursion. Maybe you will want to celebrate Ground Hog Day, National Pickle Week or Flag Day at your home. Perhaps you'll pick one ordinary day of the month and celebrate just because you wish to.

With family traditions rooted in the holidays, your child will one day look back and remember "what we always did on Thanksgiving." We *make* our memories.

43
What To Do
When Parents
Are Busy

No matter how orderly your home life, parents must sometimes cut themselves off from their children when other events take priority. If you've done a good job with the children under most circumstances, this will not be a hardship. In fact, it can be fun! The ideas in this chapter are adaptable for homes where both parents work.

You may be busy for an hour or for an entire day if you are working on a big project. Young children can't go for long without supervision, but good activities can prevent hours of television viewing.

If you are to be away for several days, a substitute parent will be in the home and life can continue along the usual lines. More likely, though, you will need projects that will keep a child busy for one or two hours at a time. Here are some ideas:

1. **Crafts.** For just such occasions, keep on hand a new craft kit, one that is completely safe and the child can do on his own. Model airplanes, mosaics, paper dolls, punch-out books, yarn kits, and coloring books are inexpensive but absorbing items.

2. **Games and Puzzles.** Monopoly and 500-piece puzzles are good for children eight to twelve.

3. **Playhouse.** Bring out a card table, old sheet and felt pens and let the children make their own hideaway by using the pens to decorate the sheet like a building.

4. **Theatrics.** Given a few ideas, two or more children can be kept busy for several hours if they have some theatrical inclination. Encourage them to bring out their record player, to make a curtain, to write a play, and practice it to show when parents aren't busy.

5. **Books.** Many children enjoy being left alone with good books. Keep in mind books your children have not read. If you need to take an hour for a nap or for making a super-special meal, an enticing book may be just the answer for your child.

6. **Huge Work Project.** In our playroom we have a floor-to-ceiling

cupboard in which each child has a shelf for his playthings. If I want to keep the kids out of mischief for a long period, I issue orders that it is time to clean the playroom cupboard and that they are welcome to play with the things as they work. Since children are usually slow, this sometimes supplies enough activity for several days. They start by bringing everything out, then sorting through it and putting it back. They are sidetracked many times; they find toys they haven't seen for months; they become interested in a sister's chemistry set or a brother's watercolors. You won't hear from them for hours!

DOUBLE DUTY TIME

Sometimes when I am very busy, I can do two things at once: accomplish my own work and still maintain contact with the children. If I have been out all day and return home just in time to cook supper, I can have a good chat with Mark, my supper helper; supervise Kent's homework by having him work on it in the kitchen; test Wendy on her spelling while cooking the asparagus, and listen to Karen's dramatization of the day's events as she helps me set the table.

Although I prefer privacy when getting ready to go out, some tasks can be combined with chatting with the children. In this regard it's a good idea to adopt the 30-minute rule.

THIRTY-MINUTE RULE

When you're going out without the children or entertaining and leaving them to their own devices, plan backwards from the time when you must part from them. If it takes you 30 minutes to get ready to go, start an hour in advance. The last 30 minutes then become the children's time. It gives you an opportunity to companion with them at their supper or to check the progress of their homework. The 30-minute rule gives you ample time to give the baby sitter instructions and to talk personally with each child as to what's expected of him during the party or absence. Bedtimes can be put firmly in mind, television shows approved, wearing apparel for the next day selected, good-night kisses given and children left calm and secure. This is far better than mother and father hastily rushing out the door shouting good-byes and warnings to their children.

When you are entertaining, the 30-minute rule gives you time with the children to enjoy the beauty of your home as it stands ready for guests. It never looked better! To be able to chat with one's spouse about the menu, events of the party and guest list leaves you both poised and ready for your friends' arrival.

Your child may get disgruntled when you are busy because you don't explain what's going on. You can secure your child's compassion and aid if you tell why you are behind schedule.

We were to entertain friends one Saturday afternoon when I arrived home late from a business luncheon where I'd been unavoidably detained. With only one hour before the guests were to come and with food and house needing attention, I enlisted the children's help. I spent five whole minutes explaining to them the importance of the guests, why I wanted certain areas of the house to look nice, how upset I was with the shortness of the time. It was amazing how the children volunteered to sweep leaves off the sidewalk, fluff pillows, help make the appetizer, load the dishwasher, get themselves tidied up, select appropriate records for the stereo and give the house a general pick up.

Long phone calls needn't cut you off from your children. Encourage your toddler to get on his toy phone and imitate you. Communicate with older children via written notes while you phone. When I had three toddlers and a full time writing job, I had a hands-free telephone in my kitchen so I could phone, feed baby and cook simultaneously.

When you are busy, you needn't fear what your children will be up to if you have spent adequate time with them on other occasions. Your busyness is an opportunity for the children to show that their training toward independence is paying off. The success of your home education is shown by the deportment of your children when you are *not* on hand to give them guidance. You needn't feel guilty about being away from your children or ignoring them for a few hours when you have taken the time on other occasions to play ball with them, cook with them, teach them crafts, read to them or go bike riding with them. As much as we enjoy being with our children, we do have lives of our own and we should, without apologies, attend to our own activities.

With the increase of working mothers, both parents must be even cleverer in seeing that their children are not neglected. This means that when the children are inside and awake, one parent must be accessible to the children for conversation, play or guidance. If two parents work, sharing home duties is essential and the most important home duty is parenting. This also means that when the children are sleeping, parents must concentrate on those activities that require their 100 percent attention.

Let's be sure we aren't giving our children the busy signal too often. When we must put off a child's request or question to another time, note it in the family date book so you will remember to bring it up when you do have time. Some parents put their children off habitually and then wonder why the lines of communication have been broken.

One day Kent put a note on the refrigerator door. It said he wanted time with me when he came back from play. I got dinner organized so that I could talk with him at 5:30. His story was about a cheater who wasn't caught and who got a high grade on a test and much commendation by the teacher. Kent had received a mediocre mark. He was troubled. After a conversation on what he had learned from the experience, he still wasn't totally satisfied but said, "The thing I feel best about is that you wanted to listen to this whole dumb story. I feel better because by telling it to you, it didn't seem as bad. You understood how I felt. I like to tell you stuff."

Sometimes a parent just has to listen. Kent didn't expect me to solve it all for him, although I tried. Just listening was important. Sometimes our children talk to us while we are cooking, repairing, driving, bathing, dusting, folding laundry. A parent can never be so busy that he can't find time to listen!

Your Week Four Check List

Here's how to get started with creative ideas in your home. Don't try to introduce too many new activities at once. Choose one area to emphasize each week or two. Here's your list and the appropriate chapter numbers. Check them off after you've gotten started with the activity.

- ☐ Music (29)
- ☐ Art (30)
- ☐ Literature (31)
- ☐ Drama (32)
- ☐ Sports and Games (33)
- ☐ Science (34)
- ☐ Nature (35)
- ☐ Car creativity (36)
- ☐ Visiting friends (37)
- ☐ Shopping creatively (38)
- ☐ Having friends over (39)

You'll want to refer to these chapters through the year:
Clubs (40)
Birthday parties (41)
Holidays (42)

Don't give the busy-signal to your child! Remember *Double Duty Time* and the *30-Minute Rule*. (43)

Now, onward to Week Five!

Week Five

Education As A Home Responsibility

If society continues to take over more and more family functions, the only job left to parents may be to conceive, feed and clothe their children. Today we have to wage a conscious campaign to make the home a positive influence. Sadly, many parents are willing to abandon the education of their children to the schools, to the church, to the Scout leader and to television.

When a child can learn everything from science to sex in the classroom and learn it from people who are supposedly experts in the field, little is left to the novice parents at home. For this reason, many parents feel useless and inadequate and, as a result, they completely give up the job of being parents.

Education, however, is still a home responsibility. It is in the home, largely, that a child's character is formed. It should be in the home that his religious, ethical and moral training is given. It is in the home that he is prepared to face life without parental guidance. It is in the home that he receives counsel and advice that teach him to stand on his own in later years. And, most important of all, it is in the home that he finds the security, love and appreciation that no social organization can equal.

If parents do the best job possible in these home-oriented assignments, our school teachers can concentrate on academics, our Sunday school teachers can make religion practical, our Scout leaders can teach talents and crafts that are not in our bailiwick, and television can widen the horizon of our child's world.

However, when parents set no example as to true character, when they have no standard of behavior, when their lives appear to be at the mercy of the outside world and when their only advice to their children is to stop being what they are and do better, home becomes merely a hotel operation providing clean sheets, a place to hang the clothes and a few meals each day. Who but parents can give children the security of home, the love that endures "no matter what?"

217

Learning in the home is possible when parents create an intellectual atmosphere that encourages curiosity and study. When a question comes up that no one can answer, it should be natural for someone to say, "Let's look it up," whether it be in the dictionary or in the encyclopedia. The library habit should come naturally to a child. A child should be aware that his parents are still learning and that there are many things parents don't know.

Parents can make available to their children other adults who offer special learning experiences. At one time Mark was interested in the repair of a plastic boat. This was something completely beyond the scope of his Father, but a good friend had some knowledge of fibers and resins. There grew up between this adult and Mark a fine friendship plus a great deal of education that took place during the boat repair.

Education in the home has a strong base in the arts of discussion and conversation. Children should be given many opportunities to verbalize, to be responsible for interesting topics of discussion and to take the leadership in family conversation.

As for the sex education of young children, this is being rapidly abandoned to the school system. It is better for the schools to give out information than for the children to have no information at all. One of the best systems is used by our local school district. The teacher of a biology-oriented eighth grade class makes copies of the text available to the parents who are encouraged to read it in advance. At mid-semester the class has two evening meetings, one for mothers and daughters and the other for fathers and sons. This learning together takes the embarrassment out of it, makes a stronger bond and conversational link between parent and child and provides the latest in factual information. This becomes a springboard to home conversations in which the parents can reinforce home standards.

Moral and sex education should be a part of daily life. Then it is unnecessary to sit a child down and tell him "the facts of life." If we answer his questions when he is curious, if the children have pets and visit zoos, if they are given honest answers when they see a pregnant woman, they will gather basic facts when they are young. As to the specifics on reproduction, these are taught in the science classes at school. Health classes handle current questions on dating and the consequences of sexual involvement. As for the techniques of sex, no child under twelve needs information. We often err in telling children far more than they need or want to know at the time. It is equally wrong, of course, to fail to inform them of their own capabilities or to omit telling them what is normal and natural in their own sexual development. When matters of sex are presented undramatically, they take their proper place in the child's life and are kept in balance.

To educate a child, you must educate yourself—about your child, about how children learn, about what they can learn. You must be sure of your own life values. To teach, to lead, you must fill yourself with up-to-date facts and set the standard you wish the children to follow.

The home becomes an educational institution the moment the baby is born and continues as a haven after the child has left. Nowadays there is much helpful information on how to be a parent in books and parental training classes. In previous chapters, we've discussed the proper home atmosphere and the type of character we would like our children to have.

We have set the scene for education by teaching the children how to combine orderliness and obedience with spontaneity and creativity. Now let us consider specific areas of home education.

44
Concepts That Start In Babyhood

Psychologists agree that certain basic concepts are formed in a child by age three and that much of a child's learning is accomplished by age six. First, let's consider concepts we knowingly or unwittingly teach our children in babyhood and early toddler years.

1. **A sense of value.** Whether or not we admit it, we teach our youngest babes what is important in life and what is not. An executive exhibits bad temper over a typist who misspells a word in a letter. A wife is cold and distant to her husband because he fails to notice that she has washed the car. A teen-ager goes into a blue daze over the loss of a school election. A nine-year-old stomps out of the room because everyone decides to play a game other than the one he selected. The misspelled word, the clean car, the election and the game are NOT important enough to make one upset. In a world of divided nations, massive pollution, wars and riots, some things are worthy of great emotion and some things should be sloughed off.

Value sense starts to form with the baby's observation of our attitudes toward his activities. If we shout and slam cupboard doors when he dumps his milk, he is taught early in life that small mistakes are upsetting. What he needs is the lesson on how to hold the cup better. But we forget this and thus he will have to learn by trial and error. The lesson we are teaching him, unfortunately, is that two minutes of our time in mopping up spilled milk is a big deal. If we teach a toddler "no," we won't have to be frantic about precious things on the coffee table. If we read books with him and show him how much we love the book, he will be less apt to scribble in a book and tear out its pages.

2. **That we mean what we say.** While it is never too latè to try to regain the reins at home, parents often start to lose control when children are babes and toddlers. How can we expect our teen-ager to come home promptly at the required time when we have let him break other rules during his younger years? When he is little and kicked the

dog, and we have told him in advance that this behavior will merit punishment, have we come through with the punishment? If not, why will he believe us when we say that improper teen-age activity will result in restrictions? We must be faithful to our own words: "Supper will be at six," "We'll go to the beach Saturday," "Come to me when you are bothered by your little brother." You may not think your child is listening and watching your actions, but he is, and he is learning if you are true to your word. If we are setting the example for a child to get by with as much as he can, in later years the same child will bend our rules and even the civil law as far as possible.

3. **Taking care of possessions.** By about age two, a child may discern that an endless supply of amusement exists at home and that the more toys he leaves outside, breaks or throws out of his playpen, the greater our desire to keep him supplied with more. His toys and clothes are treated like tissues: when used, another always pops up. The answer is to be a home conservationist, not just recycling cans and bottles but treating clothing and toys with respect. Mark was notorious in his treatment of possessions one year. I worked with him once a week to get some order in his room and found that my conversational patter had more effect than harangues. I'd say things like: "Teddy Bear is so sad under the bed." "These crayons would take all your monthly allowance to buy." "I'll have to take time out from cookie baking to wash your Sunday shirt and pants." "Let's give this puzzle to the rummage sale so some child can really enjoy it." This wasn't too subtle but it wasn't shouting. Soon I found Mark talking to his toys: "Where are you caboose, you belong with the engine." "Oops, paint spilled on my whole tablet, not good." He did get better!

4. **Unselfishness.** Babies learn quickly that crying and fussing will bring more food, attention and coddling. Granted, there are times when babies require attention. On the other hand, much of the early years' senseless tears and tantrums, which result in willfulness in the later years, come from parents who refuse to stand firm. The first time a child says "I won't" and stomps his little foot or the first time he cries and pleads in a store for some purchase, he should be shown quickly and impressively that this sort of selfish behavior will not bring results even once.

A child can quickly learn to put himself first —selfishness —or to care for others —unselfishness. Parents can help by conversational reasoning in child-like terms: "You are making all the shoppers in the grocery store sad because you are noisy and crying." "We will play the game of your choice next time." "What can YOU do to make everyone happy?"

Wendy, then a kindergartener, was helping me choose groceries one day. A mother with a cranky child was in the same aisle. Suddenly Wendy stopped pushing my cart and said to him, "Do you have to go to the bathroom?" He shook his head no. "Don't you feel good?" He shook his head no. "Do you have a bad mommy?" He shook his head no. "Then talk quiet and help her and don't come in my aisle if you're going to be bad." I was a little awed, and so was the other mother, but harmony reigned at the supermarket from then on.

5. **As you sow, so you reap.** It is up to the parents to teach clearly that praise and inner joy are the results of doing good and that stern words and unhappiness are the results of doing wrong. As soon as we confuse the results, ignore good and let evil go unnoticed, we have failed in this most important lesson.

The computer business has popularized the term "GIGO" — "garbage in, garbage out." If misinformation is fed to the computer, it will return misinformation. The computer cannot give a right answer if it has been programmed incorrectly. Likewise, a child should early be taught that what he gets out of life is directly proportional to what he puts in and, that the choice is *his,* each day, actually each moment, whether to feed garbage in and thus get garbage out or instead to perform acts of true value that result in blessings and rewards.

6. **Patience.** In a world of self-cleaning ovens, frozen dinners and instant art, patience is difficult to teach. We've raised a generation that wishes everything to happen quickly, that is not interested in negotiation, in step-by-step progress or in anything that cannot be capsulized. The good old words, "Just wait a moment" have become offensive. Patience in some way has become opposed to one's individual rights. To require patience, they say, is to curtail spontaneity. On the other hand, many aspects of life cannot be speeded up. Much true progress is made on an inch-by-inch basis. We cannot snap our fingers and wipe out slums, ignorance and world oppression. Perhaps the older generation has been slow to make progress against the world's ills. But the pendulum has swung too far in the direction of instant answers to all these questions. There still must be the meeting of the minds and the give-and-take of thoughtful resolutions. There is much merit in teaching tiny children to wait, to do one thing at a time, and to have compassion for those who are not as quick to move.

Too many parents "jump" to fulfill child wants. And sometimes we find that those wants fade fast and we've wasted our time or money to fulfill them. Thinking about something, planning for it, waiting for it, saving for it, considering solutions, coming back to a problem at a later time — all these functions require patience. This should be the method of home activity, rather than instant gratification.

"Right idea, wrong time" is a saying that is meaningful to children. "It isn't that we don't want to go to a movie, it's just that tonight is not the right time. So, let's plan it for Saturday night." Is there a better way to improve one's own patience-factor than to deal with young children?

7. A sense of accomplishment. So much is going on in the world nowadays that a child scarcely has time to savor one event before he's off on the next. In many ways it is good for a child to have a variety of experiences. Yet, the joy of accomplishment, of finishing what has been started, of completing a big task, is a great satisfaction, too. In our effort to get out the door we button buttons. In an effort to get to TV time, we write sentences for the child's composition. In an effort to see a completed model, we do the gluing for the child. "Finish it later," "Work faster," "Let's get on with this project," these are all phrases that rush children from one activity to another without letting them thoughtfully bring a task to a satisfying conclusion.

8. A sense of importance. The inadequate in this world far outnumber the self-important. Often, those who appear to be self-centered and self-important are merely covering up for a feeling of inadequacy. Yet within each of us lies the talent and ability to contribute to home, community and world, if we have the confidence to step forward and do it. This confidence, this feeling of being needed and important in the large plan of things, originates when a child is small. We listen to him, though his speech is faltering and his vocabulary inadequate. We appreciate his child-like attempts to please; we take time for games and activities that are greatly beneath our own abilities. How careful we should be not to make him feel as if he is a burden to us, time-consuming, stupid, slow or of no value until some hazy future time.

Let us then put the baby years in the proper perspective. Let us give our child a sense not only of being loved and appreciated but also of being part of a far greater picture in which he needs to be unselfish and patient. Let us show him what things are important materially and mentally and how to achieve them. It's not impossible to achieve this delicate balance.

These words of John Henry Newman might form a code of conduct for parent and child:

"God has created me to do Him some definite service; He has committed some work to me which He has not committed to another. I have my mission...I am a link in the chain, a bond of connection between persons. He has not created me for nothing. I shall do His work."

45
What You
Can Teach
A Toddler

At ages three and four a child is being prepared for his first solo experiences. He has ten basic skills to master during these years.

1. **Bathroom etiquette.** This skill so upsets almost every parent that one would think that the control of one's elimination processes was a major issue in this world. But few people grow up without having mastered this simple function. So let's keep it in its proper perspective. To be socially acceptable, however, a child must learn when and how to control himself and the niceties of remembering to wipe clean, lift seat (if a boy), flush the toilet, put the seat and lid down again, and when in public to express in discreet terms his need to go to the bathroom.

2. **Please and thank you.** A little child can be messy, interruptive or confused but the simple graciousness of "please" and "thank you," when requesting and receiving, cover a multitude of minor mistakes and are pleasant words for those around him. "Please" and "thank you" should become so automatic in a child's vocabulary that he needn't have to be reminded.

3. **Simple table manners.** If you wish a quick education in what is required in this field, serve as room mother in a kindergarten or pre-kindergarten class for a year. Help out during the lunch hour and you will see an assortment of table manners that will lead you to believe that our youngsters are only slightly removed from the animal level. Simple table manners should become automatic. Elbows off the table, the proper way to hold a fork, where the napkin goes and how to use it — these little skills, learned early, will save you much effort in later years when many teen-agers lounge on the table and stuff their mouths full of food while continuing to talk.

Children should also be encouraged to try new foods. This is not a question of will they or won't they; it is a question of how much. Teach them that everyone tries every new food. At our home we use the phrase "courtesy serving." Even when guests are present, our children know that when their plate is being prepared, they may ask for a "courtesy serving" (which is about one mouthful) and that they will be expected to eat it. Many foods start out on the "courtesy serving" basis and later graduate to be favorites.

4. **How to dress oneself.** Take pity on the nursery school teacher or kindergarten teacher when you select your child's clothing. Little boys' shorts with elasticized waistbands are better than zippers and snaps. Dresses that button in front are better than dresses that button in back. Be sure boots and rubbers are big enough to go on easily. By age three, a child should be fully capable of dressing himself and following it up by a look in the mirror to see if his appearance is as he wants it.

Be patient with bizarre combinations of pants and shirts, mismatched shoes or misbuttoned garments. Start by laying out desirable combinations so he can dress himself. This way the child learns to control his arms and legs, buttons and snaps.

5. **Name, address and telephone number.** Learning this can be a game. You ask the question, the child gives the answer. The child asks the question, you give the answer. It's wisdom that a child not leave home alone or go down the street to play until he has mastered this basic information.

Here is a little poem that is easy for a very young child to learn. Fill in your child's name, telephone number, age and address. Say it once or twice a day for him starting when he is eighteen months or two years old. He will soon repeat it with you and then by himself.

Suzy Smith is my name;
I'm really not so tall,
But if you want to talk to me,
1234567 is what you call.
Did you know I am *four years old?*
That's the age I give,
And *1234 Main Street*
Is the place I live.

6. **Taking turns.** At home the child has learned that he is king. However, he is quickly going to learn that thousands of other children suffer from this same misapprehension. Hence, parents must teach their child to share. Sharing is difficult with an only child but can be practiced with young friends or parents.

7. **Numbers and colors.** Three- and four-year-old children can be taught six or eight basic colors and also how to recognize numbers up to nine.

8. **Left and right.** In preparation for following directions at school, these two words should become part of a child's vocabulary. Parents must not make it easy for their children by saying, "this side" or "that side," or "this hand" or "the other hand," or "the cupboard near the door." It makes

life more difficult at first but knowing left from right is essential.

9. A love of books. Since toddlers have fifteen to twenty years of book-learning ahead, books should become beloved friends. Teach a child to handle a book with care. While we should not force a child to learn to read, children must develop an appreciation for literature and a thirst for knowledge. Recognition of certain letters of the alphabet sometimes comes automatically from a love of books.

10. How to throw and catch. This is not an easy skill since it involves eye-hand coordination. Children will work on it for years to come, but those who start early to learn to throw and catch a ball will master it sooner. They may even avoid the anguish of being last chosen for ball games!

GAMES FOR TODDLERS

Jeanne Wood and Helen Clarke have written a delightful little book called *Children's Games Around the World*. It is available at bookstores or from the Dietz Press, 109 East Carry Street, Richmond, Virginia. It gives you hundreds of simple game ideas for children under twelve. Make sure that your three- and four-year-olds have played enough games so they are not shy in taking part in organized activities. The five most common games for this age group are:

1. London Bridge is Falling Down
2. Ring Around the Rosy
3. Follow the Leader
4. Hide and Seek
5. Tag

A child should also be able to sit down for ten to fifteen minutes and play a quiet game.

TOYS FOR TODDLERS

During these active years creativity and imagination are budding. See that your youngster has toys in these areas:

1. Automotive. Wheels to ride on — wagons, trikes or toy cars.
2. Building toys. Blocks, simple puzzles and other put-together items.
3. Imagination toys. Simple puppets, dolls and animals. You may wish to create a small doll corner in the child's bedroom or playroom.
4. Simple crafts. Crayons, paints and lots of plain paper plus a big apron.
5. Aim-at toys. These are toys that exercise the child's ability to give direction to his own force. Balls, pounding sets, pails and shovels fall into this category.
6. Rhythm toys. A drum, triangle or sticks are good for beginners.

When choosing toys, it is often more economical to purchase a good make of long-lasting and imaginative toys for children. They cost more, but many are so sturdily built that those we purchased for Wendy are still being used by Mark. In purchasing toys, remember that what appeals to us is not necessarily what will attract the child. At this age minute details on toy cars are not as important as their ability to roll smoothly and to last for more than a day.

BOOKS FOR TODDLERS

Although tastes in literature change through the years, certain basic books come to be loved by almost every toddler. You may wish to consider these books as a basic library.

1. An alphabet book. Hilary Knight's *ABC Book* is one of the best.
2. The *All-By-Myself* books available for little boys and little girls.
3. *A Child's Garden of Verses* by Robert Louis Stevenson. Choose an edition with handsome pictures and it will be a life-long possession.
4. Books by Dr. Seuss and P. D. Eastman. The extraordinary characters in these books and the humorous incidents will make them read and reread. Choose the simplest for toddlers.
5. A book of nursery rhymes. I recommend Marguerite de Angeli's *Book of Nursery and Mother Goose Rhymes.* This is a large, beautiful volume well worth the investment.
6. *I Made a Line* — Kessler.
7. The *Curious George* books — Rey
8. *Mr. Gilfump* — Howard
9. *A Little House of Your Own* — de Regniers
10. *The Doll and the Kitten* — Wright

GETTING READY FOR NEW EXPERIENCES

To prepare your toddler for social situations, give him experience in following directions. His future teachers will not always be able to check that he has understood directions, so teach him to speak up if he doesn't understand what he has been told to do. Also give him experiences in group play and in being both leader and follower.

As soon as your child starts to play near streets or at playgrounds, teach him how to handle emergencies and how to deal with strangers. By covering these situations in advance in a matter-of-fact way, you will not frighten your child but will emphasize the importance of keeping calm and thinking carefully in special situations. Teach your child what he should do if offered candy or a ride by a stranger. Be explicit as to what you want him to do if he is lost.

The toddler is eager and anxious for new experiences and thus is easy to teach since he wants to learn the skills that will give him greater freedom. Be sure to stress to him the many things that he *can* do rather than the things that he is too young or too small to do.

46
Preparing
To Love School

For three to six hours of each day your child will soon be on his own and under the direction of another adult. Again, a few basic skills will help him take part in school activities and concentrate on the important new learnings.

    1. **To print and recognize his own name.**

    2. **To understand the sizes and values of currency and coins.**

    3. **To paste.**

    4. **To dress himself,** even to lacing shoes, tying bows, putting on winter attire.

Lacing comes easily to children when you point out that they are making X's with the laces. Bow tying takes a bit more patience. While I read a book, one of our children practiced tying bows around the leg of the chair in which I was sitting and soon mastered the task! For a child who doesn't catch on immediately, let him learn one step each day and practice it to his heart's content. When taught this way, most children can learn to tie a bow in about three five-minute sessions. This is a good project for children to work on in the car with an older child teaching a younger one.

    5. **To talk in a group and to speak up loudly enough to be heard.** Mark told a sad story of a kindergarten friend of his who had lost his lunch money and was afraid to tell the teacher. Somehow in the excitement of eating time, the teacher did not notice that he had neither home lunch nor school lunch. So this child went hungry for his inability to speak up and tell what was wrong.

    6. **To nap or at least to rest quietly.** Most nursery schools and kindergartens have a required rest period each day. Parents are wise to have continued a rest time through the toddler years. Every child needs a quiet time and if a child does not sleep, he can certainly spend an hour in looking at books in his bed. Many parents make the excuse that their child just will not settle down. (You usually hear this from parents who are under the child's control.) The answer to this problem is to tell a child

that he should either sleep or pretend to sleep until you give him permission to be up. You'll be surprised how many pretenders fall asleep.

7. To listen quietly for fifteen-minute periods. This is easy for a child who has been read to by his parents during his pre-school years or who has been given time for quiet book-looking.

8. To use scissors. Five- and six-year-olds should be able to cut fairly well on a pre-described line and should also know how to carry a scissors with the point downward. Buy left-handed scissors for "lefties."

9. To care for possessions away from home. This carries over from home practice. Most preschools and kindergartens give a child a shelf, cubbyhole or box in which to put his belongings. Whenever you visit school, make it a point to inspect the box and praise good housekeeping or suggest improvement.

10. To go and return. Many five- and six-year-olds are responsible for getting themselves to and from school. They need the skills of how to cross streets, what to do if the carpool is late, what to do if lost, what to do in case of rain, and a firm understanding that they are not to accept rides or go near cars of strangers.

11. To tell time. Learning to tell time comes most easily when the clock has a full set of twelve Arabic numerals, not dots or lines replacing the numbers. Once the child has learned to tell time on a clock with numerals, he'll be able to transfer this talent to the more modern clock faces. You can buy clock toys but you can also make a simple cardboard clock.

When a child knows numbers to twelve, let him start telling you where the small hand is pointing. Don't involve him in more than this at the time of his first interest. Let him know that he is learning to tell time and can already tell you what hour it is. Later you'll show him how to tell exactly how many minutes it is, too. Make him feel useful by asking him the hour several times a day.

From this point you add the intricacies of the minute and second hands. A kindergarten teacher told me that only ten percent of children entering kindergarten are able to read a clock and that this would be a most helpful home lesson for pre-schoolers.

There are two additional home skills that your youngster should fully understand at this age: answering the telephone and the door.

THE TELEPHONE

Answering the phone should be a great privilege and a pre-school child should not be permitted to do so until he can do it properly. Children should answer the phone in the approved family manner. Let them practice on a toy phone and show you that they can do it right before you let them be your telephone answerers. Since they also have the privilege of making telephone calls, set up certain rules about early and late calls, the length of conversation and whether they need to ask permission to use the telephone.

As for answering the telephone, many families prefer some standard greeting such as "Smith residence, Susy speaking" or "Susy Smith here" or "The Smiths" or the telephone number or merely "Hello." If the call is not for the person answering, the child should put his hand over the mouthpiece before calling or bellowing for the recipient. The telephone answerer is responsible for seeing that the proper person gets to the phone. Nothing is more exasperating than being left at the other end of the line with the feeling that no one is ever going to come.

Often the child answering the phone must take a message. First and second graders should know that messages are always written and put in one established place: under the sugar bowl, on the table, on your desk, on the tablet next to the phone, wherever the whole family has agreed. When a home has more than one phone, it's especially important that all messages be collected in one spot so that you don't have to hunt all over for them.

A child should make note of all incoming calls even though no name is left. In this case the message is simply "4:00 p.m. lady called for mother," or "7:30, boy called for Wendy — will call back." When possible, the child should write down the name and telephone number of the caller. A child should be taught to ask for the name and not hesitate to have the number repeated.

Teach the child early that the telephone is a powerful servant, not a toy, and that telephones should never be played with or used for pranks.

ANSWERING THE DOOR

Sometimes it's expedient to let the child answer the door when you are at home. Your family rules should make it clear when children may open the door and when it must be answered by an adult. Teach young children whether they are to open the door whenever the doorbell rings or whether they are to ask first who is ringing. This, of course, depends on where you live and whether your front door has glass in it so the visitor can be viewed. If you wish the child to open the door, then you must teach him what to do with the caller. If the caller is known, he will invite the person to sit in the hall or living room. It is bad manners to leave friends standing on the doorstep! However, if the caller is unknown, you may wish to have the child say, "Can I tell my parents who is here?" Under these circumstances it is permissible for the child to leave the visitor on the doorstep and ask you what to do next.

BOOKS FOR KINDERGARTENERS AND FIRST GRADERS

The following is a list of books that children will enjoy having read to them.

1. Riddle books. This is the know-it-all age and they enjoy trying to outguess the book and later entertain others with the riddles and jokes.
2. *Mary Poppins* — Travers
3. *Hail Stones and Halibut Bones* — O'Neill. This is one of the most exciting books on color and will be a creative favorite for years to come.
4. The *Oz* books — Baum
5. *A Bear Called Paddington* and others in the series — Bond
6. *Now We Are Six* and *Winnie the Pooh* — Milne
7. *Lona* — Wright
8. *Prove It* — Wyler and Ames
9. *Chitty-Chitty Bang-Bang* — Fleming
10. *Henry and Ribsy* — Cleary
11. *The Petunia Books* — Duvoisin
12. *Harry, (The Dirty Dog)* series — Zion
13. *The Little Bear* series — Minarik
14. *Danny and the Dinosaur* — Hoff
15. *Frog and Toad are Friends* — Lobel
16. *Good Night Moon* — Brown
17. *Are You My Mother?* — Eastman

GAMES FOR KINDERGARTENERS AND FIRST GRADERS

Kindergarten games are an introduction to the more competitive games of older children. Basic kindergarten games include:
1. Leap frog
2. Blind man's bluff
3. Red rover come over
4. Hide and seek
5. Tag
6. Hopscotch
7. Circle chase (often called Drop the Handkerchief)

While success and failure are involved in these games, the importance of winning and losing is slight. They teach team activity and competition in preparation for more competitive games later.

TOYS FOR KINDERGARTENERS AND FIRST GRADERS

In addition to those toys mentioned earlier, the following six areas of toys include ones that you will want to purchase to support activities in the school.
1. Musical toys. Simple musical instruments which develop a child's sense of tone and rhythm; if possible, a phonograph.
2. School-oriented toys. A ruler, activity book, notebook, sticker books.
3. Number toys. Dominoes, follow-the-number games and games

involving dice where children learn to move markers a specified number of spaces.

4. Outdoor play equipment. Simple and inexpensive outdoor equipment such as rope ladders and hanging bars.

5. Building toys. Wood, plastic and cardboard blocks are essential to the creative development of the child since these toys have no entity of themselves but are merely what the child makes of them.

6. Coordination toys. Jump ropes, hula hoops, ring toss, tops and balls.

HAVE A GOOD DAY

Although parents want to be loved and sometimes missed by their children, few want a child who screams, kicks and cries through his early school days. Proper preparation can avert much of the unhappiness over going to school. First days at school should be natural experiences. If a child has an older brother or sister, the transition is much easier for he has visited school and heard talk about school life. If possible, visit the school the spring before and show him the kindergarten.

For a first child, the transition need not be painful. In the year before the school experience begins, parents should provide the child daytime opportunities to be away from them for an hour or more at a time. This can be either at a playground or at a friend's home. Like school, the playground gives the child an opportunity to play with different children. The first time the child is left at a playground, it might be well for a parent to stay nearby.

If you have been working in small educational pursuits with your child, it will be natural to tell him that soon he will be old enough to be taught by the expert, the teacher. Thus your child can look forward to the new learning experience and all the equipment and toys he will have at his disposal.

The purchase of school supplies should be a togetherness experience between parent and child. The child should label and pack them up himself and pick out exactly what he wishes to wear the first day of school whether it be an old favorite or a special new outfit. If possible, the child should see the school several times before school begins, to familiarize himself with the school buildings and playground.

Many kindergartens have an indoctrination program that starts the child with a 30 minute visit and works up to a full schedule. Many a crying child is afraid of school because he has caught the fear in a parent's voice. If you properly prepare your child for school, he need not fear this adventure. The child should be taught that school is his right place and that because you love him, you will not remove him from his right place merely by his suggestion of unhappiness or tears. A few children are truly unhappy and ill-adjusted to the school program but the great majority of the fussers are evidencing improper preparation or the fears of the parents. Be firm and cheerful when parting with your child and be clear as to when and where you will pick him up.

A proper send-off in the morning is essential to your child's happiness in school. Breakfast should be served early enough so he isn't stuffing down the last mouthful as he goes out the door. His hour before school should be as calm and uneventful as possible. This is not a time to reprimand or criticize him. Remind him to take all the proper equipment with him until he is old enough to remember for himself. Your final words should be cheerful and encouraging. "Have a good day." "See you after school." "Remember, I love you." "Have fun."

At the end of the school day be ready to listen to his account of his experiences. Older brothers and sisters may find this discussion boring but they should be encouraged to be attentive and appreciative of the achievements of the younger child. These hours away from home are the most important events in this child's day and we must give them their proper importance at home.

While stressing the positive aspects of school, the new skills being learned and the fun of making new friends, be tuned in to his minor complaints lest they become major issues. By working with your child and his teacher, minor personality problems, difficulties with other children and skills that seem hard to master can be worked on and corrected. However, he should be taught that there will be a few tiring or boring areas of work and that he should accept these and carry them out as quickly as possible. If he knows that the major part of school will be satisfying, he will be able to contend with those study areas that are less appealing.

Let your child tell relatives and friends the small but exciting experiences that happen to him at school. If he builds up a backlog of pleasant school memories, he will be eager to continue his education.

The most important thing a kindergartener can learn is that school has value for him both for personal enjoyment and for enlightenment. When he sees the benefits of attending school, he will be as eager to go as his parents are to have him go.

47
Forming
Habits
Of Study

During the first years of school, a child forms his attitudes toward academic pursuits. He begins to develop likes and dislikes that correspond to his talents in reading, math and science. Home support at this time can often help him overcome prejudices and other stumbling blocks to learning. Parents can improve their child's school achievements in four ways: First, by stimulating interest at home; second, by supervising homework; third, by working with the teacher; and fourth, by encouraging grade improvement.

STIMULATING INTEREST AT HOME

As a little test for yourself, see if you can name the subjects your grade school child is taking. Most parents find they are aware of only half of them. If you find out what he's studying, you can stimulate interest and support his school learning by referring him to newspaper articles and home reference materials.

Your daily question, "What's doing at school?" has more behind it now since you can ferret out information on key topics. If you know your child had a test in spelling today, you can inquire how it went. Thus you show that you feel school is important and that you care what he is learning. Many children think conversation on school subjects is dreary, but through that conversation they realize their older brothers and sisters and even their parents had to learn how to spell, to study their country's history and to know the definition of a triangle.

HOMEWORK

It's a good idea to find out from each of your child's teachers what you can specifically do to support homework. Some teachers don't want mothers or fathers looking over any of the work done at home. Others take the middle view that parents should review the work without telling the child what is wrong but indicate to the child that there are mistakes on the page. Still others will give permission for parents to mark specific questions or problems with an X if they're wrong so the child can correct them.

Once you know the teacher's preference, you can proceed to enhance the value of homework time. Homework is generally a drill on material covered in the classroom. As a rule it's not new work. The purpose of homework is to perfect a skill. It is not a test of what a child knows. Testing comes in school. Homework grades usually have less importance than tests.

Make sure your child does his homework after he has had sufficient activity to be ready to sit down and work. If homework will take more than 60 minutes, break it into two or more sessions. Keep a school atmosphere during homework time. With several children doing homework, you may be able to create a study hall situation. This quiet study atmosphere reinforces the great need among this age group to concentrate for longer periods and to stick to a particular subject. You may wish to check the study hall regularly or to keep an eye on it while preparing supper.

Your child may need your encouragement to work on his long-range school projects. Children are often assigned a project such as a model or long report due later. Encourage your child to talk about these projects and be sure he has the equipment and ideas to make the projects worthwhile. These special assignments set the scene for later, more serious research.

Take time to drill your child on facts. Many children receive poor grades because they do not have the simple number facts at their fingertips. Homemade or purchased drill cards on addition, subtraction, multiplication and division are great for polishing and refreshing facts. We purchased these drill cards when Wendy was small and each of the children has used them in turn. Start a little drill late in August so that number facts grown hazy over the summer can be recalled in time for the opening of school.

The same goes for spelling. Here you can note on the calendar the date of the next spelling test and drill your child on the words. Some children enjoy competing against themselves to see their own progress. For example, Kent found that he went through the subtraction drill cards with seven mistakes the first week, three mistakes the second week and none the third week. Your child gains a feeling of accomplishment if he can see how he is improving.

KNOW THE TEACHER

With busy teachers and busy parents, you may meet your child's teacher only when there's a problem. School interviews are infrequent and most parents have contact with the school only two or three times a

236

year. When the report that the child is doing poorly comes, it's sometimes too late to make a correction.

Each autumn we ask our grade school children's teachers and spouses to a simple supper, with the host child choosing the menu. The invitation is stated so the teacher knows that the entire event will last no more than about two hours. One benefit of these suppers is that the children often take their teachers to their own rooms to see their collections or study areas. Once Kent's teacher noticed a horse figurine on his top shelf and the ensuing conversation showed that she knew something about equestrianship and the old West. Kent's estimation of his teacher went up and she, recognizing his special knowledge in this field, had him share it with the class. He would have been too shy to volunteer but with the teacher's introduction, he was eager to talk. In turn, other children had a greater appreciation of him and his special interest. If you don't want to make it supper and conversation, you can arrange another time to get together with your youngster's teacher.

When your child appears to have completely misunderstood some area of instruction, write a note to the teacher. Perhaps others in the class are equally misinformed. If you are in doubt about a particular assignment, write a note to the teacher, who will be pleased with your interest.

In your note always ask what you can do to help your child at home. We found at one time that Mark was doing very poorly on speed tests on number facts. Since the tests were given on duplicated sheets, the teacher was happy to supply us with an additional two dozen. Each day at homework time, Mark used one of these sheets to race against the clock. He was amazed to see how he improved in speed and accuracy in three weeks.

Sometimes when a child is not working as well as he should in a subject, he can raise his grade by doing a special research project. Wendy was not particularly interested in the subject matter of her science class one year and was getting just average grades. Since this was unusual for her, I asked the teacher if she might do an extra report to improve her understanding of the material. The teacher was most agreeable and worked out a project with Wendy that captured her interest and was valuable enough for her to present to the entire class.

GRADES

Grades are not the be-all and end-all of an education, but they usually are a good indication as to whether the child has grasped the material taught and is able to convey it to the teacher in satisfactory form. Grades have been played down lately but no one can deny that a grade usually shows whether the child is paying attention and getting the facts.

Some children test more poorly than their capabilities because they are fearful of tests, are tired or upset when they take them, or come from a different background from the test writers. Still, in the course of the school experience, most parents are given some indication as to the range of interests and capabilities of their child. With these factors, set different standards for each child. For one child to bring home a C grade would show an absolute lack of interest in the subject and a complete disregard for its mastery. However, for another child, we may rejoice in a C grade in the same subject because his interests lie elsewhere.

In our family we work to help the child avoid a failing grade. The minute a grade hits the C minus level, that child is given special help at homework time and there is possibly a curtailment of extra-curricular activities. It may sound very strict but we allow no TV Monday through Thursday the first half semester in the autumn. The only exception would be a program tying in with a school subject. This gives each child every opportunity to get his grades to the proper level while still enjoying outdoor play and hobbies. At the end of October when the first grades come out, those children who have acceptable grades are given some television privileges. Those with unacceptable grades then know they have to work harder in order to be granted television privileges.

Some children need shorter spaces between reviews. Mark was once surprised to get a poor grade in math. Each Friday for the next half semester, I sent a note with him and asked the teacher about his work attitude and weekly grade. This told us whether Mark was improving on a week-to-week basis. We found that this method brought about slow but steady improvement and the grade was up the next marking period.

Children may argue that grades are unfair and do not show exactly what they are learning. But we have to face this fact: if we cannot put down on paper what we have learned, we probably didn't learn it.

A great furor exists over whether children should be paid for their grades. Several years ago I read an article on this subject and found this supporting argument: we are paid in our careers on the basis of our achievement; so since school is a child's work, there is nothing wrong in giving a monetary reward for grades. Until I read this, I had been firmly against paying for grades. Now I find that for some children the monetary reward does bring about better grades. I also pay a bonus for an improved grade and deduct for any grade that slips at the end of the year. This puts a premium on self-improvement. For satisfactory reports on the children's work habits and attitudes, I also pay a small bonus.

BOOKS FOR EIGHT- AND NINE-YEAR-OLDS

Children of this age are ready to read for themselves. Librarians find that books read a generation ago by children age ten to twelve are now being read by children as much as two and three years younger. This is due to their increasingly better vocabularies, which we can probably attribute to television learning. The following "classics" are ones that many children of this age recommend highly.

1. *The Singing Tree* and *The Good Master* — Seredy
2. *Heidi* — Spyri
3. Books by Louisa May Alcott
4. *The Yearling* — Rawlings
5. *Kon Tiki* — Heyerdahl
6. *The Little Prince* — de Saint Exupery
7. *The Jungle Book* — Kipling
8. Andersen's and Grimms' Fairy Tales
9. *A Little Princess* — Burdette
10. *Where the Wild Apples Grow* — Hawkins
11. *Engines and Brass Bands* — Miller

GAMES FOR EIGHT- AND NINE-YEAR-OLDS

At this age children begin to have a greater feeling of competition and team games become important.

1. Dodge ball, kickball and tetherball
2. Baseball
3. More complicated forms of tag
4. Jump rope and jacks
5. Four square and hopscotch
6. Box games
7. Computerized games

TOYS FOR EIGHT- AND NINE-YEAR-OLDS

By now children are able to work with their toys by themselves and are interested in more sophisticated forms of play. Kits and scientific toys take on prominence. Consider the following areas when purchasing gifts for this age group:

1. Art and craft toys, including mechanical design makers.
2. Scientific and space toys — kits for spaceships, planes and boats.
3. Tops, kites and jacks.
4. Miniatures of adult equipment such as toy kitchens and workshops.
5. Electrical toys including record or tape players, walkie-talkies and transistor radios.

The early grade school years are a time of discovery. Children at these ages have minimum homework and many free play hours. During these years the wise parent gives some direction to the child's free time.

48
Studying Alone And Researching

By grade four the child's study habits are fairly well formed. In school he is being put more and more on his own and so at home he should be permitted more self-government in the area of homework.

THE FORTY-EIGHT-HOUR RULE

It was a Thursday night and Wendy was doing her homework when we got an unexpected phone call from friends who were in town for only this evening. We had two hours before we were to meet them. This seemed like sufficient time for everyone to finish his homework and for us to have some supper. But Wendy was glum and grumpy. We soon learned that she had a report due the next day—one she had not even started!

Out of this unhappy experience came the Forty-Eight-Hour Rule: any school project or paper assigned in advance is to be finished *not* the night before it is due *but the night before that*. This gives an extra day for emergencies and, if needed, the extra evening of work in case the project isn't quite ready to be turned in — time to correct spelling errors, messy writing, poor illustrations.

Grade school children are usually given one or two of these long-range projects each year. Put them on your calendar so you can remind your student to work on the project a little each day. Four or five days before the project is due, note in your date book or on the family calendar that the project should now be in rough form. If it isn't, it is time to enforce work on the project. Then, 48 hours before it's due, ask to see it to make sure that it is acceptable. You may spot small things that can be done to put the finishing touches on the project. Your bonus is that you will really learn from your child's research!

The Forty-Eight-Hour Rule can carry over into many activities. If you are to present a report at a meeting, you may wish to follow the Forty-Eight-Hour Rule yourself. If Wendy is sewing a dress to wear at a certain party, she strives to be ready 48 hours ahead. The Forty-Eight-Hour Rule helps avoid tears, shouting and gray hair. Since the project has to be done eventually, there is no reason it can't be done a couple of days before deadline.

Many schools have initiated research programs in which children as young as second grade select a topic for independent research in the library. They prepare either an oral or written report. This independent study teaches the child to scan reference material for ideas, to read quickly, to take notes on three-by-five cards and to organize the material.

We can bolster these skills at home by giving our children periodicals to scan — rather than to read. We may offer them a magazine article and tell them they can look it over to pick out of it what interests them. We can teach them to read more of the newspaper than just the comics. Nine- to twelve-year-olds can develop an interest in world affairs by scanning newspaper headlines plus conversing with their parents.

When your child is to give an oral report, encourage him to try it out loud in his own room a day before he is to present it in school. Perhaps he will be willing to practice on one understanding member of the family. Giving it for brothers and sisters can sometimes bring about suggestions that will vastly improve it.

The greatest hazard in teaching methods that give children greater freedom of curriculum and choice of study devices is that some children will waste time. For this reason we should watch closely the amount of time a child spends on his homework. Sometimes it's well to preview what he is to achieve and schedule with him the amount of time it will take to accomplish the work. If we agree in advance that the arithmetic homework should take about 20 minutes, we should then check after 30 minutes to find out why it isn't done. This will help the child to corral his wandering thoughts and to concentrate harder on getting the work done.

When a child faces a large project, getting started is usually the biggest hurdle. This is where we parents can step in, discuss the project briefly and share some ideas on reference materials and visual aids. We can help him divide a big project into "do-able" sections. Sometimes we need to make only one or two suggestions to start the child's own creative thinking.

BOOKS, TOYS AND GAMES FOR CHILDREN TEN TO TWELVE

By these ages most children have definite tastes and interests that dictate the types of toys and books we buy for them. In school their games are beginning to take on a more adult aspect. They are beginning to take part in organized baseball, tennis, basketball, football and relays. Our toy purchases should follow this trend: sports and outdoor equipment, box games such as *Monopoly,* checkers and chess, games and toys that pertain to their special interests, whether it be art, science or sewing.

Ten- to twelve-year-olds also have diverging literary interests. Adven-

241

ture, animal and science books have wide appeal and many of them even read the *Hardy Boys* books or *Nancy Drew* as did their parents. By this age, children are usually reading on their own and need little encouragement if the proper advance work has been done. School librarians can provide a list of books that a child should read in advance of the high school years.

During these pre-teen years we begin to see our children as they will be as young adults. While we still guide them educationally in the home, they are beginning to specialize at this point. We should do everything possible to see that they have equipment and books that apply to their particular interests, interests that may be far from ours!

49
The
Social Graces
Today

When Mark was reminded about his bad table manners one day, he answered, "I'll remember them when I'm invited to a good party." This is like the auditor who says he'll study math when he gets an accounting job, the tourist who plans to learn French on the plane to Paris or the speaker who is composing his talk during the introduction.

The social graces should be part of home education so that good manners become second nature to children, something they needn't even think about. A child's first introduction to the social graces comes with teaching him "please" and "thank you." Then, he's exposed to a series of rules called "table manners." The following is a list of table manners that can be mastered by children under twelve years of age. These suggestions make good sense — they aren't merely outmoded ideas.

1. **Passing serving dishes.** When the butter or vegetable or fudge topping is passed around the table the first time, it naturally starts at one end of the table and ends up there again. Later, when passed on request, it *never* goes across the table. Passing across may work in small family groups but at dinner parties one is apt to knock over the candles or get catsup on the flower arrangement.

2. **Napkins.** A child can learn early that the napkin goes in the lap at the beginning of the meal and that for small laps it can be secured at the belt if need be. Unless he is eating some especially messy food, such as lobster, the napkin does not go in the collar. As needed and at the end of the meal, the child carefully wipes his mouth and fingers. At a restaurant he places the napkin back on the table. At home, he puts it in a napkin ring. Never is it rumpled into a ball even if made of paper. And it is never put on the plate.

3. **Waiting to eat.** In a small family all members should wait until the others are served before eating. This means that while dishes are being passed, no one is taking advance samples. At large parties when the hostess has lifted her fork and signaled the beginning of eating, those

243

who find that those adjacent to them have been served may certainly start. Occasionally at large Thanksgiving feasts when much carving is going on, young children are served first and permitted to start eating while their food is warm.

4. **Serving one's self.** When a child must take food from a buffet or from a passed serving dish, he should remember that as much as he likes french fried potatoes or hot rolls, he should not take more than his share. A child can practice this at home as an adjunct to his lessons in short division!

5. **Salt and pepper.** It's disconcerting to the cook to see someone heavily salt, pepper or catsup his food before tasting it. Salt and pepper should be added unobtrusively. When someone requests salt or pepper, both travel together. Wendy made up the rhyme, "The salt and pepper travel together; the salt won't run in sticky weather."

6. **Distasteful foods.** When a child doesn't like a particular food he's put in his mouth, little should be made of it at the time. A child should be taught how to remove it discreetly with spoon or hand and without calling attention to himself. This goes for the removal of seeds and pits also. A child should try everything on his plate and not take large portions of unfamiliar foods.

7. **Elbows and arms.** These are kept off the table at all times. If there is a conversational break between the main course and dessert or following the meal, it is permissible to rest the forearm on the table if the space between place settings permits.

8. **Gulping food, cutting food.** With good conversation at the table, it should be almost impossible for a child to devour his entire meal in five minutes. A child who dumps a whole glass of milk down his throat or who noisily eats all his food in a few short gulps should be taught to slow down, to chew well and to contribute to the conversation. Of course he must be told to swallow before speaking. He should also be taught that only very small children have their entire portion of meat cut into bite-sized pieces in advance.

9. **Requesting more food.** When seconds are desired, a child should be taught to name the person adjacent to the serving dish, follow the name with the request and include the word "please." Thus: "Karen, will you please pass the mashed potatoes?" In family circles (but not at parties) Karen is free to ask in return, "May I please have some on the way?" The answer to this question is always "yes," but we go through the drill of asking the question.

10. **Silverware.** When Mark went off to kindergarten, we thought he had fairly good manners but we noticed during the first few weeks that his dinner table manners got increasingly worse. He was unable to manage a fork and chose a spoon instead. We soon discovered that an excessively large kindergarten that year had resulted in a shortage of

244

forks. The kindergarteners ate their entire lunch with spoons!

Children should know the uses of various items of table service besides the traditional knife, fork and spoon. They should become familiar with a soup spoon, a dessert spoon, dessert or salad fork, butter knife and seafood fork. If they are at a meal where they are not sure which tool to use, suggest they keep an eye on parents or host.

Prior to our first trip to Europe with the children, we practiced eating with the silverware we would find in hotels abroad. This information bored them at home but abroad they were thrilled at the very first dinner when they found nine pieces of silver for each of them. They were so proud as they worked their way through the meal and used all the silver.

11. **Suitable conversation.** Although the child may have a cast iron stomach, others at the table may not. Children should be taught that certain topics are not brought up while others are eating: scabby knees, loose teeth, car accidents, squashed bugs, garbage cans, toilet training, horror shows, etc.

12. **Jumping up and down from the table.** If you decide to assign one child the job of cook's helper and waiter, this eliminates much moving around during the meal. That child is the one to refill milk glasses, to replace a dropped fork or to bring replenishments from the kitchen. Unless a child is the supper helper, he remains at the table until he is excused.

13. **When children serve.** Serving dishes should always be presented at the left of the person being served. This has reason since it's much easier for a right-hander to serve himself. Left-handers like Mark just cope. Removal of plates was once done only from the right, but today the entire operation may be done from the left if that is more convenient.

14. **When finished eating.** A child should be shown what to do with food scraps on his plate at the end of the meal and how to place silverware at the diagonal of four to ten o'clock so that the plate may be cleared without forks and knives tumbling to the floor. He should also be taught not to shove his plate away or push his chair back from the table in order to lounge until time to leave the table.

EATING OUT

Eating out with your children should be a pleasure. No parent gets up-tight when taking his child to a hamburger place. This is because the child knows how to eat hamburgers and is familiar with what is expected of him. Eating in a more formal atmosphere can be equally enjoyable if we teach the child what is expected of him in this situation. Before going to a restaurant, instruct your child in the following areas:

1. Who follows the waiter to the table.
2. How to seat adults in a restaurant if the host does not do so.
3. When to put the napkin in the lap (not in the collar).

4. How to hold and read a menu (and check with parents for suggestions).
5. The importance of noting prices.
6. How to order.
7. What to do while waiting for food to come — conversation in a well-modulated voice.
8. How much filler (crackers, celery, etc.) to eat without ruining appetite.
9. How to respond to waiters who will be serving.
10. A brush-up on the use of silverware.
11. Suggestions on what to do when not eating but still at the table.

During my youth families did not eat out as much as they do now. From this stemmed my desire to create at home a restaurant-like atmosphere. With the help of my mother, "Blueberry Hill" was born. This was an at-home restaurant which served only our family and any friends who happened to be invited. I typed menus, made aprons and arranged flowers to give "Blueberry Hill" a touch of class. Our eating area could be completely closed off, and I made everyone wait awhile before I took them in and seated them at the table.

My cooperative mother — a superb cook — was able to come up with several choices for appetizer, beverage and dessert while holding to one main dish. I ran my small restaurant several times a month. I know the cooking was good, the price was right, and the fun of being waitress never seemed to fade.

One day I was telling all this to Karen. She thought it sounded great and so we've carried the idea into the next generation. When she and her younger brother create a restaurant-like atmosphere at our home, no one, but no one, is allowed to enter the kitchen during the preparation. Since it isn't done very often, everyone enjoys the pseudo-formality and it is good training for the children.

We were assessing our family life one day when we realized that we ate with haste and did not have very much variety in the foods served. We decided that every Thursday night we would have a special family dinner and share it with another family with children of similar ages. We would all come in nice shirts, jackets or dresses and would eat dinner in a more civilized manner than usual. The meal would have three or four courses; some of the dishes served would be new. Thus I could experiment on some good friends and some good food.

Since we have it on a school night, everyone knows dinner is at 6:00 and the event is over by 8:00. I like the freedom from the old tradition of having the big meal of the week on Sunday. Now if we have a ham or roast on Thursday night, we benefit from the good leftovers on the weekend. This eases the cooking load when the family is at home and demanding attention.

Table manners are not the total training of a socially graceful child. Let's consider some other areas where we can teach our children simple manners. First, though, we should remember that equal rights for women has made some women feel that no one should seat them, open a door, etc. Of course, the aged or handicapped deserve help. But why should an able-bodied young woman have her coat held? It isn't a matter of sex, it is a matter of being helpful. *Someone* has to push the chair in, *someone* has to hold the elevator door open. But if there is no one with a special need, who does it? If there isn't some plan we'll all be falling over one another. So, we let boys and men do these things. If this bothers a woman, she can consider it a fair exchange for some of the services she performs. There is much more to being liberated than seating yourself! So good manners continue.

1. **Elevators and doors.** Boys should be taught to hold doors of buildings, houses and cars for girls, and girls should be taught to step forward quickly through revolving doors, into elevators and into cars. Boys and girls, in turn, should be taught to give adults or someone with a special need this attention.

2. **Air travel.** As a mobile nation, more children are appearing on airplane flights, sometimes even alone. It is wise to teach children the etiquette of air travel in advance of the trip. They should be taught to keep their chairs upright unless sleeping — and not to use them as toys. They should be reminded not to dig their feet into the back of the chair in front of them and thus into the back of the occupant. They should not stand on their seats and peer over into the row behind them. Voices should be kept down and food should be eaten as neatly as possible. This doesn't mean the children can't have fun on airplanes but it does mean that airplanes are not playgrounds. Others may be reading or resting, and childish antics can be offensive if carried beyond their own seats.

3. **Contradictions and interruptions.** Most family conversation is so casual that we hardly notice when we interrupt one another. However, it is objectionable to be with children who talk incessantly without waiting for a pause in the conversation. Children should be alerted against monopolizing conversation. And, above all, children should be taught that contradicting their elders in public is strictly taboo.

4. **Compliments.** Teach your child how to graciously accept a compliment on his behavior, his clothing or his piano playing. Many children just hang their heads and blush or refuse to speak when an adult makes a complimentary remark. It need be nothing more than, "Thank you very much. I'm glad you like it." But it is good manners to respond to compliments.

5. **Church and formal occasions.** Many events in the lives of children require them to act in a formal way. These might be church services, baptisms, funerals, weddings, concerts, etc. The child who is always

allowed to run loose around his home, who never settles down to finish a project, who is not given an opportunity to sit quietly and read for 30 minutes, who is never required to stay at the table until the meal is over, is apt to be restless under more formal conditions. It is well to tell the child in advance that it may be difficult for him to sit quietly for one hour but that you will sit next to him and remind him if need be.

A basic set of rules is essential for small children: no talking during church services, no taking off of shoes, no playing with the hymnals or programs and dropping them on the floor, no whispering or loud comments during the concert, no laughing. This doesn't make these events sound like much fun. Frankly, until children are of an age to appreciate the event, they are better left at home. This doesn't mean that we excuse our small children from all formal occasions. Children's attendance at church services and other occasions where they must be quiet and attentive is good training for their later years if not carried to excess. Sometimes you can stimulate their interest by telling them that at the end of the hour you're going to ask them questions to see if they have listened and observed. Young children usually like going to weddings. Here, especially, they should be reminded that they are not the focal point of the event and that it is a privilege to be asked to attend.

6. **Letter writing.** A child should be instructed that in accepting a gift he also accepts the responsibility for writing a thank-you note within 48 hours. How to write these letters has already been described in detail in Chapter 12.

7. **Introductions.** Introducing one person to another often throws adults into a tizzy so how can we expect our children to do it with good grace? Start with the very young and insist that you be introduced properly to his playmate. When our Campfire group had a Mother's Day tea, we rehearsed with the girls the proper introductions for mothers to other mothers, mothers to teachers and mothers to daughters. Once children understand the system, they find it fun and satisfying.

Insist on introductions around the house and your child will grow up to take them in stride. Little children have just two basics to remember: first, the younger person is introduced to the older; and second, a man is introduced to a woman. Of course there are many variations and exceptions that adults will note in the field of introductions, but for children these two rules are sufficient.

The phrase, "May I introduce," is rather formal and so children can be encouraged to use instead "This is." Thus, when Karen is playing with a seven-year-old friend and her aunt is in our home, she would say, "Aunt Elaine, this is Mary Jones." This is an example of the younger person being introduced to the older. Kent, at a Scout meeting, wants me to meet his leader. He would say, "Mother, this is Mr. Lee, my Scout leader." This is an example of a man being introduced to a woman.

You may say, "Why should I bother to teach young children manners? They will be able to pick them up when the occasion calls for them." However, good manners should become so natural that a child is not even aware that he is using them. Manners become crucial in the teens. A youngster at a social function needs to have his or her mind free for conversation and not cluttered with concern over when to put napkin in lap or which fork to use. These things should be second nature to your child and they will be if during the early years you help to make good manners as automatic as possible.

50
Money
Sense

When we think of children and money we automatically think of allowances. However, in giving a child the necessary home education concerning money, we must go far beyond this. The need for budgets, the value of savings and some concept of the cost of supporting oneself — these are essential parts of his education.

The young child's first lesson is to understand our forms of currency. He can trace the coins and learn their names. You can tape each of the small coins to a piece of cardboard and put it on his bureau. A child can learn to differentiate between the various denominations if you let him put money in parking meters and pay for small items you buy.

ALLOWANCES

When a child is about four years old, he is ready for his first allowance. At our house the purpose of an allowance is not to pay for work done. It is the child's own money for being a member of the family. He does his home helps free of charge. If he does a special large job, we may pay him for it. We may choose to pay a child for baby-sitting at home if he could be earning that money elsewhere.

Rather than give a child a weekly allowance, we prefer a monthly allowance for two reasons. First, it provides the challenge of making the money last for an entire month. Second, it gives him the opportunity to spend a larger sum of money at one time rather than weekly on small useless items. You may wish to compromise and pay an allowance on a twice-a-month basis.

How much allowance should a child receive? This depends on the finances of the family, on the child and the life he leads. Paying allowances on a monthly basis, we use the rule that a child gets 50 cents for each year of his age. His allowance is increased annually on his birthday month. Thus, a four-year-old gets $2.00 a month to spend, a seven-year-old $3.50 and a ten-year-old $5.00. We have used this system for many years and found it to be adequate, but inflation may change it. (Teen-agers' allowances are entirely different.)

Allowances vary due to the items they cover. The child should early learn that the demand, "Buy that for me," is not part of his vocabulary. The essentials of life will be provided by his parents; he must add the frills. Thus the model car kits, batteries and other little toys a child finds so important must come out of his allowance. These we call his *wants*. Next come the *treats*, the candy bar on the way home from school, the package of chewing gum, etc. Besides wants and treats, the third item to come out of his allowance is the purchase of family gifts. When we pay a child his allowance, we alert him to his gift needs for the next two months.

Some parents have children pay for the Saturday afternoon movie from their allowances. In this case, the allowance would have to be increased to cover a movie once or twice a month. When a child is eight or nine years old, his church contribution can be added to his allowance. Thus, if he is to give $1.00 a week in Sunday school, his allowance should be increased by $4.00 a month. It is good training for the child to remember that part of the money you've given him on the first day of the month is already spoken for and must last the entire month. At first, check on church mornings to make sure he has his Sunday school contribution and compliment him when he has the specified amount the last Sunday of the month.

At age twelve, a child's school bus fares, if any, can be added to his allowance. At this age many families establish the child's clothing budget and gradually launch him on the purchase of his own clothing. This takes advance financial planning but in about 30 minutes once a year you can figure out with your child what his clothing needs will be, divide by twelve and give him this additional amount. Some twelve-year-olds can't handle this much responsibility but if they are not started then, they should be by fourteen.

For children under twelve, the allowance usually does not cover school supplies, clothing, bus fares or school lunches. We have made one exception. If the child has been supplied, for example, with a notebook and gym shoes and carelessly loses them, he should contribute to the replacement of them out of his own money. When a child realizes the cost of what we give him, he'll take better care of those items.

TWO "DON'TS"

1. Don't refuse to let your child spend his money as he chooses. His allowance is his very own and you must let him have the experience of spending and even wasting it. You can counsel him about the fragility of a toy he is about to select but he must decide. He will quickly learn a sense of values if given his head concerning the spending of his allowance.

2. Don't issue credit or advances on allowances. Few items are so essential that their purchase can't be postponed until next month. An exception might be made when a child receives an unexpected invitation to go with a friend to a movie. Rarely make an exception and then make a big point of it. Living on credit will be a lesson he will learn all too soon as an adult. We needn't encourage it at the juvenile level.

Gifts for birthday parties are usually paid for by the parents until the child is twelve, when the sum is budgeted into his allowance.

FAMILY FINANCES

A child who understands the cost of toys is ready to understand a little of family finances. Don't hesitate to let your children know the weekly grocery bill, the price of going out for dinner, the cost of taking several children to a movie. Don't stress these so the child feels guilty about social events but let him know how much these cost the family.

If the family takes a two-week vacation, the child should be aware of the general cost of such an adventure. Let him calculate how many miles we get on a gallon of gasoline and what it costs to run the car.

By the time your child is ten years old, he should know the cost of homes in your neighborhood and also what your monthly mortgage payments are. The year Wendy first went to camp, she was impressed with the high cost. The day I took her shopping for her camping supplies, I had her keep a list of what we spent for blue jeans and horsemanship equipment so she would know the complete cost of this important experience.

The high and rising cost of home repairs can be made pertinent to a child. Perhaps he will then deal more kindly with television sets and toys and even be inspired to learn how to fix them!

BUDGETS AND SAVINGS

Giving the allowance on a once or twice monthly basis teaches the child restraint in not spending it all at once. This is a lesson he must learn for himself. Let him blow his allowance on the second day of the month. He will soon learn the importance of budgeting his funds.

By the time the child is nine or ten, he can prepare a simple budget for his allowance. If he has about $5.00 to spend each month, you can show him how he can spend $2.00 for an airplane kit, $2.00 for a movie matinee and still have $1.00 left for other treats.

Children should have the opportunity to earn additional money if they choose, through paper routes, baby-sitting and even home tasks for which you are willing to pay. When grandparents give money gifts for birthdays or Christmas, counsel your child to spend these windfalls wisely. A crisp ten-dollar bill is exciting to spend and can be frittered away on fifty-cent items. Encourage the child to spend it on one worthwhile gift.

When a child receives this much money at one time, it is easy to introduce him to the concept of a savings account. Few children can save anything out of their monthly allowances, but when one has a ten-dollar bill, setting aside ten percent in a savings account is not hard. When a child is seven or eight, a small savings account makes a superb birthday gift from parents or grandparents. Children enjoy the excitement of going to a savings institution, having their own passbook and seeing how their money grows. If a child is given money for his grades, it should be understood that ten percent of these special funds be added to his savings account.

Don't hesitate to let your child use money from his savings account, especially for a major item such as a bicycle or tape recorder. Some children can save enough money to pay for a week of camp. With a goal, a child will save much more quickly. However, if we never let him spend his savings or part of it, he may become discouraged and disinterested. We can set an example as parents when we save as a family for a particular goal: a special trip, furniture or a canoe.

By the time a child is eleven or twelve, he is ready to take a small interest in the larger picture of finances. The cost of running the government in his city, the budget of his nation, the cost of a jet may not be fascinating but these items in the news will begin to give him some perspectives on finances beyond the family level.

Many parents feel that mentioning money to children places an unnecessary burden on them. However, keeping children financially naive is a great unkindness and does them harm in later years. Young people going off to college at seventeen or eighteen are in control of large sums of money, as is the high school graduate on his first full time job. Advance financial training before we turn them loose is essential. I recall in college a fine young woman who was attending school on the insurance money that came to her as a result of her father's death. She had no idea how to budget. The excitement of being able to buy fur coats and other luxuries was soon dampened when she realized she had spent half the money in one year. Happily, she got a grip on things (and a job) but it was a hard lesson.

However, we must not stress the cost of everything so that our children see existence in a dollar-and-cents framework. If our lives demonstrate that intangible values are uppermost, we can afford to be frank about dollars and cents and keep money in its proper perspective.

51
Education
For Future Homemakers

Toddlers to teens can benefit from home instruction in gardening, auto care, home economics and home maintenance. Let's consider a few areas that will be important in any child's future...boys and girls.

HOUSECLEANING

It's important to let a child know what's involved in cleaning a home. Even pre-school children can dust flat surfaces and some of them are quite exceptional in working on those hard-to-dust places such as the intricate legs of tables.

When a child has made a mess, such as spilling a glass of milk, he can learn to wipe it up properly. Now is the time to familiarize him with the pail and mop but don't make cleaning a punishment. If a paper-cutting project has left many tiny scraps on the floor, let the children know that they are welcome to use the vacuum cleaner. Show them how to plug it in and use it. Once you feel they understand it, give them blanket permission to use it when necessary.

A child can be his own housekeeper in his own room. An adult may do the vacuuming, but let the child dust his shelves and furniture and even wash his own windows, if it's safe to do so.

While most cleaning is an expected contribution to the home, you can pay for extra tasks. One busy spring I made a list of all the cupboards, bureaus and closets in the house and offered our children, who were short of spending money, the opportunity to help with the housecleaning. They would get paid if they followed these rules:

1. Inform me that they were emptying a particular cupboard.
2. Carefully remove the contents and wash all the shelves with a prescribed detergent and two rags, one to wash and one to dry.
3. Set the pail on several thicknesses of paper.
4. Install new shelf paper and call me to inspect it.
5. Leave the contents of most shelves for me to sort out and reorganize.

I was pleasantly surprised with the children's gusto in tackling this project. The coins it cost me were small in comparison with the skills they developed and the free time I got in return.

Let children also clean the car — glove compartment, windows, carpets and floor mats. If you have a place where they can use hoses, this can be a popular assignment if you don't mind absolutely drenched children.

HOME REPAIRS

Pre-school children can learn the names of tools and serve as helpers and retrievers for dad or mother when it's home repairs time. They should be taught what each tool does, how to carry and use it safely. Safety can be taught without fear. Simply explain good usage without negatives. As soon as a child is old enough to be careful with electric sockets, he can be in charge of changing light bulbs.

If you include the children in the repair of toys, in the gluing of doll dishes and the intricate work of replacing missing wheels on little cars, you will find they often take better care of their possessions.

Children can do simple painting and carpentry with supervision. We have friends whose eleven-year-old boy replaced several broken screens for the family. Another boy replaced all the faucet washers in the house.

LAUNDRY EQUIPMENT

For some reason little boys enjoy running the laundry equipment much more than do little girls. Teach a child the importance of sorting clothing properly before loading the machine. Boys should not be exempt from the knowledge of clothes sorting. Had my husband been given proper training, he would not have put a green rug in with white diapers and thus our first child would not have had pale green diapers the first year of her life!

During the summer let children do a load of their own wash by themselves and fold their own clothes. Show them how to run both the washer and the dryer. With most clothes permanent press today, you can let them practice ironing on a simple dress or shirt for the experience.

SEWING

Don't teach sewing to a child by assigning him the mending. Buttons, yes, but mending, no. Let him work on something that gives him a sense of creative achievement.

Even boys are fascinated with the capabilities of the sewing machine. Kent once stitched up a shirt for his GI Joe doll. Children as young as eight or nine are ready for a sewing course. If you are not adept at teaching sewing, community groups usually offer classes. Whether your youngsters go on to make their own clothes is not important although the teen-age desire for a vast wardrobe can be most easily satiated if the teen-ager knows how to sew. The older children in the family can often teach the younger. We have a seven-year-old neighbor who has already produced two very respectable A-line shifts. On his mother's machine, a teen-age boy cousin made new plastic seatcovers for his secondhand car.

COOKING

If you set up your household chores so that your child is an assistant at supper, he will naturally take an interest in doing more of the creative work in the kitchen.

By age four or five, a child, with supervision and prior safety instruction, should be able to turn the burners on and off for you. Children of this age can make jello, simple puddings and toast. By kindergarten age they can fry bacon and cook frozen vegetables. As soon as they can read, they are ready to follow recipes, first the slice and bake cookies, then cake mixes and finally "scratch" recipes.

By eight or nine they should be able to make some dishes entirely by themselves. These include the warming of prepared and canned foods and the making of simple box meals such as macaroni. By age ten most children should be liberated enough in the kitchen to use a cookbook with little guidance. Fine children's cookbooks are available for step-by-step instruction.

When I married I didn't know how to cook. Every day I had to call my mother for menu ideas and detailed cooking instructions. For this reason I have insisted that our children know what goes on in the kitchen. Granted, some of the things we serve are not too tasty, but it's all in the learning process. And now, with microwave cooking, our children are good cooks — and fast.

The following two recipes are typical of what your younger children can do without your being in the kitchen. I have written these in a simple style so that young children can follow them.

Wendy's Cheese Fluff

What to use: Four regular pieces of white or wheat bread
One pound of cheddar cheese, sliced
½ teaspoon of dry mustard
One teaspoon of salt
One cup of milk
Two eggs
Butter or margarine for greasing

How to:

Grease a round casserole with the butter. Break the bread into pieces about one inch in size and put in the bottom of

256

the casserole. Lay the sliced cheese over the top of the bread. Scatter the salt over the cheese. Scatter the mustard on top. With a hand beater, mix the eggs and then add the milk to them. Mix again. Pour this liquid mixture into the casserole. Cover the casserole and let it sit for one hour. Set the oven for 350 degrees. Place the casserole in the oven on the middle shelf and bake uncovered for 45 minutes. This should serve a family of four.

Kent's Seven Layer Cookies

Put half a stick of margarine or butter in a rectangular cake or lasagna pan. Place this in the oven as the oven preheats to 350 degrees. When melted, put the following evenly on top of the butter in this order:

> 1 cup graham crackers — you can use the pre-crushed variety or whirl crackers in blender or food processor. Pat these into the butter.
> 1 six-ounce can coconut
> 1 six-ounce package of chocolate bits
> 1 six-ounce package of butterscotch bits
> 1 cup of chopped nuts

Then pour a can of sweetened *condensed* milk over the top. Bake at 350 degrees for 20 to 30 minutes. Cut these into squares while they are still warm.

This is an ideal recipe for young children since it is made right in the pan and requires no mixing. Even children too young to be involved with the oven can make Seven-Layer Cookies once you have melted the butter for them.

When children have made part of a meal, praise them for their work and let them present their dish with flair to the family. Such skills should be encouraged and the occasional flops overlooked.

Even though a cake falls, a shirt shrinks or a toy breaks again after a child repairs it, remember that only through practice and home education will the child reach perfection in these household talents.

52
Educational Experiences In The Community

Even the smallest community has places that can offer education to a child. It's up to us as parents to get the child to these places and to encourage him to take advantage of them. The following list will start you thinking about your community's free facilities that can enhance your child's life.

1. **The library.** Besides lending books, many libraries offer educational programs and story hours. Many also lend art prints, records, films and cassettes.

2. **The art museum.** Visits to the art museum may lead to classes for artistically inclined children.

3. **Science museums and planetariums.** Depending on your location, you may tour scientific research centers concerned with oceanography, ecology and botany.

4. **Historical sites.** A knowledge of local history can increase a child's pride in his community and nation. Children should be aware of local historical places and patriotic organizations.

5. **Government.** Children of age seven or eight are ready to understand the basics of government and will enjoy a trip to the town hall, city hall or state capital. Our school system invites legislators to school events; the children write to legislators on current issues, good practice for the future.

6. **Police and fire stations.** Many schools take pupils on tours of police and fire stations. If yours doesn't, you will find these services most eager to explain their duties to your children. Cities near the water have fire boats and children are invited to go aboard to see the fire-fighting equipment.

7. **Gas and electric companies.** While the intricate operations of these companies are usually beyond young children, they offer some useful services: material concerning the functions of home appliances, cooking and baking ideas, even cooking classes for children.

8. Social services. Y's and Boys' and Girls' Clubs may fit into this category and offer classes for children. Also include visits to places such as the Seeing Eye Dog Center and the Humane Society. Even if you are not in the market for a dog, children need to be aware of the services offered by animal protection agencies.

9. Conservation. If you are near parks or fish and game sanctuaries, you and your children will find the talks and walks provided by the rangers worthwhile.

10. Businesses. Ice cream plants, dairy farms. factories and banks often have tours. Some stores provide educational activities and classes for children. Our local shopping plaza recently sponsored a children's art contest. One large department store has a yearly poise course for eleven-year-olds. Group tours behind-the-scenes in supermarkets, department stores and plazas may be available.

By the time a child is age seven or eight, he is beginning to realize that his world goes beyond his family, that he is part of a large society with responsibilities and problems. Help him to become familiar with his community, how it functions and how it serves and protects him.

53
Being
Our "Brother's Keeper"

The Bible tells us that we are our "brother's keeper," a concept that can be instilled in very young children. A child's first opportunities to do something for someone else often come in school when he makes gifts for Mother's Day or Father's Day. However, many schools are now aiming their service projects toward the more needy. Scout and Campfire groups are finding that children seven, eight and nine years old can work in service projects for the less fortunate.

What home support can we provide for this important concept of taking a genuine interest in our neighbors? By our own attitudes when helping others, we teach our children generosity, compassion and humility.

WORKING THROUGH ORGANIZED GROUPS

Most school, Scout or Campfire groups have a yearly service project. If you are in a position of leadership, remember that at Christmas and Easter the aged, ill and underprivileged are generally deluged with favors and for the rest of the year are unfortunately forgotten. Thus an occasional service project that is not tied to a holiday is a good idea. Here are a few suggestions:

1. Small dried flower arrangements for hospital trays.

2. Place mats for hospitals or senior citizen homes. Make these out of old sheets cut with pinking shears. The children color them with crayons, then seal them between two pieces of waxed paper with a hot iron to make them more durable.

3. Tiny toys. For children's hospitals, fill tiny boxes with ten or twelve very small toys, purchased or handmade. Spray these treasure boxes gold and label with each patient's name.

4. Scrapbooks. Make inexpensive scrapbooks containing cartoons, pictures to color, puzzles and other items of interest depending on the age of the recipient. Sunday newspapers are valuable sources of material.

5. Entertainment. Children's groups are often welcome to bring their music to hospitals and homes at any time of year. I know of one senior citizens' home that has open house for young children each Thursday afternoon. Children's groups come and play checkers and other games with the residents. Many of these people, cut off from contacts with children the age of their own grandchildren and great-grand-children, find this a joyful experience.

6. The Twelve Days of Christmas. One of the most rewarding service projects I was ever involved with was the creation of the Twelve Days of Christmas for a local Shriner's hospital. For the 40 children in the hospital we prepared 40 bags into which we placed twelve individually wrapped gifts, one to be opened on each of the Twelve Days of Christmas. This gave the young hospitalized children something to anticipate each day. The twelve gifts were inexpensive. We cut large coloring books into six-page sections to give each child along with several crayons. Another gift was a candy treat approved by the hospital staff. Still another was a small paper doll that we had made with a cone shaped skirt and a marble to make the doll roll around on their bed trays.

GIVING SERVICE IN THE NEIGHBORHOOD

You cannot legislate generosity or selflessness. However, by example and encouragement, young children will surprise you in their desire to do something for a neighbor. Some suggestions are:

1. Care for a young child while his mother shops. The "sitter" should be at least ten or eleven and responsible.
2. Rake leaves for an older couple.
3. Bake cookies for a new mother or for a busy person.
4. Telephone a shut-in.
5. Send a card to someone who needs a pen pal or friend.
6. Help a busy, childless neighbor with tasks around the house.
7. Make a casserole for a neighbor on moving day.
8. Teach a sport, like skating, to a younger child.
9. Give a new-in-the-neighborhood child a back yard get-acquainted party.

HOLIDAY GIVING

For several years Kent was asked each Thanksgiving to bring canned goods to school. The project was so poorly explained that the class never knew why or to whom they were giving. Obviously, we often cannot see the recipient of our giving but still we must instill in our children the desire to give.

It is a tradition in our home that we "adopt" a needy family for Christmas. In our community we are permitted under certain circum-stances to make direct contact with the recipient family. Out of our own

Christmas budget our children buy a small tree and simple decorations. We then go together to the grocery store and select a holiday meal, items that are not perishable. To this we add one "spectacular" which might be a small turkey or ham.

One year it so happened that our Christmas family's children and our children were almost identical in sex and age. We shopped for a suitable new gift for each member of the family. Then, I left it up to the children as to just what extra thing they would like to give. Wendy not only selected some clothes that she had nearly outgrown and a few that she didn't like; she also chose one particular dress that I knew she liked very much. She found it especially satisfying to give something she was enthusiastic about. It's far too easy to be unselfish when we are not personally affected.

Kent's idea of sharing was to collect lots of his nails, wire and extra tools and also to start a wood project for his counterpart. Karen, who has somewhat of a miserly reputation around our house, surprised everyone by deciding that she would take several months' allowance and buy an extra toy for her friend.

Even when we have not personally delivered our Christmas items to the family, we have discussed the family's problems and what social government agencies can provide to alleviate their condition. When we have been permitted to take the materials to the family, our children have seen government housing and welfare in action and have made some firsthand observations of their own.

When children are directly involved in giving to the community, they are far more understanding of the volunteer hours and evening meetings of their parents. In this regard, it's well to talk with the children about the service you give and the good it provides for the less fortunate.

54
Travel
As An Educational
Experience

When planning a vacation with your children, home education will make the experience much more rewarding. Whether the trip is of 50 or 5,000 miles, familiarize your children with the geographical location through map study. Write for brochures and mount them where the children will see them often. Check out travel and tour guidebooks at the library. Spend mealtimes talking about what you will see.

If the trip is for more than a week, earmark a large envelope for each day and let the children put into it pictures of what they hope to see, brochures and other information. These envelopes also provide a place to keep receipts and other papers picked up during the trip. On the front of each envelope the children can register where they are going that day, what sights they plan to see, what they wish to buy and where they are staying overnight. A child interested in maps can also list the proposed routes and mileage.

PACKING

Include the children in the packing. Wash-and-wear clothes, things that look good a second day, clothes that don't mind crushing make for good traveling. Avoid clothes that MUST be dried flat or drip-dried. Sometimes there just won't be time for such things. Sturdy clothes, well-sewn buttons and hems, and new shoelaces make for less on-the-scene maintenance. Each child should be responsible for seeing that all his belongings are in his case each morning when the family moves on to the next stop.

Distribute the suitcases to each child's bedroom in advance of the trip so they can pack special items. Show the children tricks of good packing. To keep your own sanity, help pack all children's cases in the same manner. For instance, put all socks in the lefthand pocket. Stack the dress-up clothes at the bottom, the moderate clothes in the middle and the play clothes on top. In a plastic bag put the items that are needed each night:

pajamas, robe, slippers, toothbrush, hairbrush, etc.

Give each child a little carry-along case of his own — an airline flight bag is ideal. The car (or plane or train) will not become a shambles if each child has a place to keep personal things for day use. Items in the carry-along case should be selected on the basis of long interest value under mobile and possible solo conditions. Standard items for carry-along might be these:

1. A sweater
2. A new book
3. A snack that will not melt
4. Hairbrush and other necessary daytime cosmetics
5. A small toy
6. A notebook and pen
7. A small scrapbook, jar of paste and blunt-tip scissors
8. A plastic bag for gathering such things as rocks, flowers, shells, etc.

Once when we took a once-in-a-lifetime European trip with the children, I listed every item each had with him and pinned the list to the inside cover of each case. At the top I printed, "Did you see these items today when you packed?" We traveled for five weeks with four children and lost only one headband. Halfway through that trip, Karen's case got quite messy. When we next went through a border crossing, the customs official looked at all our luggage, picked out Karen's, opened it and shook his head. When he hesitated a moment before filling out the forms an electric feeling swept over the children. They thought that because Karen's case was so bad we might be detained at the border! Of course, this was not so but from then on when anyone's case got disorganized, we would playfully threaten customs incarceration!

Each child should have a small cloth or plastic bag for soiled clothes. I've found it best to have sufficient clothes to go five or six days, then stop at a laundromat. However, some families like to do a little wash each night.

A JOURNAL AND SCRAPBOOK

Provide each child with a small notebook in which to keep a trip diary and a scrapbook in which to paste travel items. The journal and scrapbook will keep the children busy at boring times in the car or in the evening when the entertainments of the day are over. Then, as programs, scenic place mats, admission tickets, etc. are accumulated they can be put right into the book in the right order. If you wait until you get home, this scrapbook will never get made and the material will sit on a shelf until it's no longer useful. Make the scrapbook en route and it's much more meaningful, especially for end-of-the-day reviews. Children who prefer a scrapbook to a travel journal can, with a ballpoint pen, write the day's events on the page opposite the mementos.

STOP OFTEN

On cross-country travel, hundreds of miles day after day, travel with young children is more pleasant if it begins early in the morning. Since youngsters are generally early risers, you might as well travel for an hour before breakfast. Often little ones will fall back to sleep in the car for another hour or more. The later breakfast gives you a breather after a couple of hours of morning travel and affords everyone a chance to look for the right restaurant or spot for a breakfast picnic.

Using this system, you next stop mid-morning for gas, at eleven o'clock just to let everyone get out and run up and down a hill, and at noon for lunch. By three o'clock you can be at your day's destination with a good portion of the time left for sightseeing, or if it's just an overnight stop, for a walk, a movie or a dip in the motel pool.

There is much merit to letting children work off some steam on a long car trip. A game of tag in a field adjacent to the road or turning off into a gravel road to run a few relay races will do wonders for everyone's disposition. Use this as an opportunity to rearrange everyone in the car. At least it gives everyone a new person to talk with.

CAR ASSIGNMENTS

Giving the children responsibilities in the car also helps to make the ride more fun. One can be song chairman, another food chairman, a third in charge of safety. The safety chairman's job is to make sure that the people are always seated, strapped in and not hanging out windows or unlocking doors. The song chairman can call for any song he chooses and the food chairman has the right to recommend where or when to eat.

If you have a station wagon, create different activity areas within the car. The child who wants to speak with mother and dad can have the middle spot in the front seat. Those who want to read can be in the library or second row. Game players can be in the rear section. You may also wish to create a "kitchen" area where food is kept and snacks are prepared. On a day-long trip, a car may need to be divided at different times into different sections including a quiet sleeping area. If traveling children must arrive somewhere refreshed but insist they cannot sleep in the car, tell them they need only pretend to doze. A good pretender often falls asleep!

CO-PILOT

Most children exult in being co-pilot in charge of telling the driver where he is and where he's going. The co-pilot sits in the front seat and is in charge of the map. He needs to know at all times the route number on which the car is traveling and the next route to be taken.

The child co-pilot determines the number of miles to the junction and by gauging how long it takes the car to cover a certain number of miles, he can estimate times of arrival at towns and scenic points. The co-pilot is in charge of announcing items of interest along the way and enlisting the help of others to look for scenic spots and important junctions. Your lessons on map reading and local geography take on immediate practical value.

A child who can add a column of figures can keep the trip financial log. This can be a simple list to cover food, entertainment, gas, purchases and lodging. It's a good education for children to know the costs involved on a trip of more than a day or two.

Another child can be in charge of the guidebook. As sights are about to come into view, he can read to everyone what's to be observed. Although it's well to discuss significant spots prior to a trip, it certainly helps to refresh a child's memory in the hour before he is to visit an important battleground, mountain or church.

One of the least enjoyable but most essential jobs on a car trip is that of custodian. This is the person who picks up all the scraps and paper napkins, empties the litter bag, puts the games back in the toy bag and leaves the car tidy for the next event. If you rotate the job of co-pilot, historian, snack preparer, etc. among the children, also rotate the job of car custodian.

EATING EN ROUTE

When you travel for many days with children, it's to your advantage to avoid three daily restaurant meals. Stopping at a grocery store for some peanut butter and jam, a loaf of bread, fruit, cookies and milk or juice breaks the restaurant routine. On a trip such as this you may want to carry a cooler for perishable items and cold drinks. Get as many things in individual packages as possible, especially drinks, so you don't have to pour from a bottle at 55 miles an hour.

In the glove compartment of your car keep a few rolls of mints and extra paper napkins. Most cars are equipped with a tissue dispenser and a litter bag. For a really long trip with toddlers, take a portable toilet. Include a package of lotion-saturated tissues that let you refresh your face and hands at a moment's notice. One of my vivid recollections of childhood travel was a Mason jar filled with about two inches of soapy water and a wash cloth. This was my mother's method of sponging the jam and chocolate off of us on a long trip.

Another item to keep tucked under the seat of your car is a set of trays. These are ideal for lunches in or out of the car, for writing and for games.

The end-of-the-day dinner is often the long, expensive meal where your children practice their table manners and conversational abilities. If you are going to another country, tell the children about the food specialties they can try. It's often just the *name* of a food that scares them. Our children thought wiener schnitzel, strudel and oxtail soup sounded awful until they tasted them. They soon became favorites.

Consider split orders for young children. Nothing is more discouraging to them and to your wallet than wasted food. Include the children in selecting restaurants. When you arrive at the day's destination, drive up and down the main street and through outlying areas, check your guidebooks and let the children help choose the spot for the evening meal. If no entertainment is scheduled after dinner, give children some exercise — a walk to look in shop windows, a romp through the park or even blind man's bluff in the hotel room.

TOYS AND GAMES

Before going on a long trip, buy a new collection of inexpensive books, games and toys for the children. Wrap and label these for each day of the trip. Then when someone's temper is short or everyone is bored with road games, have each child take a turn reaching down into the "if all else fails" bag and coming up with some new goodie. A felt marking pen, one of those little hand puzzles where you try to get the metal ball into the little hole, a punch-out paper doll book, a book of crossword puzzles and other easy to handle items can keep everyone in the car happy for a long time simply because of their novelty. Avoid toys with sharp corners, any that require scissors, and those with small, losable pieces. A few paperback books and a pillow will help make car travel more enjoyable.

SHOPPING

Each child traveler should take some of his spending money and perhaps some of his savings. If shopping will be a prime feature on the trip, advise children to save or earn extra money. If you travel yearly with your children, suggest they specialize in some item they wish to collect, such as a music box from each spot visited, a charm, a doll, a wood carving.

We also let it be known that we will purchase one item for each child on the trip. Knowing that they will get only one free gift, the children are very careful in selecting that most important remembrance.

In the days before the trip, let the children print the names and addresses of their friends on small labels. Then as they buy postcards along the way, they will have only to stick the label on the postcard, write a message and send it off.

It's best to be frank with children when they are caught in a souvenir shop. Teach them to ask themselves these questions: Is this item worth it? Will I play with it? Can I get it better at home? Will it fall apart? Tell them what the specialties of the area are so that they will not buy junk.

HOTELS AND MOTELS

When the signing-in ceremony at a hotel or motel is over, turn the children loose for awhile with the understanding that they are to quietly explore the location. This gives you a chance to unpack your luggage while the children collect information as to where the mail chute is, what time the dining room opens, where the laundry is, etc. If children are to stay in a room separated from the parents, let them take turns being in charge of room neatness, safety, cleanliness and quietness. Alternate the jobs so there won't be antagonism. Connecting rooms are best but sometimes not available.

MAKING THE TRIP FUN FOR CHILDREN

A married couple traveling together has entirely different tastes from a family on vacation. While you don't want the children to run the vacation to the exclusion of your interests, you still want the trip to be educational fun for the children. Children enjoy simply stopping along roadsides, romping in parks and playing with other children. If you are visiting friends along the way, bring your children up-to-date on these friends and their children. When the visit is over, see what new things your children have learned from them. If you cross borders, ask your children to keep a list of foreign words they have used. Make children feel essential on the trip. Let them be the postcard writers and mailers. Help each to become an authority on mileage, mountains, special trains, etc.

Occasionally take in some program that is strictly for children such as a marionette show, boat ride, zoo or carnival. As a special treat, let them visit a toy store, even if without purchasing. When they will be staying up later than usual for an evening entertainment, forewarn them that they will be expected to nap.

Encourage them to be outgoing, to get to know other children on the trip, to talk with and understand the people who are living in that area. Help them to be observant as to what is different from home.

BAD TRAVELERS

For children who are obstreperous or ornery on car trips, it's best to explain in advance the difficulties of being in close quarters with several people over many hours. Ask the child for ideas on how to make the event a smooth one. If he realizes that he *is* going on the trip, that there's nothing he can do about it and that it is up to him whether it is a treat or a trial, he may pitch in to make it more fun. If you have several mischief-makers, pick the most disruptive and make him chairman of peace and harmony.

THE REWARDS OF TRAVEL

In our travels with the children, I have noted these gains:
1. A better understanding of the size of our country and the world.
2. The realization that other people in other areas have their own

dignity and are nice to know.

3. A recognition of different lifestyles in hot and cold climates.
4. An appreciation of other foods and other ways of eating.
5. An awareness of architectural differences in various parts of the world and within the United States.
6. Growing evidence of responsibility and flexibility. (You are not "taking" your children on a trip; they are helping to lead.)
7. An understanding of history.
8. The ability to talk about a trip, to verbalize and to meet strangers with poise.
9. Better decision making — what to buy, what to eat, where to go.
10. More naturalness, happiness and good behavior in public.
11. An expanding vocabulary that includes regional or foreign words, place names and names of unusual foods.

12. The education that new experiences bring. When we lived in Hawaii and Mark was just six, we made a very special trip to Switzerland. When we landed and our guide met us, I noticed that Mark was looking sad. I asked him what the matter was. "The people on this island don't really like us. They haven't brought us a flower lei." He quickly learned two lessons: that all visitors everywhere don't receive leis and that everyone in the world doesn't live on an island!

Parents must face the facts: if children don't know right from wrong at home, if they fight constantly with each other, if they can touch everything in the local shops, if they have no manners, if they don't know how to talk or think for themselves, no one can expect them to act differently on a trip. Children often become excited on a trip and don't always behave as well as we expect them to. However, we can tell when our children are ready for travel by their responsibility and actions on the home front. Home training and home education make the difference between a memorable trip and a nightmare.

Kent's teacher asked him to write a summary of the Swiss trip when we returned home. He was to tell how the country was different, what he liked better, what he would like to do again. He wrote, "I would like to go skiing again when my hands are bigger and warmer. I would like to live where I can hear cow bells in the morning. It isn't too hard to learn a foreign language. Let's have wiener schnitzel at home. I wish I had a tram car to go to school on. America isn't the only good place."

Your Week Five Check List

Here are six assignments to tie in with home education.

1. Find the chapter that corresponds with your child's age and compare his basic skills, literary tastes and abilities with games and toys.
   Toddlers —chapters 44 and 45
   Five- to seven-year-olds —chapter 46
   Eight- and nine-year-olds —chapter 47
   Ten- and eleven-year-olds —chapter 48
   Take action to improve his abilities in these areas:
2. Start observing table manners and other social graces. Introduce the ideas from this chapter one at a time.
3. Discuss allowances. Learn what your child plans to do with his money and how he will budget, spend and save.
4. Introduce both boys and girls to homemaking—and home repair —skills.
5. Enable your child to give service through an organized group or an informal neighborhood project.
6. With the help of the family, make a list of nearby places to visit — recreational areas, museums, historical and government sites. Plan to visit one each month.

When you have your next vacation, re-read the chapter on travel.

Now, onward to Week Six!

Week
Six

6
6
6
6
6
6
6
6
6
6
6
6
6
6

Problem Solving:
Planning And
Explaining Ahead

If you feel that your children's formative years are a series of problems, think of them as opportunities to teach children how to settle differences, to live in a group and to plan ahead so as to *avoid* problems. Children function best when there are certain basic rules that they understand and follow and when they know that certain actions will be taken if their behavior is undesirable. In problem-solving a family can reason together over possible solutions to specific conflicts. However, some decisions must be made by parents alone and others must be properly made by the child. Teaching a child to think for himself and to solve his own problems prepares him for temporary absences of his parents and for emergencies.

55
The
Family
Council

Even a one-child family should periodically sit down together to chart the direction it's going or to settle some common problem. This may be done informally; but a large family may require the calling of a family council meeting. Such a get-together can be very casual, but if the matter is a serious one, it's well to treat it on a dignified and serious basis.

We have a weekly meeting at which we consider matters of current interest to the entire family, events of the upcoming week, plans for the future, unsolved problems as well as some ethical or religious question. The family council is democracy in action in the home. Before presenting a problem to the family council, the parents must agree that it is one they wish the entire family to decide. Sometimes a subject is brought up but it must be decided by parents only or children only. For once the question is posed, the parents must be willing to abide by the group's decision. Once the decision has been made, it's up to the parents to see that it is carried out. At a family meeting, expect the unexpected!

Sometimes when children are angry with one another, it helps to list the details of the gripe. Kent insisted on a family meeting to consider his multitudinous complaints against Wendy. Since he does not speak as effectively as he could, he wrote down his complaints in his inimitable handwriting: "Wendy made a servant out of me. 1) She made me pick up the game we were playing, 2) She told me to shut the door, 3) I had to bring her a potato chip on a plate."

While this may seem like a small item, Kent was very upset. It also pointed out a trend we parents had just become aware of. After Kent read his paper, we asked Wendy if this was true and she admitted it was. We then discussed how we would feel if the roles were reversed. Next we considered what was fair among brothers and sisters. In a friendly way without shouting and threats, the older children concluded that they must not boss the younger. The point was made and that was the end of the problem.

274

On another weekend the children were being extremely cantankerous and unloving to each other and to us. We called a family meeting, gave everyone paper and pencil and asked them to write down an idea on how they felt family harmony could be restored. Wendy wrote, "The day seems so long today. Let's have something to look forward to." It was the middle of a three day weekend for which we hadn't done any real planning. Although certain days can be fun when they just develop on their own, on this holiday the children felt at loose ends. We suggested a hot dog supper on the beach with another family. The children agreed. Since the idea of planning something to look forward to was Wendy's, this became her afternoon project, with the aid of her brothers and sister, and harmony reigned.

Kent wrote on his paper, "Karen needs to talk more sweetly." Since he could think of no examples when she did not speak sweetly, I gave him my Campfire leader whistle to wear around his neck and told him to blow it anytime he heard her speaking unkindly. Alerting her to the importance of gentle language, we heard the whistle blow only once during the entire afternoon.

On Karen's list were several points that everyone quickly agreed on: "Take turns, do your share, be a peacemaker, give in sometimes, stay out of my room."

Creating a forum for discussion of problems and fears is wise. Sometimes we do not know what our children are really feeling. We will never know what upsets and hurts them unless we give them a quiet opportunity to tell us. At one time we considered and discussed disbanding the family meeting. Wendy said: "It's nice to be together and everyone be able to talk equally and be heard." Kent: "When you're in trouble, you need someone to comfort you and talk you out of it." Karen: "I used to be scared of some things until we began talking about them." Mark: "I can talk just as much as the bigger children and sometimes I have a good idea." We did not disband.

At a family council meeting courtesy and democracy must prevail. Everyone must be heard and decisions should be made on a majority basis. Family meetings shouldn't be called only when things at home become disagreeable. They should be called to discuss future plans and joyful events also. Sometimes the family standing rules cover the situation, but at other times it's up to the family council to decide on corrective measures.

Mark once broke a family eating rule, compounded it by making a large chocolate stain on a white carpet and then further compounded the problem by lying about it. A family meeting was called and the facts presented. Since this offense deserved some punishment, we asked the children what they felt it should be. Their ideas clued us in on what punishment they considered severe enough for breaking rules, spoiling property and lying. The children were candid in discussing how lying reduced their opinion of someone and that it would be awhile before they could believe him again. This made a far deeper impression on Mark than such a statement by us. They felt he should have to pay for the cleaning of the carpet but that since he didn't have sufficient funds to cover it, he should work around the house to pay for it. Mark was quick to suggest some projects which were really fun. However, his sisters and brother felt he should do some work no one liked. Mark weeded one hour a day for one week.

Other than disciplinary action, family councils can discuss values in a changing society, world situations, what to do on the coming holiday, how to resist temptations, desired changes in family life, thoughts while falling asleep, Bible stories, ways of spending free time. These are topics we've considered. We also use our family council meetings as planning sessions before trips. On a regular weekly basis we use them to extend religious training beyond the format provided in Sunday school and church.

As children grow older, have more friends and go more places on their own, many families find that a family day or a family hour is essential to keeping their identity. Some families we know set aside one evening a week for family activities.

One of the greatest purposes of the family get-together is to avoid problems by discussing them before they occur. By positive exploration of ways to achieve desirable behavior, we can make these educational sessions preventive rather than curative. Most important, they keep the lines of communication and discussion open.

A survey of parents shows five areas where most think they could improve their relations with their children:

1. Communicating, being able to find the time and the topics to talk with their children.
2. Expressing patience and understanding to their children.
3. Following through on discipline with children.
4. Having time to enjoy children in a recreational way.
5. Giving the children responsibilities that would help them grow.

56
When
Parents
Must Decide

Parents must make, on their own, certain basic rules, decisions that are not up for consideration by the children. These basic rules may be discussed at family meetings but the final decision rests solely with the parents. These decisions might include the age when a child can cross a street alone, whether children are to open the doors of the house to strangers, at what age a child may stay overnight with a friend, at what age a child may go to a movie with someone of the opposite sex.

Many parents are afraid to make a decision and stick with it. They allow so many exceptions to the rule that the rule does not really exist. If you make a rule, let it be known what the rule is and what the consequences will be if it is broken.

Parents often wisely consult their children on future plans even when the final decision rests with the parents. These decisions include where to go on a vacation, when to move into a new house, what sort of car to drive, whether mother is to return to work, whether junior is to attend summer school, if the family can afford camp for the children. While children's opinions should be respected on these issues, these decisions are usually made by the parents.

If parents consult *with each other* about family problems, they can often see certain trends developing in the children and can either encourage or discourage these. Parents should avoid arguing in front of the children. This makes youngsters feel pressured to side with one parent or the other, not a healthy situation. If you think your child should go to summer school and your spouse doesn't, this question should be settled between the two of you first so that your child is presented with a unified decision.

This brings up the question, are parents always right? Of course we know they aren't! It's important for our children to know that parents aren't always right. Children should be taught from babyhood to see life as a progressive experience, moving toward a fuller expression of their

277

God-given perfection and to realize that the older and more experienced we are, the fewer mistakes we make. This is why parents are in charge of children, not children in charge of parents. Parents should be willing to admit when they have made a mistake and to show the consequences. Children need to know that their parents are human while respecting the decisions parents make.

57
When
Children
Must Decide

Life must not be so organized and outlined for children that they do not find themselves facing frequent choices. Making a decision and reaping the consequences of it is an important part of growing up. Even toddlers can be taught to make choices. Children should early learn to choose what they wish to wear each day, with whom and where they wish to play, and what they wish to do. It should be pointed out to them that they have regular daily choices, and those choices are not always beween right and wrong but between good and better or between better and best.

Children should be given as many choices as possible:

"Of these three vegetables, which one do you want for dinner?"

"Would you like to go to movie A or movie B?"

"Would you like to stay up late tonight or tomorrow night?"

Children like to feel they have had a part in deciding the general rules to live by. At a time when Kent was being obstreperous, I asked him to write a set of rules he felt he could live by. The following is what he wrote. Only the spelling is corrected.

I have decided I could be happy and do the following:

1. Finish with snacks by four o'clock.
2. Snack in the kitchen only until further notice.
3. Ask permission for candy.
4. Use only my own toys unless I ask.
5. Bring inside toys back in at night.
6. Knock on a door when it is closed.
7. Ask if I can see TV.
8. Remember to ask to be excused from the table.
9. Don't invite friends over when parents aren't home.
10. Don't speak sassy to Karen.
11. Do my helps first.
12. Try to appreciate what mother does.
13. Remember that daddy works hard.

14. Don't open house doors without asking who's there.
15. Write down phone messages.
16. Don't waste paper and paint.
17. Don't play around daddy's desk.
18. Remember boy's special bathroom rules.
19. Be mad at myself when I am wrong.
20. Erase, don't scribble over homework.

He created all these rules by himself and I was proud of him. In fact, we discussed them with the other children and he was honored to think that his code of behavior could be useful to others in the family.

At church one Sunday, Mark seemed to do everything possible to distract himself and those around him. When we got home, I asked him to write his *own* code of behavior for church. He wrote:

DON'T
Talk to the person next to me — save it
Rest my head back 'cause I'll snore
Play with the hymn books
Not listen to what's going on

DO
Close my eyes when it is prayer time
Sing when it is singing time
Try to read some of the words in the responsive reading
Put the money in the collection basket
Fold hands and not let them do finger games
Try to remember one thing I learned
Pray that I will be gooder next week

The whole purpose of home education, discipline and planning with a child is to teach him how to act on his own. Thus, we should not feel sad when our children begin to need us less and when they are able to act and decide on their own. When children are left to think for themselves, we should be sure to appreciate their own decisions:

"You did the right thing to open the telegram when it came and we weren't home."

"How smart of you to realize in school that we were going to be out tonight and you would have to do your homework at recess."

"That was a good decision to wash that mud off yourself with the outside hose before coming in."

By being aware of what a child is doing, we can reinforce his confidence in himself and we can give him opportunities to decide things all on his own. All our efforts are contributing toward that time when the children will not have the benefit of our constant presence and advice.

58
What To Do
When One Parent
Is Away

Many fathers work long hours, take business trips and find their home time with their children very limited. In these cases it's up to the mother to create and maintain a two-parent picture even when the facts seem quite contrary. Mother can often speak of "what Daddy and Mother would like." This keeps Daddy in the conversation and in a position of authority and shows his interest in the children even when he is not present. (The same thing applies when father is home and mother is away.)

The at-home parent should avoid deferring all unpleasant situations concerning the child until the other parent's arrival. When a father has limited time with the children, the mother should create pleasant experiences for them together. Mothers should see that the children's homework and daily chores are scheduled so that when father comes home there is time for them to enjoy each other's company. She may find that they enjoy checkers or chess together, home repairs, sitting and reading together or running errands. Whatever those special things are that father enjoys doing with children should be left to them as opportunities for the father to be with the child. In turn she should leave him completely out of those areas in which he is disinterested. If he is not the type to be a Scout leader, then it's up to mother to take on the work as den mother. If he is no good at math, she should take over this aspect of study with the children — or find someone who can.

Since many fathers come home when dinner is over, a father can take over the "tucking in" ceremonies. This gives him a quiet period to talk with each child. A child may wish to have a special welcome home time when dad returns. Some children enjoy helping dad change his clothes, getting his newspaper, bringing him a glass of juice and reading the funnies with him.

When fathers are out-of-town for long periods of time, letters, tapes and cassettes can keep the family close together. A mother's own attitude of respect and appreciation for the father's contributions to family life will help maintain the father image at home.

59
When
Both Parents
Are Away

Parents should not feel guilty about a proper amount of time away from their children. Such times can benefit your children in three ways:

1. The children learn to respect the authority of someone other than their mother and father.
2. The children learn to make decisions on their own.
3. The children can show their parents how well they function in their absence and how the home training has paid off.

Certainly you should prepare your children in advance for your absence. If you are going away on a trip, it helps your children to know where you are going to be, whether it will be a business or a pleasure trip, what you will be seeing and doing and exactly when you will return.

Daily letters and postcards will keep you in touch with your children. Sometime you may wish to leave short letters for the children to read at breakfast each morning to remind them about lunch money, dental appointments, tidying rooms and having fun in your absence. It doesn't take long if you're going to a five-day convention to compose five brief letters of loving support to your children.

The person in charge of the children during your absence, whether it be for an evening or for a week, should understand the children's schedule. I keep a typical schedule on the kitchen bulletin board. Sometimes children will try their "keeper" the first day to see how much they can get by with. The keeper or sitter should be aware of what's expected of the children in the way of daily duties and daily fun.

On the same bulletin board I keep a list of special things to remember, such as: eating is okay in the kitchen, play rooms and outside; no getting out of bed after tucking-in time; no messy play in the living room; always tell where you are going and when you will return; keep out of mom's and dad's desks; don't use other's toys unless you ask; hang up your wet swim suit; shut the door when you go out. Things to remember can be reviewed with the sitter in the presence of the children.

When instructing the person who will care for the children, it's wise to have the children present in case questions arise. My sitter instruction sheet includes telephone numbers of neighbors, friends, relatives and also emergencies and repairs. Such a list takes time to compile but is repeatedly useful. Especially if you are going on a trip, it's essential to list exactly who to call for repair of washer, freezer, car, television, etc.

Rules for the baby-sitter should include:

1. How to answer the telephone
2. How to take messages
3. How long the sitter may use the telephone
4. Information concerning the children's bedtimes
5. Where parents can be reached
6. Not to give out information over the phone unless the caller is known
7. Whether doors are to be opened in your absence
8. Whether the children are to play in the house, in their own yard or in neighbors' yards
9. What to do in case of storms
10. What to do in case a child is injured
11. What television programs may be viewed by the children
12. What the children can eat

Many children view the absence of their parents as an occasion to do exactly as they please. For this reason when I am to be gone for more than an hour, I speak with each child before leaving to find out what he thinks he will be doing while I'm away and also to give some suggestions of things to do. Then upon returning I can see what the children have accomplished. When going out for an evening, I try to organize myself so I can spend the last 30 minutes with the children — I may just sit at the table as they eat their supper, read to them or talk with them. Thus they don't feel that I am always busy and out of their reach or that they are deprived of my attention and counsel.

60
Learning
To Cope
With Emergencies

As soon as a child can navigate by himself, parents should be alert to remove from his reach potentially harmful items. These of course include matches, knives, poisons and sprays, as well as toys that come apart easily or have small pieces.

As a child gets older, you cannot keep harmful items out of his reach and so you must teach him how to avoid them or use them so as not to get hurt. When a child is five or six, he can be taught to slice cucumbers and use a knife safely. Later he can be taught how to use dangerous tools. Even at a simple meal we burn candles. A child of five is ready to learn to light a match properly: by closing the box, by striking the match away from him and by holding it parallel to the table, rather than downward and thus burning his fingers.

It is ignorance that harms children and so it is our job to see that this ignorance is counteracted by intelligence. Because so many things come in spray cans today, we must alert our children to watch the direction they are spraying. Deodorants, hair sprays, insect repellents and paints are potentially dangerous if used improperly.

But what do we do if, despite our care and training, a child does some damage to himself or to a friend? Teach children early to be calm in emergencies. Unless a child should not be moved, it's well to take him away from the scene of the accident and from the presence of other children. In this way we can calm him more easily. This is the time for reassuring talk from parents and for immediate action. After wounds have been washed and bandaged, encourage the child to go right back to what he was doing unless he's been incapacitated.

Make as little as possible of these experiences. Retelling doesn't make less of them. Pity and unnecessary special care don't make a whole and healthy child. Band-aids and mercurochrome are not toys and children should not be painted and decorated with them. Keep a container of bandages in the bathroom, kitchen, playroom and car. Teach children how to use them when they are five or six years old but also insist they report bruises or damages to you so you can be sure the wound is clean and healing properly.

Teach children that the best reaction to a crisis is to *think:* What is the most important thing to do in this emergency? This is the best training. When a half gallon of milk has been dumped off the counter, a child should not sit down and cry or run for the pail or shout for help *until* he has righted the carton and stopped the spilling. If he has spilled red paint on the carpet, he should call for help immediately rather than trying first to clean it up. If a child has broken a quantity of glass around him, he should be taught that his first concern is to extricate himself, especially his bare feet, then call for help.

The preventive is far more important than the curative. Although it takes time to give children the proper warnings, we can save them and ourselves much grief by urging caution in advance. Teach children to respect electrical appliances, to keep forks out of toasters and hands off hot dishes. When riding in cars, show how safety belts are to be buckled, doors locked and door handles left untouched while the car is in motion. In public places train children to keep hands out from between elevator doors and revolving doors. When children are learning to ride bicycles, enroll them in a bike safety course, often given by your local police department or school.

In crossing streets, teach your children to err on the side of being overcautious. In water sports or games, the buddy system should be a standing rule. Before children work with tools, give them a few moments of instruction to save fingers from being hammered or pinched.

Train your child through example and conversation to ask what he can do to be of help in an emergency. Crying, shouting, screaming, condemning and panicking have no merit and compound the trouble. Children should know the phone numbers of their parents at work, the nearest neighbor, the doctor, the police and the fire department.

"What would you do if" is one way of covering many situations with children. When you take your young children out in public, use this line to cover the possibility of their becoming separated from you. Make sure they know that they are either to stay where they are or meet you at a certain place or report to a policeman or salesclerk the fact that they are separated from their parents.

A neighbor once told me that she was running a bathtub for her youngest child when she decided to make a quick trip to a neighbor's house with some cookies. She had been there only a moment when her nine-year-old son came over to say that the bathtub was overflowing. She ran back to the house with him and found that what he said was absolutely true. However, in his haste to let her know of the emergency, he had failed to think ahead and turn the water off! Emergencies are unexpected and we can't cover the proper response to every emergency with our children but we can teach them that the most important response is to *think*.

Talk over with your children how the family could cope with floods, fire, unemployment, war, etc. Prepare your comments ahead of the discussion and don't frighten the child. Assure him that despite emergencies the family continues and so does the parents' love and concern.

When a child is not well, this emergency can have a bright side. He can enjoy home during the day, reading and quiet play. If he can have company but must remain in bed, assign sisters and brothers 30-minute play sessions with him. If he can be up, use the opportunity to talk and work together. So that the day doesn't seem long and boring, make him a schedule such as:

  9:00 Read
10:00 Snack and watch TV
10:30 Rest
11:30 Read mail with parent
12:00 Lunch
12:30 Do homework
  1:30 Call grandparents
  1:45 Rest
  2:45 Read
  3:15 Snack
  3:30 Here let the sisters and brothers take over

Encourage a child to get well. Make his home stay pleasant but serious. Do *not* turn the TV on and forget him! Send him back to school only when he is perfectly healthy — and that can be soon.

61
TV—
No Substitute
For Parents

The argument over television continues. Those in favor of the tube say it improves a child's vocabulary, opens new horizons and educates him. Those opposed say that it makes our children willing nonparticipants, inactive dwellers in a dream world of violence and fantasy.

The true value of television falls somewhere between these two opinions. It can be a useful education and entertainment media but it is no substitute for culture, life, people and real experiences. Thus, as parents we have to see television in perspective and see that it does not take over our children's lives.

The future probably will bring a much greater use of television with, hopefully, more constructive programming. The TV set will become a combination encyclopedia, newspaper, data processing center and game arcade. We can't go back to pre-TV days and we don't want to. Every invention has its usefulness and TV can be the source of great good to children and parents alike. But that good comes with selective useage.

When all the new programs come on in the fall, review the listings with your children. Watch with them any new program you think you would want them to see. After one viewing, you should have a fairly good idea as to its suitability.

Tell the children you will consider programs that they place on a list for your approval. Leave the list-making and the burden of getting the programs approved up to them. With their list in hand, discuss with the children which programs are their real favorites and which they just put on the list as filler.

Set a time limit for viewing each day. It is amazing to think that the *average* child sees TV for 43 hours a week! A more rational approach might be one hour on school nights after homework is under control and two hours on Fridays, Saturdays and Sundays. This makes a total of ten hours a week. In addition to this time control, children should be permitted to see fine specials.

If Saturday morning is your sleep-late morning, you may wish to let your children view the children's shows but make sure that they understand that they are *children's* shows, not shows that are stupid or violent. Children should understand that usually homework and home helps are done before television viewing time and that slipping grades cancel television privileges.

Children with enough active interests don't need their TV time legislated. They will be so involved in play, hobbies and sports that they won't have much time for TV. Even during winter's cold and rainy months there should be attractive alternatives to television. Many families have found that when their television set went out of order, they hardly missed it. You might want to purposely try a TV-less week sometime. You will be surprised at the variety of ways you can spend your time when not being entertained by the tube.

But if TV is to remain a part of family life, introduce news programs, documentaries and cultural television programs to the children. Spend some time looking at these programs as a family. In many communities the movies are undesirable for young children. Yet many fine old movies appear on TV. When a good movie is to be shown on TV, let the children take a rest in the afternoon. Then "go to the movies" with the same preparation as you would if you were driving to the local theater. Line up comfortable chairs or cushions, make popcorn and have your favorite drinks on hand.

Parents often ask, how do you control TV? Simply by saying that the television may not be turned on without a parent's permission and that anyone doing so will watch no TV for a number of days. Children quickly learn to say, "I've finished my homework, Mother, and I've loaded the dishwasher. May I look at TV?" Your answer is, "Yes, as long as you look at one of the shows on the okay list."

If you have fortitude and are in control of what your children do, you are not afraid to walk into a room and simply turn the TV off. Remember that even though television would like to take over the bringing up of your children, you have the right to turn the knob when garbage is being aired or when your child has become stupefied by the set. But you can't fight something with nothing. Attractive home life and suitable alternates such as family-oriented entertainments, books and hobbies will keep your children from an inordinate amount of tube watching.

Television is taking notice of its tremendous impact and is beginning to use its potential for enriching our lives. It's the parents' jobs to help their children discriminate between what is mindless and what is enlightening.

62
Building
Memories

Most of us live too fast to savor our experiences. One event follows another like boxcars in a train and we have little time to anticipate or analyze our lives. Anticipating an event can enhance its joy and in many cases the remembrance can be just as rewarding as the event itself. If we are to build memories for our children, we must do memorable things. Our lives cannot be filled with mediocre events. This doesn't mean every day must be a spectacular. Valleys make the peaks stand out.

The building of memories takes conscious effort and parental planning. Some memorable things *do* just happen; others are part of one's creative planning. In our employment, we look ahead, set certain goals and make plans for the success of our jobs; but at home we so often let things develop without any master plan. Then we look back on mediocrity, drab days, uneventful years, when, with little or no extra expense, we could have created happy memories.

Sit down some evening and ask your child what he remembers of his early years. You'll get a good idea of the types of things that thrill him and make him happy. You may also find that some of the memorable events were catastrophes. Childhood is supposed to be the most joyful time of life and in the 18 or 20 years that our children are living with us, we have thousands of hours for creating memories.

One night the power failed and we completed dinner for 24 guests with the use of candles. Our children were assigned to groups of guests to see that they found powder rooms, places to sit for dinner and finally, a candlelighted song fest. A near-catastrophic social event became a memorable one for our children.

Family holiday traditions are very important. Friends with extensive Thanksgiving traditions have a handmade-by-mother Thanksgiving tablecloth and a set of spectacular turkey serving dishes. The children use these happily each holiday with the understanding that when they have their own homes these Thanksgiving trappings will be divided among them for their families.

Memories are built when families have time to spend together: weekends, holidays or vacations. Our children visit friends around the neighborhood during the week or after their Saturday helps are done, but we have always kept Sunday as a family day, a day to be together, an ideal day for creating memories.

Our children visited cousins years ago and one of their happiest memories was of Sunday evening suppers consisting of crisp apples, pop corn and hot chocolate, eaten on the floor in front of the fireplace. This was a far cry from our heavy Sunday dinners. We adopted this particular tradition and there is still much joy over recalling the memories that it brings back.

Special foods at special times can bring back memories. A tradition of ours is the farewell chicken picnic we give house guests or a particular kind of cake we make to show our appreciation to friends.

When you have taken time to create a memorable party, holiday, evening or trip, build on these events; keep them growing and glowing as happy memories. Remembering travel is easy for we can recall it through our pictures and scrapbooks. Mementos of trips help build memories, too. Wendy collects music boxes for major events in her life and from places she has visited. Even small children who do not collect anything of value can bring back something to remind them of their adventures. Mark can remember California's giant Sequoias because he is reminded of them by a toy logging truck he bought on that trip.

Reinforce pleasant memories by actually reliving parts of them. If one of the most exciting memories you have is a jeep trip through the mountains of a distant state, investigate the possibility of a similar trip nearer home. If we look back nostalgically upon the songs sung after supper around the campfire, sing those songs again at home around the fireplace. Verbally reliving these experiences, whether it be around the dinner table, the fire or at some quiet family time, brings the family close together and makes the most of the experience. Evenings of "do you remember" can reinforce memories as each child tells his part of the fabulous story. Encourage letters to relatives telling about memorable events. If you have a writer in your house, have him compose a poem or saga in honor of an event. Make a wall in the kitchen or the door of the refrigerator into an ever-changing bulletin board for mementos and maps of memorable events, programs from choral concerts or circuses.

When Kent first went to camp, he did not enjoy being away from home or the boyish rough-housing. In "do you remember" sessions, however, his recollections got better and better, happier and happier, to the point that he became eager to go to camp again.

Simple things can be memorable. Karen loves rain and remembers going out in her swim suit to stand in the rain or, if the weather was cool, putting on her raincoat to sit under an umbrella and read a book.

Memories need not be expensive; the cost is our own creative thinking. We can even build happy memories out of adversity. One of our homes was on a street that often flooded knee deep. Our children remember the rainy days when they sailed small boats and boards in the murky waters of the closed-off street. When we lived in an area where tidal wave alerts were not unusual, we sometimes moved to high ground in the middle of the night. Our children didn't fear tidal waves because their memories were of happy mountainside picnics at two in the morning or of doubling up with neighbors and doing calisthenics while waiting for the all-clear signal.

Sit down some evening with your spouse and talk about the fun you had in the "old days." Make a list of the memorable events of your growing up years. Times haven't really changed so much! Why not plan to repeat some of those experiences with your own children — walking in a field, making caramel corn, reading a mystery by firelight, having foot races on the driveway, going to a movie on the spur of the moment, building a snowman? Make a family fun list and keep adding to it as you cross off memory-making events.

63
Looking Ahead To Teen Years

A friend with four teen-agers calls the teens the years of the four D's: dating, driving, drinking and drugs. When our children are ready, we favor the first two D's but strongly oppose the last two. Coping with the four D's doesn't mean a "serious chat" when the child is twelve. Helping our children handle the temptations of teen-age life starts when they are toddlers and continues as long as they are under our roofs.

DATING

If you give your child natural opportunities to be with the opposite sex and if you regularly say that he *will* be allowed to go on a date at a mutually-acceptable age, the first date won't be an earth-shaking experience. In the grade school years we point up the fun and naturalness of being with young people of *both* sexes. We tell them that the time *will* come when the opposite sex is no longer considered "yuck."

Families with both boys and girls are fortunate in being able to have more interaction between the sexes. Studying or playing with one another becomes natural. However, while it is desirable to encourage a wholesome attitude about the body, children in grade school should be given privacy at bathroom and bath-taking times.

Children ten to twelve are often ready for parties with both sexes, trips to the beach or movies with several families of children. Prepare your youngster by indicating the proper social behavior during such events.

Movies and television often portray boy-girl relationships in an unreal way. But they do provide an opportunity to bring up the subject. After a few dad-and-mother dialogues on proper relationships in front of the kids, children will gradually make these values their own and reinforce one another. This is an opportunity to strongly influence our sons and daughters about the physical and mental harm they can do to themselves and others through pre-marital sex.

Again, the parent's example is important. Affection of parents for each other shouldn't be hidden from the child. Love isn't mysterious and confined to the bedroom. Let it be a natural progression — the right boy-girl activities at the right time. Most important, don't be anxious to prove that your child is acceptable to the other sex. Many parents push their children into boy-girl relationships long before they are interested or prepared.

DRIVING

A friend lets his toddler sit in his lap to "help steer" the family car. This is NOT the kind of driver education a child needs. As soon as your child is interested, usually when he starts school, begin your preparation for the time he will be driving. Tell him about seat belts, makes of cars, traffic laws, defensive driving, being a good walker, jogger, bicyclist, judging distances, the reasons for speed laws. This sort of education means you have to know the rules, too.

Much of this can be accomplished through car games: telling what the shape of signs means, being the first to note the speed limit, estimating the right time to activate a turn signal. Let your child sit in the center of the front seat and monitor your speed. This will make a better driver out of you, too. Stress that the car is not a toy but a means of getting places.

At license renewal time, our dinner talk includes a discussion of new laws and also ideas from the driver's test handbook. Eventually the oldest child in the family is in a driver education class. Let him tell the younger ones what driving is all about. In our state, you're permitted to take your graded test home. Younger children love to see if they can answer the questions as well as mom or dad!

Help to prepare your child for that important day when he takes the test and becomes a careful, accident-free driver. There is no need for the new driver to have even one accident. Here again, parental example is important. If we treat our cars carelessly and they look as if they have barely survived a riot, our children learn that cars are expendable. However, if we include a child in car care, — checking fluids, making minor repairs and taking him along when the car must go in for major work, — he learns respect for this large investment.

DRINKING AND DRUGS

Mark brought a friend home after school one day. I suggested that the friend phone home to say where he was. He said it didn't matter. I found out later that he was right — the home parent was an alcoholic and not interested in the child.

Alcohol, nicotine and drug addiction start with the first drink, puff or shot. These hard-to-break habits are the greatest blights on our growing generation. And it is in grade school that children now have their first smoke, toke, drink, upper or downer. To them these are symbols of "growing up." After all, when they see adults doing these things, they assume that they are fun.

Frank discussions should fortify children with reasons not to take part! Sometimes we can accomplish this by commenting on something we see on the street, on TV or in a movie. Sometimes we may have to sit down and deliberately talk it all out. Too often parents are afraid to know what is going on, so they don't bring up the subject.

When our children were in the pre-teens and young teens, we found the Consumer Union book *Licit and Illicit Drugs*. Dad read the book and excerpted from it important parts which were shared with the family at supper. This scientifically sound view of the long-term effects of nicotine, caffeine, alcohol and other chemical substances was an eye-opener to us and the children. Some of it was pretty grim reading. However, the information was very worth sharing and it debunked some old wives' tales. We read a little and talked a little, taking up only one drug at a time. The children were encouraged to share what they had heard about the subject. Without telling tales, they told what their friend's experiences were.

Out of these serious discussions came a strengthening of values that helped them when everybody-is-doing-it pressures came. Kent said in summing up his reaction to drugs, "I could never treat my body that way. I have too much self-respect." Wendy commented, "If I can't be happy without artificial things put into me, I'd better work harder on me." Karen and Mark listened quietly but one night when a TV show portrayed drinking and drugs in an attractive way, they were quick to point this out to us.

KEEPING THE CHANNELS OPEN

Parents can't be shocked over what pre-teens say or do. And they can't win with scare tactics. While parents may not always approve and sometimes will have to discipline, they should always be ready to listen. Make some good strict rules here — make them early and talk about them often. Be prepared for these rules to be challenged. Open the matter for discussion whenever it is brought up. Listen to the experiences your children have — and the ones they say their friends are having. Sometimes you will know that the "friend" mentioned is your own child! Listen, talk, argue, be prepared with facts. Admonish, educate, love, forgive — but stand firm for what you believe.

The years from birth to twelve are the *formative* years. As children near the teens, they should be helped to see that their personal habits, study habits, academic interests and hobbies are pointing the way toward college and career — making them into either interesting and useful adults or boring and unsatisfied members of society.

GOALS

Children ages seven or eight can learn to set goals for their futures. Quarterly, at our family meetings, we set goals for ourselves, parents and children alike. Then when the three-month period is over, we look over our goals to see what we have accomplished. In a free-for-all discussion, each family member comments on how close he has come to achieving his goals. Then we give our opinions. Here are some typical goals:

FOR WENDY
1. Sew four outfits
2. Be more even-tempered
3. Practice music each day
4. Write six letters

FOR KENT
1. Raise spelling grade
2. Set example in Sunday school for younger children
3. Cooperate with baby-sitters
4. Take more photographs

FOR KAREN
1. Show more love to Kent
2. Do needlework kit
3. Brush teeth better
4. Be in two plays

FOR MARK
1. Try to tell the truth more
2. Learn to catch a ball four or five times in a row
3. Be a good sport
4. Hang up pants

Even parents make goals and post them on the family bulletin board. These might include:
1. Have four of seven nights each week at home
2. Show more appreciation to the children
3. Make the family travel scrapbook
4. Read a book a month
5. Lose ten pounds
6. Weed the front yard

Goal-setting time is a good time for self-analysis. You may think that Karen's goal of showing love to Kent or Kent's goal of raising his spelling grades were prompted by parents. They were not. As soon as children are able to stand back and look at themselves to see where they need to improve, they set appropriate and often demanding goals for themselves. This is far better than having it legislated from above. A child who has *realized* what needs to be changed is well on the way to *making* that change.

If I could say in two words the best advice to parents of a young child, I would say *love him*. Love him impartially, recognizing his differences. Love him confidently, seeing value in him right now and in the future. Love him appreciatively for what he is able to do. Love him wisely, knowing sometimes that love chastens. And love him expansively, letting creativity and spontaneity be an essential part of his life, and yours.

Your Week Six Check List

Plan to hold a weekly family meeting for the next four weeks. (They're so much fun, you'll probably continue!) Consider some of these items for your agendas:

1. Plans for the coming week
2. Rules for the baby-sitter
3. New bedtimes
4. Allowances
5. The children's list of approved TV shows
6. Individual and family goals for the three months ahead
7. Gifts hoped-for at birthdays or Christmas
8. Places to visit
9. Rearranging bedrooms
10. Children and adults to invite over
11. What to do on the next holiday
12. Games to play as a family
13. Music to listen to
14. How school is going
15. Activities of parents
16. Home conservation of energy
17. Books that could be read at supper
18. How helps are going
19. Foods that should be served more often
20. The best thing that happened last week

Now don't put this book away! In a few weeks, look over the most pertinent chapters again. Use the index to find answers to current problems. Then read the book again when the children are older. It won't give you all the answers, but you'll find useful items you missed the first time. What is more, you'll continue to develop your own good ideas. Onward!

NEW BEATITUDES FOR CHILDREN TO MAKE EACH DAY BLESSED AND HAPPY

1. Blessed are the peacemakers, for they shall play joyfully all day long!

2. Blessed are they who do more than required, for their cup will run over with good!

3. Blessed are those who play safely and come home promptly, for they are both creative and responsible!

4. Blessed are they who tell the truth "no matter what," for they are honest and forgiven!

5. Blessed are those who are clean and bright, for they shall be especially huggable and kissable!

6. Blessed are those who eat gracefully, for they shall have fun and friends at parties!

7. Blessed are those who care for their possessions, for they show gratitude for good received!

8. Blessed are those who do their homework willingly and thoroughly, for they shall have wisdom for the future!

9. Blessed are they who go to bed cheerfully, for they rest sweetly in God's loving care!

10. Blessed are they who pursue the truth, for theirs is the kingdom of heaven right now!

Acknowledgments...

To
Claire,
Chris,
Carrie
and Cameron
for being themselves and
to Cliff
who helped them grow joyfully

With special appreciation to Elaine Waller Hunter
for her editorial expertise

And Sheila Kinder and Robert Hunter for
their mechanical know-how

Index

A

Absence, of Parents, 211-214, 281-283
Accomplishment, 14, 223
Affection, Love, 32-35
Air Travel, 247
Allowances, 250
Aloneness, 81-84
Anger, 66-67, 74-76
Animals, 166-169
April Fool's Day, 72
Arguments, 74-76
Art, 145-149
Astronomy, 168
Authority, 59-65, 220
Auto Trips, 170-172

B

Babyhood Education, 220-228
Bathroom Etiquette, 224
Beatitudes, 299
Bedrooms, 19
Bible Study, 101-105
Biology, 166-169
Birthdays, 191-198
Books:
    for children ten to twelve, 241
    for eight- and nine-year-olds,
        238

for kindergarteners and first
    graders, 231
for toddlers, 227
literature, 150-154
Bully, 74-76
Busy Times, 211-214

C

Calendar, 9, 119
Calmness, 42
Car Trips, Carpools, 170-172
Character Building, 27-106
Charity, 260-262
Charts, 122-128
Christmas, 207
    shopping, 181-182
Church, 101-105, 247
Civic Activities, 258-262
Cleaning,
    closets, 46
    house, 254
Clothes, Shopping, 178-179
Clubs, 188-190
Comics, 152
Communicating, 213, 294
Compliments, 57, 247
Confidence, 13-17, 40-45
Conversation, 41-44
Cooking, 256
Correction, 129-134
Council, Family, 274-276

303

To order additional copies of
Six Weeks To Better Parenting
for yourself or as gifts

Tear out and mail to:

Belleridge Press
Box 970
Rancho Santa Fe, CA 92067

Please include check or money order
$8.95 plus $1 for shipping and handling
(California residents add 54¢ tax per book.)

PLEASE PRINT OR TYPE
Send to:

_____
Name

_____
Street address or P.O. Box

_____
City   State   ZIP CODE

☐ No Gift Card   ☐ Gift Card to read _____

PLEASE PRINT OR TYPE
Send to:

_____
Name

_____
Street address or P.O. Box

_____
City   State   ZIP CODE

☐ No Gift Card   ☐ Gift Card to read _____